READINGS IN ANCIENT SOCIETY AND SOCIAL ISSUES

READINGS IN ANCIENT SOCIETY AND SOCIAL ISSUES

R.N. Dhar

CYBER TECH PUBLICATIONS
4264/3, Ansari Road, Daryaganj, New Delhi-110002 (India)
Ph.: 011-23244078, 011-43559448 Fax: 011-23280028
E-Mail: cyberpublicationsdelhi@yahoo.com
Website: www.cybertechpublications.com

READINGS IN ANCIENT SOCIETY AND SOCIAL ISSUES

R.N. Dhar

First Edition 2010

Published by : Asian Offset Printers

G.S. Rawat for **Cyber Tech Publications**
4264/3, Ansari Road, Daryaganj, New Delhi-110002 (India)
Ph.: 011-23244078, 011-43559448 Fax: 011-23280028
E-Mail: cyberpublicationsdelhi@yahoo.com
Website: www.cybertechpublications.com

Preface

Indian Society, as we see it today, has come through the ages. In this long journey towards development and progress it has transcended ancient, medieval periods and running through to the modern period. During this process of transcendence, the culture and civilisation of each period had great bearing on Indian society. Many civilisations became extinct in this developmental process but their art, archaeology and cultural heritage still remains and reminds us of those golden days of history. History and civilisation of India has seen many foreigners, faiths and religions coming in close contact with Indian society. Being of generous attitude, Indian society assimilated all these faiths and religions enriching and depicting its secular nature.

The present work aims at understanding the nature and features of ancient Indian society during different historical phases. The evolutionary approach has been applied in order to analyse the changes took place in various social institutions and refutes the claim of those who see the ancient Indian society as unchanging. Alongwith various internal and external factors responsible for the occurrence of numerous social changes, the economic developments, the role of heretical religions such as Buddhism and Jainism, the incursion of foreigners and its impact on brahmanical social order have also been specifically examined. This book also examines the steps taken by the classical thinkers for restoring their deteriorating traditional social order and the declining hegemony of their managerial class in the society. Among such remedial efforts, enacted as laws as well as social prohibition applied by them the origin of Pauranic Hinduism and the doctrine of Kalivarjya have also been specifically analysed in this work by the author.

—*Author*

CONTENTS

1

Introduction

Indian culture is an ancient and dynamic entity, spanning back to the very beginnings of human civilization. Beginning with a mysterious culture along the Indus River and in farming communities in the southern lands of India, the history of the sub-continent is one puncuated by constant integration with migrating peoples and with the diverse cultures that surround India. Placed in the center of Asia, Indian history is a crossroads of cultures from China to Europe, and the most significant Asian connection with the cultures of Africa.

Indian history, then, is more than just a set of unique developments in a definable process; it is, in many ways, a microcosm of human history itself, a diversity of cultures all impinging on a great people and being reforged into new, syncretic forms. The most striking element of Indian geography is the natural barrier formed by the mountain ranges in the north of India. For India is a continental plate that is crashing into the Asian continental plate. As it does, both continental plates push up the earth where they meet into a forbidding range of mountains. The central mountain range, passing across in the shape of a sword near the northern edge of the Indian subcontinent, is the Great Himalayas. These northern mountains, which are less of a barrier in the west, have naturally isolated India from its neighbors.

All along the southern edge of this great mountain wall are rich soils that are generously rained on; even though this region lies in the temperate zone, it is lush and subtropical. To the south are the extensive flood plains of the Indus River in the west and the Ganges in the east. With rich soil renewed every year by river flooding and with generous summer rains, these plains in the north are among the richest agricultural areas in the world. It was here that Indian civilization first arose, in the fertile flood plains adjoining the Indus River. This vast stretch of flood plain has been the home of the great Indian empires as well, the Mauryans and the Guptas.

The southern portion of India is a large peninsula with a forbidding mountain range all along the western coast and a large flat plateau called the Deccan in the center of the sub-continent. The eastern coast is flat land and affords many opportunities for harbors; from this area Indian culture had the widest contacts with foreign peoples. The western portion, however, being walled from the sea and hard to reach by land, subsequently became the seat of the powerful empires of the south, such as the Muslim kingdoms.

India is one of the most culturally, linguistically, and ethnically diverse regions one can imagine. Four major peoples, distinguished by the languages they speak, make up the population of the region. The majority of the population are Indo-European speaking a variety of languages related to European languages such as Greek, German, or English. Precisely when these peoples arrived is subject to much debate, but they seem to have arrived somewhere between 2000 BC and 1600 BC, and they brought with them their own religion and social system. The bulk of Indian religion and almost all of its literature is Indo-European. Second to the Indo-Europeans, but more ancient in India than the later immigrants, are a people who speak languages from the Dravidian family of languages. While we cannot be certain, the Dravidians were probably the authors of the great Indus River civilizations contemporary with the Mesopotamian civilizations to the west. In addition, the peoples in the northern mountains speak languages related to Chinese, Tibetan, or Mongolian. Finally, the smallest group, but most likely the oldest inhabitants of India, speak languages from the Australoid family, which are the languages spoken by indigenous peoples scattered throughout southeast Asia and Australia. Australoids are still present throughout the mountainous forests of the Deccan, but their traditional way of life, which was still vital only forty years ago, is beginning to die out.

Each of these peoples speak a bewildering variety of languages; each region of India is dominated by a single language. The major languages, most of which are Indo-European, are:

- Hindi
- Urdu (which is very closely related to Hindi but uses Arabic script)
- Bengali
- Marathi
- Assamese
- Sindhi
- Oriya
- Punjabi
- Kashmiri
- Nepali
- Telugu (Dravidian)
- Tamil (Dravidian)
- Kannada (Dravidian)
- Malayalam (Dravidian)

Wow. Despite this variety of languages, Indian culture is remarkably fluid and the contacts between peoples frequent and productive. Very few cultures are so tied into the overall geography of their region; Hinduism requires frequent pilgrimages as part of one's spiritual perfection, so the intercourse between different peoples has been constant throughout Indian history.

In the north, the great mountain barrier. To the south, the great river plains of the Indus and the Ganges, and the large, high plateau of the Deccan. This is the stage on which a complex history took place, and the first act began along the Indus River.

Although agriculture seems to have come late to India, arriving sometime around 5000 BC, India was one of the first regions to give birth to civilization. Only a few centuries after the first Mesopotamian cities sprang up, a people living along the northern reaches of the Indus River discovered urbanization, metalwork, and writing. It is a mysterious civilization and one with no discernible continuity, for it thrived for just several centuries and then disappeared. The Indo-European immigrants who settled the region did not adopt most of the aspects of this civilization, and what precisely they did adopt is difficult to ascertain. So while Egypt, Mesopotamia, and the Yellow River civilizations lasted for millenia and left their mark on all subsequent cultures, the Indus River civilization seems to have been a false start.

For the overwhelming majority of human history, this early culture was truly a lost civilization. The mounds which stood where great cities once thrived excited interest in observers, but no one in their wildest dreams could have imagined that beneath those large mounds lay cities that had been lost to human memory.

In the 1920's, excavations began on one of these mounds in Harappa in Pakistan. While the archaeologists expected to find something, they did not imagine that a city lay beneath the earth. Archaeologists would later discover another large city to the recovery of at least eighty villages and towns related to this newly discovered civilization. They named it Harappan after the first city they discovered, but it is more commonly called the Indus River civilization. While we have stones and tools and fragments and bones, we really have no one's voice or experience from the bustling days of the great Harappan cities. We don't know who the people were who built and lived there. We don't know, either, when they first built their cities; some scholars argue that Harappan civilization arises around 2250 BC, while others argue that it can be dated back to 2500 BC or earlier.

Like the civilizations in Mesopotamia, Egypt, and Greece, Harappa grew on the floodplains of a rich and life-giving river, the Indus. The original cities and many of the towns seemed to have been built right upon the shores of the river. The Indus, however, is destructive and unpredictable in its floods, and the cities were frequently levelled by the forces of nature. Mohenjo-Daro in the south, where the flooding can be fairly brutal, was rebuilt six times that we know about; Harappa in the north was rebuilt five times.

The Harappans were an agricultural people whose economy was almost entirely dominated by horticulture. Massive granaries were built at each city, and there most certainly was an elaborate bureaucracy to distribute this wealth of food. The Indus River valley is relatively dry now, but apparently it was quite wet when the Harappans thrived there. We know this because the bricks that they built their cities with were fired bricks; since sun-dried bricks are cheaper and easier to make, we can only assume that over-abundant humidity and precipitation prevented them from taking the cheaper way out. In addition, many of the Harappan seals have pictures of animals that imply a wet and marshy environment, such as rhinoceroses, elephants, and tigers. The Harappans also had a wide variety of domesticated animals: camels, cats, dogs, goats, sheep, and buffalo.

Their cities were carefully planned and laid out; they are, in fact, the first people to plan the building of their cities. Whenever they rebuilt their cities, they laid them out precisely in the same way the destroyed city had been built. The pathways within the city are laid out in a perpendicular criss-cross fashion; most of the city consisted of residences.

Life in the Harappan cities was apparently quite good. Although living quarters were cramped, which is typical of ancient cities, the residents nevertheless had drains, sewers, and even latrines. There is no question that they had an active trade with cultures to the west. Several Harappan seals have been found in excavations of Sumerian cities, as well as pictures of animals that in no way could have existed in Mesopotamia, such as tigers. There is not, however, a wealth of Mesopotamian artifacts in Harappan cities.

We know nothing of the religion of the Harappans. Unlike in Mesopotamia or Egypt, we have discovered no building that so much as hints that it might be a temple or involve any kind of public worship. The bulk of public buildings in the city seemed to be solely oriented towards the economy and making life comfortable for the Harappans. We do, however, have a number of tantalizing figures on various seals and statues. What we gather from these figures (and we can not gather much), is that the Harappans probably exercised some sort of goddess worship. There is, however, some sort of male god (maybe) that has the head of a man with the horns of a bull. In addition, we believe from various artifacts that the Harappans also may have worshipped natural objects or animistic forces, but the circumstances of this worship can only be guessed at.

We know that the Harappans were eventually supplanted by waves of migrations of Indo-Europeans. These new peoples, however, did not seem to adopt the religious practices of the Harappans, so it is not possible to reconstruct Harappan religion through the religion of the Vedic peoples, that is, the Indo-Europeans who constructed the rudimentary Indian religion represented by the Vedas.

Right at the heart of the mystery, like a person speaking behind sound-proof glass, are the numerous writings on the artifacts that have been unearthed. Harappan writing was a pictographic script, or at least seems to be; as of yet, however, no one has figured out how to decipher it or even what language it might be rendering. The logical candidate is that the Harappans spoke a Dravidian language, but that conclusion, which may not be true, has not helped anybody decipher the script. Like the rest of Harappan civilization, the writing was lost to human memory after the disappearance of the Harappans.

And finally they disappeared. And they disappeared without a trace. Some believe that they were overrun by the war-like Aryans, the Indo-Europeans who, like a storm, rushed in from Euro-Asia and overran Persia and northern India. Some believe that the periodic and frequently destructive flooding of the Indus finally took its toll on the economic health of the civilization. It is possible that the periodic changes of course that the Indus undergoes also contributed to its decline. All we know is that somewhere between 1800 and 1700 BC, the Harappan cities and towns were abandoned and finally reclaimed by the rich soil they had sprung from.

The Indus Valley Civilization, beginning sometime around 2300 BC, developed in two major city areas along the river valleys of the Indus, Ravi, and Sutlej, just beneath the Himalayan Mountains in modern Pakistan and Northeast India. Though these two cities have been excavated and exposed to the world, much is still unknown of the culture of Mohenjo-daro and Harappa. The Indus people did not engrave inscriptions on stones or place papyrus scrolls in the tombs of their dead; all we know of their writing is derived from the simple inscriptions on their seals. Several efforts have been made to decipher the Indus seals, but none have truly succeeded this far; there is some notion that these seals could have been used as markers in trade situations, or that some may have represented family names.

What we do know of this civilization comes from the intense archaeological excavation of the area (Basham 1963:14). Anthropologists do know that these cities were highly developed for their period in history; the structure of their cities were so far advanced that it was not surpassed until the late nineteenth century in Europe (Heinz 1997:68). The genius behind the advanced architecture of the Indus civilization carried over into a thriving agricultural and trade based economy. The Indus people used the plentiful rivers surrounding them much to their advantage, the Indus the most spectacular of the three rivers.

How did this civilization make its living? Like the older civilizations proceeding Indus in Egypt and Mesopotamia, these ancient people farmed. The people of Indus prospered on the foundations of an agriculture based system of irrigation and fertility, maintained by silt-bearing floods (Hawkes 1973: 267). Wheat and six-row barley were grown, as were melon seeds, oil crops like sesame and mustard, and dates (petrified dates have been found in the excavation of the Valley). As for vegetables, the only apparent source was the field pea. The earliest traces of cotton known anywhere in the world have been found in the Valley. The people of Indus may have cultivated rice on the west coast, though this is not exactly certain (there is not enough evidence to prove this statement entirely true). They domesticated a number of animals from local wild species, including dogs and cats, zebu or the humped cattle, short-horns and buffaloes, and possibly pigs, camels, horses and asses (the later three used as transport). They may have domesticated the elephant too, but the evidence for this is also vague; the elephant was represented on several of the excavated Indus seals and its ivory was used for crafts (Wheeler 1966:64).

From every crop that a farmer grew, a large portion of it had to be paid into public granaries. At the Mohenjo-daro site, there was a high loading platform above a lower spot intended for carts where the farmers would dump their grain. It is assumed that this cart was small and powered by an ox or bullock, similar to those used in the area today. Terracotta models of bull driven carts have been excavated from the Mohenjo-daro site, and it appears that these carts have changed very little over some 4000 years. This cart would be taken and unloaded at a central granary where all farmers of the city gave up their wheat and barley. There are guesses that this centralized granary might have been the economic equivalent of our modern State Bank. This system is not found in Harappa; grain was brought into the city by boat (Hawkes 1973:267).

It appears that the people of Indus did in fact hunt the abundant wildlife in their midst. It is impossible to know if these people fished on a full time basis, but there is evidence that fish were caught with barbed hooks and line, and nets. Many of the local animals (including elephant, tiger, rhinoceros, buffalo, antelope and gharial) were represented on the seals so readily that they must have been a significant part of these peoples' diets. According to Hawkes, it is reasonable to believe that tigers may have taken the place of lions "in providing the sport for the princes...

One seal shows a Gilgamesh-like figure standing between two upreared tigers and another a man tackling a buffalo with a barbed spear" (1973: 268). In any respect (along with the grains, vegetables and fruits grown), animal meat was a factor of the ancient Indus diet.

Aside from the subsistence of agriculture and hunting, the Indus people supported themselves by trading goods. Through trade, the Indus Civilization expanded its culture, coming into regular contacts with far away lands. The long coastline and many rivers provided the people of the Indus territories with consistent trafficking by water. Archaeologists have turned up imports including gold from southern India, copper from Afghanistan, jade like fuchsite probably from southern India, and turquoise from Iran. Trade with Mesopotamia has been noted, as Indus pottery has been discovered in the ancient city of Tell Asmar (Wheeler 1966:64).

A number of typical Indus seals have also been found in Sumer, seals dating back to between 2300 and 2000 BC. The finding of Indus seals in Mesopotamia suggests that people of Indus may have resided in this territory; possibly merchants who were keeping up a constant trade with the Mesopotamian people (cotton was a staple export of Indus, and could have been the crop that brought these two civilizations into contact). As mentioned before, these seals are thought to have been a representation of personal names. With these seals turning up in some many locations, it seems that in spite of the totalitarian casts associated with the Indus state, trade may have been in the hands of private merchants rather than regulated by a form of governmental authority (Hawkes 1973:270).

The Indus seaboard has been commended by anthropologists for its efforts of oversea commerce. According to Hawkes, the people of Indus sailed in "high-prowed, single masted" boats, sound for carrying the trafficked goods (Hawkes 1973:270). The excavated site at Lothal (another ancient city within the Indus Valley) has revealed harbour works, and the Harappan people may have been more advanced in their nautical skills than was originally perceived. It is probable that the people of Lothal were in regular contact with peoples much farther south. As for the Harrapan culture, it is plausible to assume that their influences touched people as far as south India (Barham 1963:19).

Nearing the end of the Indus Valley Civilization, the cities began to wither and the strong economy slowly deteriorated.

It was most likely the intermittent floods that tore apart and put and end to this civilization. Floods wiped out the irrigation system that supplied water to the crops, and many of the buildings were smothered. The people lost their drive to keep the cities orderly and prosperous. The constant flooding simply broke them of their morale as a proud people of such an advanced civilization. If it is true that the Aryans invaded the Indus Valley at the time when the civilization was withering, it was no wonder that they had no trouble forcing the people of Indus out of the area. But, it is certain that these people were powerful, determined, and advanced; easily seen through their strong willed and successful economy (Wheeler 1966: 76-9).

They called themselves the "noble ones" or the "superior ones." Their names are lost; their tribal names are lost. But when they found themselves conquerors, they gave themselves the name "superior" or "noble."

They were a tribal and nomadic peoples living in the far reaches of Euro-Asia in hostile steppe lands barely scratching out a living. They were unquestionably a tough people, and they were fierce and war-like. Their religion reflects it dominated as it is by a storm-god or sky-god that enjoins warfare and conquest. This god was called something like "Dyaus," a word related to "Zeus," "deus" (the Latin word for "god"), "deva" (the Sanskrit word for "god"), and, of course, the English word "divine." Their culture was oriented around warfare, and they were very good at it. They were superior on horseback and rushed into battle in chariots. They were a tribal people ruled over by a war-chief, or raja (the Latin word "rex" (king) comes from the same root word, along with the English "regal"). Somewhere in the early centuries of the second millenium BC, they began to migrate southwards in waves of steady conquest across the face of Persia and the lands of India.

There, they would take on the name "superior" or "noble" to distinguish themselves from the people they conquered. Their name is derived from the Indo-European root word, "ar," meaning "noble." In Sanskrit, they were the "Aryas" ("Aryans"); but that root, "ar," would also serve as the foundation of the name of the conquered Persian territories, "Iran." This concept of nobility, in fact, seems to lie at the heart of Indo-European consciousness, for it appears in another country's name, "Ireland," or "Eire." You can bet, however, that when a people go around calling themselves superior that it spells bad news for other people.

And there is no question that they were bad news for the southern Asians. They swept over Persia with lightening speed, and spread across the northern river plains of India. Their nature as a warlike, conquering people are still preserved in Vedic religion, the foundation of Hinduism. In the Rig Veda, the collection of praises to the gods, the god Indra towers over the poetry as a conquering god, one that smashes cities and slays enemies. The invading Aryans were originally nomadic peoples, not agricultural. They penetrated India from the north-west, settling first in the Indus valley. Unlike the Harappans, however, they eventually concentrated their populations along the Ganges floodplain. The Ganges, unlike the Indus, is far milder and more predictable in its flooding. It must have been a paradise to a people from the dry steppes of central Asia and Iran, a paradise full of water and forest. When they arrived, the vast northern plains were almost certainly densely forested. Where now bare fields stretch to the horizon, when the Aryans arrived lush forests stretched to those very same horizons. Clearing the forests over the centuries was an epic project and one that is still preserved in Indian literature.

The Aryans, or Vedic civilization were a new start in Indian culture. Harappa was more or less a dead end (at least as far as we know); the Aryans adopted almost nothing of Harappan culture. They built no cities, no states, no granaries, and used no writing. Instead they were a warlike people that organized themselves in individual tribal, kinship units, the jana. The *jana* was ruled over by a war-chief. These tribes spread quickly over northern India and the Deccan. In a process that we do not understand, the basic social unit of Aryan culture, the *jana*, slowly developed from an organization based on kinship to one based on geography. The *jana* became a janapada, or nation and the *jana-rajya* , or tribal kingdom, became the jana-rajyapada, or national kingdom. So powerfully ingrained into Indian culture is the *jana-pada* , that Indians still define themselves mainly by their territorial origins. All the major territories of modern India, with their separate cultures and separate languages, can be dated back to the early *jana-padas* of Vedic India.

The earliest history of the Aryans in India is called the Rigvedic Period (1700-1000 BC) after the religious praise poems that are the oldest pieces of literature in India. These poems, the Rig Veda, are believed to represent the most primitive layer of Indo-European religion and have many characteristics in common with Persian religion since the two peoples are closely related in time. In this early period, their population was restricted to the Punjab in the northern reaches of the Indus River and the Yamuna River near the Ganges. They maintained the Aryan tribal structure, with a *raja* ruling over the tribal group in tandem with a council. Each *jana* seems to have had a chief priest; the religion was focused almost entirely on a series of sacrifices to the gods. The Rigvedic peoples originally had only two social classes: nobles and commoners. Eventually, they added a third: *Dasas* , or "darks." These were, we presume, the darker-skinned people they had conquered. By the end of the Rigvedic period, social class had settled into four rigid castes: the caturvarnas, or "four colors." At the top of the *caturvarnas* were the priests, or Brahmans. Below the priests were the warriors or nobles (Kshatriya), the craftspeople and merchants (Vaishya), and the servants (Shudra), who made up the bulk of society. These economic classes were legitimated by an elaborate religious system and would be eventually subdivided into a huge number of economic sub-classes which we call "castes." Social class by the end of the Rigvedic period became completely inflexible; there was no such thing as social mobility.

In the early centuries of Later Vedic Period or Brahmanic Period (1000-500 BC), the Aryans migrated across the Doab, which is a large plain which separates the Yamuna River from the Ganges. It was a difficult project, for the Doab was thickly forested; the Aryans slowly burned and settled the Doab until they reached the Ganges. While the *Rig Veda* represents the most primitive religion of the Aryans during the Rigvedic Period, the religion of the Later Vedic period is dominated by the Brahmanas, or priestly book, which was composed sometime between 1000 and 850 BC. Later Vedic society is dominated by the Brahmans and every aspect of Aryan life comes under the control of priestly rituals and spells. In history as the Indians understand it, the Later Vedic Period is the Epic Age; the great literary, heroic epics of Indian culture, the Mahabharata and the Ramayana, though they were composed between 500 and 200 BC, were probably originally formulated and told in the Later Vedic Period. Both of these epics deal with heroes from this period and demonstrate how Aryan cultural values, as we can understand them from the *Rig Veda* , are being transformed by mixing with Indus cultures.

What did the Aryans do with their time? They seem to have had a well-developed musical culture, and song and dance dominated their society. They were not greatly invested in the visual arts, but their interest in lyric poetry was unmatched. They loved gambling. They did not, however, have much interest in writing even though they could have inherited a civilization and a writing system when they originally settled India. We do not know exactly when they became interested in writing, but it may have been at the end of the Brahmanic period somewhere between 650 and 500 BC. Still, there are no Aryan writings until the Mauryan period—from Harappa (2500-1750 BC) to Maurya (300 BC) is quite a long time. The script that the Mauryans used is called "Brahmi" script and was used to write not only the religious and literary language of the time, Sanskrit, but also the vernacular languages. This script, Brahmi, is the national alphabet of India.

The Vedic period, then, is a period of cultural mixing, not of conquest. Although the Aryans were a conquering people when they first spread into India, the culture of the Aryans would gradually mix with indigenous cultures, and the war-religion of the Aryans, still preserved in parts of the *Rig Veda,* slowly became more ritualized and more meditative. By 200 BC, this process of mixing and transforming was more or less complete and the culture we call "Indian" was fully formed.

In 331 BC, Alexander the Great of Macedon began one of the greatest conquests in human history. After conquering Egypt and defeating the Persian Empire Alexander had pushed his army to the very limits of the world as the Greeks knew it. But he wanted more; he saw that the world extended further. By conquering the ancient lands of the Mesopotamians, he came into contact with cultures to the east, such as Pakistan and India. After almost a millenium and a half, from the period of Harappa (2500-1750 BC), to the end of the Brahmanic period, the peoples of India entered into no commerce or trade with the Mesopotamians. But starting around 700 BC, the Indians began to trade again with the Mesopotamian cities, and by the time of Alexander, that trade was dyanmic. Partly out of curiosity, and partly out of a desire to conquer the enitre world within the boundaries of the river Ocean (the Greeks believed that a great river, called Ocean, encircled all the land of the world), Alexander and his army pushed east, through northern Iran and all the way to Pakistan and India. He had conquered Bactria at the foot of the western Himalayas, gained a huge Bactrian army, and married a Bactrian princess, Roxane. But when he tried to push on past Pakistan, his army grew tired, and he abandoned the eastward conquest in 327 BC.

Alexander only made it as far as the region of Gandhara, the plain which lies directly west of the Indus River. Alexander himself seems to have had literally no effect on Indian history, for he left as soon as he reached the Indus. Two important results, however, arose because of Alexander's conquests: first, from this point onwards Greek and Indian culture would intermix. But most importantly, the conquest of Alexander may have set the stage for the first great conqueror of Indian history, Chandragupta Maurya (reigned 321-297 BC), who, shortly after Alexander left, united all the kingdoms of northern India into a single empire.

CHANDRAGUPTA MAURYA (321-297 BC)

He was an adventurer rather than a king. Like Alexander, he began with almost no army whatsoever; with this army he seized the region of Magadha just south of the lower Ganges and then steadily conquered the whole of the Ganges basin.

Chandragupta Maurya had started his empire. When Alexander the Great departed from Gandhara, a power vacuum was left in western India which Maurya took advantage of. Marching westward, he quickly conquered the whole of the Indus Valley, and eventually gained Gandhara and Arachosia (the mountainous region west of the Indus) after defeating the Greek rulers of Persia and Bactria, the Seleucids.

Hand in hand with this ambitious conqueror was a shrewd and calculating Brahman named Kautilya. While Chadragupta Maurya built his empire by the force of his arm, Kautilya designed the government. Together they created the first unified state in Indian history. The government Kautilya and Chandragupta created strictly regulated economic activities. The laws were harsh and the death penalty was applied to a myriad of offenses.

BINDUSARA (297-272 BC)

Chandragupta's son Bindusara extended the conquests even further by setting his sights south to the Deccan. By the end of Bindusara's reign, the Mauryan Empire included at least a third of the peninsula and stretched all the way from Bangladesh to the Hindu Kush mountains.

ASOKA (272-232)

Of the great conquering kings of the Maurya Empire, the only one we know much about is Asoka, for it is in the reign of Asoka that the first samples of Indian writing since the fall of Harappa appear. Asoka kept careful records of his edicts, so we have an excellent source for the history of his reign.

He seems to have been forged from the same mold as his illustrious fathers. Once he rose to the throne, he began an aggressive campaign to conquer the remainder of the subcontinent. The last major regions yet to be conquered were the Dravidian regions in the far south and the Kalinga in North India.

The conquest of Kalinga, which extended Mauryan rule to its farthest boundaries, seems to have been a tremendous shock to Asoka. War and conquest are always bloody and cruel, and the experience of massive homicide is often an experience that shakes people to their very souls. Asoka was so troubled by the conquest that he underwent a religious conversion. In the latter years of the Brahmanic period, several religious movements arose in reaction to the power and abuse of power by the Brahmans. The most significant of these religious reactions was Buddhism, which is discussed in more detail in the chapters on the religious history of ancient India. Buddhism was really much less of a religion and more of a philosophy—or, better yet, a philosophical therapy. Its founder, Siddhartha Guatama, the "Buddha," or "Awakened One," was the son of a noble who, when he first encountered death and sickness, resolved to find a way to end human suffering. After years of struggle and meditation, he "awakened" to the truth of things: that all human suffering is caused by human desire and that human desire can be quenched when one understands the impermanence of all things, including the self. Unlike Brahmanism, Buddhism eschews elaborate rituals and magic; unlike the Rig Veda, Buddhism advocates a non-striving, non-coercive and meditative life.

The Buddhist way of life was a way out of Asoka's crisis. He converted to Buddhism and strove to achieve the Buddhist "middle way" between extremes. He became a vegetarian, renounced all warfare, and attempted to build a state based on Buddhist principles. First and foremost, the state would strive for nonviolence, or ahimsa; in place of violence, the state would rule by "law" or "right" (dharma).

Asoka, of course, could not put all of these reforms into practice. He found that some level of violence and retribution was necessary and declared as much. Although he made the laws less harsh, they still involved physical punishment and, in some cases, execution. Still, Asoka began a process of transformation in Indian society. He represented first and foremost the possibility of exemplifying religious idealism in a lived life rather than in a merely formal position. Although he took the vows of Buddhism and even joined the order, he chose to remain active in the real world and exemplify his religion in his actions as king. He also demanded religious toleration; under Asoka, all competing religious systems were allowed to co-exist peacefully. The stunning ability of Indian culture to tolerate competing religions throughout its history begins with Asoka. Finally, although he could never really fully translate Buddhist ideals into government, he began a process of cultural transformation that would completely remake India. By the start of the Gupta dynasty, the bulk of Indian society had become vegetarian and no laws carried the death penalty.

His greatest achievement, however, was cultural. For he was dedicated to his new religion and fervently patronized its expansion. Under Asoka, Buddhist monks were sent in every compass direction: to Burma, Tibet, Nepal, Persia, Mesopotamia, Syria, and Israel. The eastern evangelical missions were extremely successful; Buddhism spread very quickly from Nepal and Burma into Tibet and China where it was fervidly embraced. The western missions, however, were less successful. However, Buddhism left traces in Middle Eastern and even European culture. For instance, one of the Catholic saints of the Middle Ages and the Renaissance was Barlam, whose life is based on that of Siddhartha Gautama, the Buddha. Not only is this Catholic saint the Buddha, but one of the stories of Barlam is the conversion of a cruel king, Iosaphat; this king, in many ways, corresponds to Asoka, who is presented as intolerant and cruel before his conversion in the Indian epic, *Asokavadana*. So there is tantalizing evidence that Buddhism has had some influence on Christianity, though we are not quite sure to what extent. Needless to say, the spread of Buddhism under Asoka greatly influenced the religious history of Asia. Asoka's conversion also produced the first written literature in India; it was not Vedic literature but the Buddhist scriptures that were first committed to writing. Finally, Asoka's zeal in spreading Buddhism beyond the borders of India ensured its survival, for when the Muslims defeated the Hindus and took control of India, Buddhism is destroyed as an organized religion in India.

Asoka was the last of the great kings of the Mauryan dynasty. His successors were less energetic and capable; in 184 BC, the last of the Mauryan kings was assassinated, and the first empire of India came to an end.

Before the Guptas

When the last of the Mauryan kings was assassinated in 184 BC, India once again became a collection of unfederated kingdoms. During this period, the most powerful kingdoms were not in the north, but in the Deccan to the south, particularly in the west. The north, however, remained culturally the most active, where Buddhism was spreading and where Hinduism was being gradually remade by the Upanishadic movements, which are discussed in more detail in the section on religious history. The dream, however, of a universal empire had not disappeared. It would be realized by a northern kingdom and would usher in one of the most creative periods in Indian history.

THE GUPTA DYNASTY (320-550)

Under Chandragupta I (320-335), empire was revived in the north. Like Chandragupta Maurya, he first conquered Magadha, set up his capital where the Mauryan capital had stood (Patna), and from this base consolidated a kingdom over the eastern portion of northern India. In addition, Chandragupta revived many of Asoka's principles of government. It was his son, however, Samudragupta (335-376), and later his grandson, Chandragupta II (376-415), who extended the kingdom into an empire over the whole of the north and the western Deccan. Chandragupta II was the greatest of the Gupta kings; called Vikramaditya ("The Sun of Power"), he presided over the greatest cultural age in India.

This period is regarded as the golden age of Indian culture. The high points of this cultural creativity are magnificent and creative architecture, sculpture, and painting. The wall-paintings of Ajanta Cave in the central Deccan are considered among the greatest and most powerful works of Indian art. The paintings in the cave represent the various lives of the Buddha, but also are the best source we have of the daily life in India at the time. There are forty-eight caves making up Ajanta, most of which were carved out of the rock between 460 and 480, and they are filled with Buddhist sculptures. The rock temple at Elephanta (near Bombay) contains a powerful, eighteen foot statue of the three-headed Shiva, one of the principle Hindu gods. Each head represents one of Shiva's roles: that of creating, that of preserving, and that of destroying. The period also saw dynamic building of Hindu temples. All of these temples contain a hall and a tower.

The greatest writer of the time was Kalidasa. Poetry in the Gupta age tended towards a few genres: religious and meditative poetry, lyric poetry, narrative histories (the most popular of the secular literatures), and drama. Kalidasa excelled at lyric poetry, but he is best known for his dramas. We have three of his plays; all of them are suffused with epic heroism, with comedy, and with erotics. The plays all involve misunderstanding and conflict, but they all end with unity, order, and resolution.

The Guptas tended to allow kings to remain as vassal kings; unlike the Mauryas, they did not consolidate every kingdom into a single administrative unit. This would be the model for later Mughal rule and British rule built off of the Mughal paradigm.

The Guptas fell prey, however, to a wave of migrations by the Huns, a people who originally lived north of China. The Hun migrations would push all the way to the doors of Rome. Beginning in the 400's, the Huns began to put pressure on the Guptas. In 480 they conquered the Guptas and took over northern India. Western India was overrun by 500, and the last of the Gupta kings, presiding over a vastly dimished kingdom, perished in 550. A strange thing happened to the Huns in India as well as in Europe. Over the decades they gradually assimilated into the indigenous population and their state weakened.

Harsha, who was a descendant of the Guptas, quickly moved to reestablish an Indian empire. From 606-647, he ruled over an empire in northern India. Harsha was perhaps one of the greatest conquerors of Indian history, and unlike all of his conquering predecessors, he was a brilliant administrator. He was also a great patron of culture. His capital city, Kanauj, extended for four or five miles along the Ganges River and was filled with magnificent buildings. Only one fourth of the taxes he collected went to administration of the government. The remainder went to charity, rewards, and especially to culture: art, literature, music, and religion.

Because of extensive trade, the culture of India became the dominant culture around the Bay of Bengal, profoundly and deeply influencing the cultures of Burma, Cambodia, and Sri Lanka In many ways, the period during and following the Gupta dynasty was the period of "Greater India," a period of cultural activity in India and surrounding countries building off of the base of Indian culture. This medieval flowering of Indian culture would radically change course in the Indian Middle Ages. From the north came Muslim conquerors out of Afghanistan, and the age of Muslim rule began in 1100.

2

Ancient Indian Religion

Very little is known about the religion of the Indus civilization because no written records exit. There is, however, an assumption that parts of the Harappan tradition were held in common by ancient religions of the Middle East as well as the later Hinduism. Prominent among the evidence discovered are the many seals discovered at the sites along the Indus River, as well as in Mesopotamia. Some of these seals clearly indicate the sacredness of the bull which later became a common tradition in Hinduism. Other features are the horned god. These seals have two faces in profile, and one facing forward. The figure is surrounded by a tiger, an elephant, a rhinoceros, and a buffalo. His legs are bent with his feet pressed together in a yoga position which has led some to believe that this god is most likely a proto-Shiva. Shiva is the three-faced Hindu god of death, destruction, and fertility.

Some of these sites have also yielded terra-cotta figurines. Similar, in many respects, to evidence discovered in Egypt and Iran, some of these figurines are of broad-hipped pregnant-looking females. Representative of the Great Mother or nature, these types of deities, as well as the bull, are common among early agricultural societies of Eurasia.

Excavations of Indus cities have not revealed any buildings that can positively be identified as temples. No large statues or monumental sculptures, similar to those found in Egypt, have been discovered. This lack of temples and statuary has resulted in the belief that the focus of religious life was primarily centered in the home. Anthropologists are relatively certain that the peoples of the Indus civilization emphasized ritual purity. Much of this is evidenced by the presence of drainable baths in most of the residences, as well as a great bath or pool surrounded by a pillared hall with small cell-like rooms. Scholars have surmised that washing and bathing were integral to the preservation of purity and that cleanliness was considered necessary to ward off evil spirits.

Similar to the culture of Egypt, it appears that the Indus religion recognized some type of life after death. Unlike later Indians, who practiced cremation, this civilization carefully buried their dead with their heads facing north and the feet pointing south. Included in the graves were pottery jars containing food and weapons for use in the afterlife.

The most ancient sacred literature of Hinduism is called the *Vedas*. This collection of hymns, poems, and ceremonial formulas represent the beliefs of several Aryan tribes. Initially the *Vedas* were considered so sacred that they were only transmitted orally from one generation of brâhmans to the next. The passages of the *Vedas* were eventually written in Sanskrit, we believe, near the end of the third century BC, and primarily consist of four collections called the *Rig-Veda*, the *Sama-Veda*, the *Yajur-Veda*, and the *Atharva-Veda*. Collectively, these are referred to as the Samhitas.

The first three Samhitas were used in the Vedic period by the priestly class as ritual handbooks. Containing 1,028 poetic hymns, the *Rig-Veda* was used by the *hotri* who called on the gods by reciting the hymns aloud. The hymns vary in style and length, and praise a pantheon of gods. Although Indra, the god of war and weather, is the most frequently mentioned, there appears to be no hierarchy. Agni, the god of fire, is the second most prominently mentioned deity. The *Sama Veda* consisted of various portions taken from the *Rig-Veda* and were utilized by the *udgatri* chanters. The *Yajur-Vedas* was used by the *adhvaryu* priests. This work contains specific sacrificial formulas which were recited during that form of ceremony.

The final *Veda*, the *Atharva-Veda*, is attributed to a sage, or *rishi*, named Atharvan, and consists of a number of hymns and magical incantations. Some scholars believe that this scripture may have originated with the original pre-Aryan culture of indigenous peoples, and because it deviated form the other *Vedas*, it was not at first readily accepted. Eventually it too was adopted as a ritual handbook by the Brahmans, the higest class of priests.

Although the *Rig-Veda* is still considered the most important of these ancient texts, it was still never very popular. Much of this comes from the fact of its composition by and for a religious aristocracy. In contrast, the *Atharva-Veda*, compiled perhaps as late as 500 BC, frequently refers to many lesser functional gods considered useful in the daily lives and simple rituals of the ordinary Aryan that did not need the mediation of priests.

What little we know of the Vedic Age comes from the *Rig-Veda*. By the time the oral tradition of the Aryan religion was comitted to Sanskrit, however, some of the gods mentioned had already begun to lose their importance. Nevertheless, The *Rig-Veda* represented a blend of beliefs held by several Aryan tribes.

Each of the gods, of the Vedic Period, had a primary function, or *Vrata*. Usually these functions were closely connected to the forces of nature such as light, fire, and heaven which in turn followed the cosmic order (*rta*) of the universe. The demons of darkness and chaos, headquartered under the earth, arrayed their power against the righteousness of the gods. In this dualistic approach, the demons sought to disrupt the system of nature, therefore practicing *anrtà*. During a later period, *rta* gave way to the concept of *dharma*, which could be translated as "virtue."

Although the deities of the *Rig-Veda* are not organized hierarchically, each could, in its own right, be looked upon as the supreme god. Nevertheless, Indra, the god of war and weather, receives the most attention in the ancient Vedic text, and is frequently referred to as the *eka deva*, or "one god." According to the *Rig-Veda* (6.7), creation began once Indra slew Vritra, the serpent demon, who had locked up the waters necessary for human existence in mountain caves. With the waters now released, he then placed the sun in the sky thus establishing the cosmic order (*rta*) under the god Varuna.

Varuna, then, sits in the palace of heaven and oversees the world below. As the guardian of the moral order, both earthly and cosmic, Varuna punishes the sinner with disease, or for all time by condemning them to the House of Clay following death. Aryans who practiced right deeds, or performed the proper ritual would forever celebrate happiness after death. Varuna is aided in his efforts by many spies who fly through the cosmos at his command.

Less important than Indra, but still held in high regard among the numerous deities of the Aryan religion, was Agni, the fire god. Agni descends from the darkened clouds as lightning, shines on the world as the sun, and manifests in the flame of the sacrifice. Through the sacrificial offering, Agni served as the intermediary between the gods and man, and the correct performance of this important ritual could beneficially reward the devotee. Rituals based on the fire sacrifice could be as personal as dumping clarified butter in the family hearth, to the production of soma juice. As part of the sacrificial ritual, parts of the soma plant were pressed between stones, mixed with milk, and filtered through a sheepskin. An hallucinogen, soma consumed during sacrifices supposedly produced a sense of superhuman strength and visions of the gods. Soma would later become the moon god.

The cosmic order of the Aryan universe remained fairly simple. The heavens served as the residence of the major gods and the souls of the righteous. The region between heaven and earth was called the *antariksa*. This region, where the birds flew and the clouds crossed the sky, was also home to the demigods. Below the earth, in the darkness of the House of Clay, dwelled the spirits of the unrighteousness and the demons that sought to disrupt *rta*. The concept of birth and rebirth had not yet become part of the Indian cosmology that would later be indicative of all Indian religion.

Religion during the Vedic Age revolved around the sacrifice. Within the home, the patriarch of the family daily sacrificed at the domestic hearth while the brahmans performed great rituals slaughtering numerous animals to the gods. In each case, the idea was to communicate with the gods who would descend from the heavens granting the devotees health, happiness, and success. Over time, these rituals became so complex that the brahmans, who knew the correct ritual, became indispensable.

Between 800 and 400 BC, significant changes began to occur in the lives of religious peoples in all of the civilized parts of the world. Independent thinkers, discontented with the traditional explanations of the cosmic order, and specifically man's place within that cosmos, began to develop new, more simple and rational, doctrines. Scholars frequently refer to this period as the Axial Age. There is, however, no solid explanation why such dramatic religious changes would occur throughout the world during the same period.

Prominent among the rising sages were the Greek philosophers led by Socrates. In Persia, Zarathustra extracted the elements of the supernatural from religion and created a new faith, Zoroastrianism. In China, Confucius devoted himself to teaching moral persuasion and good government, which would become the mainstay of Chinese thought. The Hebrew prophets formulated a monotheistic religious tradition notably different from the polytheistic religions of Greece, China, Mesopotamia, and India. While all of this was happening in the rest of the world, *kshatriya* ascetics, throughout India, began to challenge the proliferation of brahmin ritual that personified the Aryan religion of the Vedic Age.

During this time, the Vedas were still held in high regard, but this new generation of seekers sought a more enlightened meaning to life. This period is commonly referred to as the Vedantic Age. The collection of teachings generated by the ascetics who meditated on the mysteries of human existence became known as the *Upanishads*, and the seekers who produced the writings were called Upanishads, which literally means "sitting near" the gurus. Over a hundred *Upanishads* have survived, but only a dozen, or so, are considered authentic. To lend credibility to the teachings, they were invariably compiled as appendages to the Vedas. Vedanta, then, means the "end of the Vedas." In this respect, the Vedas are considered the foundation of the faith while the *Upanishads* are considered the vehicle whereby the devotee may attain enlightenment as to the nature of god and man's role in the cosmos.

Scholars continue to debate over the beginning of Hinduism. Some insists that this tradition began with the Indus civilization and its proto-Shiva personified by the horned god. Others point to the development of the Aryan religion of the Vedic Age as the genesis of the Hindu tradition. Still others point to the Vedantic Age, with the development of *karma* (deed), and the doctrine of *samsara* or the transmigration of birth and rebirth, as the fundamental beginning. Unfortunately, unlike many other religions, Hinduism can not be attributed to the teachings of any single individual. This sort of ambiguity naturally lends itself to debate and speculation.

Although we are unable to accurately date the beginning of Hinduism, we can point to the Vedantic Age as the period in Indian history where the Hindu religious tradition began to solidify. The principles of *karma* and *samsara* directly appealed to a populace caught in the stranglehold of the rigidity of the caste system. In this respect, one's deeds in the present life would directly effect their future as the soul passes form life to life.

Interestingly, the *Upanishads*, nor the thinkers reponsible for the new orthodoxy of the Hindu religion, ever directly challenged the Vedic beliefs, the existing gods, or the practice of sacrifice. Instead, a quiet transformation gradually occurred that formulated a new system of thought that became the cornerstone of Hinduism. Increasingly, the common people directed their faith toward lesser deities that filled their specific needs. Rising to the top of the nonexistent hierarchy of the gods, the religious practices, although still based in the Vedic scripture, decidedly shifted from Indra and Varuna to the two current sects of Hinduism which worship Vishnu and Shiva.

During the Axial Age, enlightened thinkers, throughout the known world, were developing new explanations of existence, and man's place within the order of the universe. In India, the Upanishads redefined the Aryan religious tradition. Led by ksatriya ascetics, this new development rebelled against the ritual superiority of the brahman class proliferated during the

Vedic period. This movement gradually led to an integral transformation of Hindu thought. But, while these new thinkers quietly transmuted the Aryan belief system, two other luminaries, not only challenged the ritualism of the former tradition, but openly rejected the rigidity of class distinction, forming new religions.

Similar to the seekers, who reformed Hinduistic thought, the individuals responsible for the growth of these new religions came from the *ksatryia* caste that sought a release from the brahman's domination of ritual. Also significant, in this quest for change, were the members of the *vaishya* caste. With the collapse of tribalism, India experienced great material and economic growth from which this class, which included an increasing number of merchants, craftsmen, and professional, benefited. Many of the *vaishya*, therefore, resented the privileges afforded the upper two castes, which invariably prepared them for religious ferment.

Most prominent of the two individuals seeking answers to the orthodox Vedism, and the injustice of the caste system was Siddhartha Gautama(c. 563 BC-483 BC) who founded the religion known as Buddhism. Although this tradition significantly diminished in the land of its birth, it remained a powerful force in the rest of the world. Central to Buddhist thought are the Four Noble Truths: that all life is suffering (*dukkha*); the cause of suffering is desire; escape from *dukkha* can be attained by ending desire; the path to the cessation of desire can be achieved through the Noble Eight-Fold Path comprised by right views, motives, speech, conduct, livelihood, effort, thought and meditation. Although Buddhism became more important because of its spread outside of India, Jainism, at least within the confines of the subcontinent, gathered equal support. Western scholars frequently list Vardhamana Mahavira (c. 540 BC- 468 BC), as the founder of Jainism. According to Jain legend, however, Mahavira was the last in line of twenty-four *Tirthankaras*, or those who had successfully crossed the river of suffering and attained enlightenment.

Like Siddhartha Gautama, Mahavira came from the *ksatriya* caste, and eventually abandoned his family and earthly possessions to become a wandering ascetic in search of spiritual enlightenment. After an extended period of meditation, Mahavira attained full enlightenment and became a *kevalin* (completed soul), and a jina (conqueror). Mahavira continued his teachings for a number of years accompanied by a band of naked monks. Purportedly he died at the age of seventy-two as a result of starvation.

The codification of Jain religious doctrines did not occur until nearly two hundred years after Mahavira's death, but contained many of his teachings. According to Mahavira, all living things are divided into five categories and are delineated by the number of senses they posses. The highest class, which have five senses include men, gods, and animals with higher intelligence. The second class, with four senses (touch, smell, taste, and sight), include most larger insects. The third classification, supposedly devoid of sight, contains smaller insects such as fleas and ants. Included in the second group, with only touch and taste, are worms, some shellfish, and leeches. The final class of one sensed creatures, not only includes plants, but such inanimate objects such as minerals, fire, and water. In this respect, then, everything in nature contains *karmic* matter, and *karma* is the cause of bondage. Thusly, all Jains are instructed to respect all things unconditionally, and to practice *ahimsa*, or nonviolence, towards all things. Salvation, or enlightenment, according to Jain principles, can only be attained by freeing one's soul from karmic matter to reach a level of purity.

VEDAS AND UPANISHADS

Although they did use some writing with pictographic symbols at Mohenjo-daro, they were not extensive nor alphabctic nor have they been deciphered yet, and the Indo-European Sanskrit which did develop in India is probably quite different. Nevertheless the Harappan civilization of the Indus Valley in what is now Pakistan did borrow many ideas from Mesopotamia and is considered the third civilization to develop. Two seals of the Mohenjo-daro type were discovered at Elam and Mesopotamia, and a cuneiform inscription was unearthed at Mohenjo-daro.

The pastoral villages that spread out east of Elam through Iran and Baluchistan prepared the way for the cities that were to develop around the Indus River, particularly at Harappa and Mohenjo-daro. By about 3000 BC they were building mud-brick houses; burials in the houses included funereal objects; and pottery had fine designs and the potters' marks. After 2500 BC farmers moved out into the alluvial plain of the Indus River valley and achieved full-sized villages using copper and bronze pins, knives, and axes; figurines of women and cattle indicate probable religious attitudes.

The urban phase began about 2300 BC and lasted for about six hundred years with elaborate cities like Mohenjo-daro (called locally Mound of the Dead), which was excavated in the 1920s. This city and others not yet excavated had about 40,000 inhabitants congregated in well built houses with private showers and toilets that drained into municipal sewer lines. Suffering from occasional flooding by the Indus, Mohenjo-daro was rebuilt seven times. The largest structures were the elevated granary and the great bath or swimming pool which was 12 by 7 meters. Around the pool were dressing rooms and private baths.

The people of the Harappan culture did not seem to be very warlike, although they hunted wild game and domesticated cattle, sheep, and goats. Wheat and barley were the main food supplemented by peas, sesame, and other vegetables and fruits, beef, mutton, pork, eggs, fish, and milk. Compared to other ancient civilizations, the houses were of nearly equal size, indicating a more egalitarian social structure. The potter's wheel and carts were used; children played with miniature toy carts. Cotton, perhaps first used here, and wool were made into clothing. A bronze figurine was found of an expressive dancing girl with her hand on her hip, naked except for jewelry. The numerous figurines of the Mother Goddess indicate a likely source for what later became the Shakti worship of the feminine power in India. A male god in a yoga posture, depicted with three faces and two horns, has been identified with Shiva, another important figure in later Indian religion. Phallic lingams, also associated with Shiva, have been found. A civilization that endured dangerous flooding for six hundred years very likely had a strong religion to help hold people together.

With no written histories the decline of this civilization is subject to much speculation. The traditional theory is that the Aryans invaded from the northwest. Although this is likely, the decline of Harappan culture was quite gradual and indicates problems beyond foreign conquest. One theory is deforestation, because of all the wood needed for the kilns to make the bricks used to keep out the flood waters that gradually brought about salinization of the soil, as it had to Sumer over centuries, so that the Harappan culture had greatly declined by 1900 BC.

However, a more comprehensive explanation comes from an analysis of the consequences of the extensive herds of cattle that indicate overgrazing and a general degradation of the ecosystem, including salinization of water supplies. This led farmers to move on to greener pastures, leaving behind abandoned villages and depopulated cities. Even though fodder was probably grown to feed the cattle, this would not have been enough; and the overgrazing by the bullocks and milk cows could have caused the surrounding land to deteriorate. By 1500 BC the Harappan civilization had faded away into a culture that was spreading throughout India with new ideas from the west.

The traditional theory, well documented by the ancient hymns of the *Vedas,* is that a people calling themselves Aryans conquered the native peoples of India and destroyed their forts. Because of language similarities these Aryans are associated particularly with the Iranians and even further back with the origins of the Indo-European language group. The general consensus seems to be that this culture must have begun somewhere in the Russian steppes and Central Asia about 2000 BC, though some have put their origin in Lithuania because of similarity to that language. The branch of these speakers, who came to India under the name Aryans, which means "noble ones," is the Indo-Iranian group. In fact "Iran" derives from the Persian cognate of the word for Aryan. Other branches spread into Greece and western Asia as Hittites, Kassites, and Mitanni.

A rock inscription found at Boghaz Koi dated about 1400 BC, commemorating a treaty between the Mitanni and Hittites, invokes the Aryan gods Indra, Varuna, Mitra, and the twins Nasatya (Asvins).

The ancient writings of the Persian *Avesta* and the Hindu *Vedas* share many gods and beliefs. Eventually they must have split, causing later authors to demonize the divinities of their adversaries. In early Hindu writings the *asuras* were respected gods, but later they became the demons most hated, while Ahura Mazda became the chief god of the Zoroastrians. (Persian often uses an h where Sanskrit uses an s, such as *haoma* for *soma*.) On the other hand the Hindu term for divinities, devas, was used by Zoroastrians to describe the devils from which even our English word is derived. Some scholars have concluded that the ancient Hindus did not want to admit that they came from Iran, and therefore the origin of the Aryans is never mentioned in the ancient texts, although they frankly boast of their conquest over the indigenous Dasas or Dasyus in India.

The word *Veda* means knowledge, and the *Vedas* are considered the most sacred scripture of Hinduism referred to as *sruti*, meaning what was heard by or revealed to the *rishis* or seers. The most holy hymns and mantras put together into four collections called the *Rig*, *Sama*, *Yajur*, and *Atharva Vedas* are difficult to date, because they were passed on orally for about a thousand years before they were written down. More recent categories of *Vedas* include the *Brahmanas* or manuals for ritual and prayer, the *Aranyakas* or forest texts for religious hermits, and the *Upanishads* or mystical discourses.

RIG VEDA

The hymns of the *Rig Veda* are considered the oldest and most important of the *Vedas*, having been composed between 1500 BC and the time of the great Bharata war about 900 BC. More than a thousand hymns are organized into ten mandalas or circles of which the second through the seventh are the oldest and the tenth is the most recent. The Hindu tradition is that even the *Vedas* were gradually reduced from much more extensive and ancient divine revelations but were perverted in the recent dark age of *Kaliyuga*. As the only writings from this ancient period of India, they are considered the best source of knowledge we have; but the ethical doctrines seem to have improved from the ancient hymns to the mystical *Upanishads*.

Essentially the *Rig Veda* is dominated by hymns praising the Aryan gods for giving them victories and wealth plundered from the local Dasas through warfare. The Aryans apparently used their advances in weaponry and skill in fighting to conquer the agricultural and tribal peoples of the fading Harappan culture. Numerous hymns refer to the use of horses and chariots with spokes which must have given their warriors a tremendous advantage. Spears, bows, arrows, and iron weapons are also mentioned. As a nomadic and pastoral culture glorifying war, they established a new social structure of patriarchal families dominated by warriors and, eventually with the power of the *Vedas* themselves, by priests also.

The *Rig Veda* does mention assemblies, but these were probably of the warrior elite, which may have had some controlling influence on the kings and the tribal priest called a *purohita*. The gods worshiped resemble the Indo-European gods and were headed by the powerful Indra, who is often credited with destroying ninety forts. Also popular was Agni, the fire-god considered a messenger of the gods. Varuna and Mitra, the gods of the night and day sky, have been identified with the Greek Uranos and the Persian Mithras respectively. Dyaus, who is not mentioned nearly as often, has been correlated with the Greek Zeus. Surya the sun-god is referred to as the eye of Varuna and the son of Dyaus and rides through the sky on his chariot led by his twin sons, the Asvins who represent his rays; Ushas the dawn is his wife or daughter. Maruts are storm-gods shaped by Rudra, who may have been one of the few indigenous deities adopted by the Aryans. Like the Iranian *Avesta*, the *Rig Veda* refers to the thirty-three gods.

Generally the hymns of the *Rig Veda* praise the gods and ask them for worldly benefits such as wealth, health, long life, protection, and victory over the Dasa peoples.

He, self-reliant, mighty and triumphant, brought low
the dear head of the wicked Dasas.

Indra the Vritra-slayer, Fort-destroyer, scattered the Dasa hosts who dwelt in darkness.

For men hath he created earth and waters, and ever helped the prayer of him who worships.

To him in might the Gods have ever yielded, to Indra in the tumult of battle.

When in his arms they laid the bolt, he slaughtered the Dasyus and cast down their forts of iron.

They call upon Brihaspati or Brahmanaspati, who has been related to a Hittite thunder-god, to avenge the sinner and protect them from the deceitful and wicked man. The Aryans did have a concept of eternal law called *rita*, which the immortal Agni in serving the gods is said to never break (*Rig Veda* III:3:1).

In *Rig Veda* III:34:9 Indra killed the Dasyus and "gave protection to the Aryan color." Not only did the Aryans shamelessly pray for booty in war, but they based their militarily won supremacy on the lightness of their skin color compared to the dark colors of the native Dasyus. They arrogantly proclaimed, "Let those who have no weapons suffer sorrow." (*Rig Veda* IV:5:14.)

Renowned is he when conquering and when slaying:

'tis he who wins cattle in the combat.

When Indra hardens his indignation all that is fixed and all that moves fear him.

Indra has won all kine, all gold, all horses, -

Maghavan, he who breaks forts in pieces;

Indra is praised for killing thousands of the abject tribes of Dasas with his arrow and taking great vengeance with "murdering weapons." (*Rig Veda* IV:28:3-4) One hymn mentions sending thirty thousand Dasas "to slumber" and another hymn sixty thousand slain. A hymn dedicated to the weapons of war (*Rig Veda* VI:75) refers to a warrior "armed with mail," using a bow to win cattle and subdue all regions, "upstanding in the car the skillful charioteer guides his strong horses on whithersoe'er he will." The arrows had iron mouths and shafts "with venom smeared" that "not one be left alive." Hymn VII:83 begins, "Looking to you and your alliance, O ye men, armed with broad axes they went forward, fain for spoil. Ye smote and slew his Dasa and his Aryan enemies."

Only occasionally did the authors of these hymns look to their own sins.

Free us from sins committed by our fathers, from those wherein we have ourselves offended.

O king, loose, like a thief who feeds the cattle, as from the cord a calf, set free Vasishtha.

Not our own will betrayed us, but seduction, thoughtlessness, Varuna! wine, dice or anger.

The old is near to lead astray the younger: even sleep removes not all evil-doing.

A hymn to the frogs compares the repetitions of the priests around the soma bowl to the croaking of the frogs around a pond after the rains come. (*Rig Veda* VII:103)

The basic belief of the prayers and sacrifices is that they will help them to gain their desires and overcome their enemies, as in *Rig Veda* VIII:31:15: "The man who, sacrificing, strives to win the heart of deities will conquer those who worship not." Some awareness of a higher law seems to be dawning in the eighth book in hymn 75: "The holy law hath quelled even mighty men of war. Break ye not off our friendship, come and set me free." However, the enemies are now identified with the Asuras and still are intimidated by greater weapons: "Weaponless are the Asuras, the godless: scatter them with thy wheel, impetuous hero." (*Rig Veda* VIII:85:9)

Many of the hymns refer to the intoxicating soma juice, which is squeezed from the mysterious soma plant and drank. All of the hymns of the ninth book of the *Rig Veda* are dedicated to the purifying soma, which is even credited with making them feel immortal, probably because of its psychedelic influence. The first hymn in this book refers to the "iron-fashioned home" of the Aryans.

In the first book of the *Rig Veda* the worshipers recognize Agni as the guard of eternal law (I:1:8) and Mitra and Varuna as lovers and cherishers of law who gained their mighty power through law (I:2:8). In the 24th hymn they pray to Varuna, the wise Asura, to loosen the bonds of their sins. However, the prayers for riches continue, and Indra is thanked for winning wealth in horses, cattle, and gold by his chariot. Agni helps to slay the many in war by the hands of the few, "preserving our wealthy patrons with thy succors, and ourselves." (*Rig Veda* I:31:6, 42) Indra helped win the Aryan victory:

> *He, much invoked, hath slain Dasyus and Simyus, after his wont, and laid them low with arrows.*
>
> *The mighty thunderer with his fair-complexioned friends won the land, the sunlight, and the waters.*

Control of the waters was essential for agricultural wealth. Indra is praised for crushing the godless races and breaking down their forts. (*Rig Veda* I:174)

In the tenth and last book of the *Rig Veda* some new themes are explored, but the Dasyus are still condemned for being "riteless, void of sense, inhuman, keeping alien laws," and Indra still urges the heroes to slay the enemies; his "hand is prompt to rend and burn, O hero thunder-armed: as thou with thy companions didst destroy the whole of Sushna's brood." (*Rig Veda* X:22)

One unusual hymn is on the subject of gambling with dice. The speaker regrets alienating his wife, wandering homeless in constant fear and debt, envying others' well-ordered homes. He finally warns the listener not to play with dice but recommends cultivating his land. (*Rig Veda* X:34) Hymn 50 of this most recent last book urges Indra to win riches with valor "in the war for water on their fields." Now the prayer is that "we Gods may quell our Asura foemen." (*Rig Veda* X:53:4) A wedding ceremony is indicated in a hymn of Surya's bridal, the daughter of the sun. (*Rig Veda* X:85)

The first indication of the caste system is outlined in the hymn to Purusha, the embodied human spirit, who is one-fourth creature and three-fourths eternal life in heaven.

> *The Brahmin was his mouth, of both his arms was the Rajanya made.*

His thighs became the Vaisya, from his feet the Sudra was produced.

The Brahmin caste was to be the priests and teachers; the Rajanya represents the king, head of the warrior or Kshatriya caste; Vaishyas are the merchants, craftsmen, and farmers; and the Sudras are the workers. In hymn 109 the *brahmachari* or student is mentioned as engaged in duty as a member of God's own body.

The hymn to liberality is a breath of fresh air:

The riches of the liberal never waste away, while he who will not give finds none to comfort him.

The man with food in store who, when the needy comes in miserable case begging for bread to eat,

Hardens his heart against him - even when of old he did him service - find not one to comfort him.

Yet later we realize that the priests are asking for liberality to support their own services, for the "plowing makes the food that feeds us," and thus a speaking (or paid) Brahmin is better than a silent one.

The power of speech is honored in two hymns.

Where, like men cleansing corn-flour in a cribble, the wise in spirit have created language,

Friends see and recognize the marks of friendship: their speech retains the blessed sign imprinted.

In hymn 125 of the tenth mandala Vak or speech claims to have penetrated earth and heaven, holding together all existence.

A philosophical hymn of creation is found in *Rig Veda* X:129. Beginning from non-being when nothing existed, not even water nor death, that One breathless breathed by itself. At first this All was concealed by darkness and formless chaos, but by heat *(tapas)* that One came into existence. Thus arose desire, the primal seed and germ of Spirit. Sages searching in their hearts discovered kinship with the non-existent. A ray of light extended across the darkness, but what was known above or below? Creative fertility was there with energy and action, but who really knows where this creation came from? For the gods came after the world's creation. Who could know the source of this creation and how it was produced? The one seeing it in the highest heaven only knows, or maybe it does not.

SAMA VEDA

The *Sama Veda* contains the melodies or music for the chants used from the *Rig Veda* for the sacrifices; almost all of its written verses are traceable to the *Rig Veda*, mostly the eighth and ninth books and most to Indra, Agni, or Soma. These are considered the origin of Indian music and probably stimulated great artistry to make the sacrifices worthwhile to their patrons who supported the priests. The *Sama Veda* helped to train the musicians and functioned as a hymnal for the religious rites.

The animal sacrifices did not use the *Sama* chants, but they were used extensively in agricultural rites and in the soma rituals for which the plant with inebriating and hallucinogenic qualities was imported from the mountains to the heartland of India. By this time the priests were specializing in different parts of the sacrifices as professional musicians and singers increased. The singing was like the strophe, antistrophe, and epode of the Greek chorus and used the seven tones of the European scale. By the tenth century BC the Aryans had invaded most of northern India, and once again trade resumed with Babylon and others in the near east. As the sacrifices became more complex, the priestly class used them to enhance their role in the society. Many considered this musical portion the most important of the *Vedas*.

YAJUR VEDA

Though also following many of the hymns of the *Rig Veda*, the *Yajur Veda* deviates more from the original text in its collection of the ritual formulas for the priests to use in the sacrifices, which is what *yaja* means. It explains how to construct the altars for new and full-moon sacrifices and other ceremonies. The *Yajur Veda* has two collections or *samhitas* called White and Black, the latter being more obscure in its meanings. By this time (10th century BC and after) the Aryan conquest has proceeded from the northwest and Punjab to cover northern India, especially the Ganges valley. The caste system was in place, and as the warriors settled down to ruling over an agricultural society, the role of the priests and their ceremonies gained influence and justified the Aryan ways to the native workers, who labored for the farmers, merchants, craftsmen, who in turn were governed by their kings and priests. Land and wealth were accumulated in the hands of a few ruling families, and with food scarce the indigenous people were enslaved or had to sell their labor cheap to the ruling classes.

By instituting more elaborate sacrifices for their wealthy patrons, the priests could grow both in numbers and wealth as well. The famous horse sacrifice was not celebrated often but was used by a king to show his lordship over potential adversaries, who were invited to acknowledge this overlordship in the ritual. The parts of the horse symbolize different aspects of the universe so that tremendous power is invoked. The complicated and obscure rituals were presided over by the priests - the three symbols of the lotus leaf, the frog (for rain), and the golden man (for the sun) representing the Aryan dominance over the land and waters of India and the natural powers that sustain agriculture.

The soma sacrifice was the most important and could last up to twelve years. Since the soma plant was imported from distant mountains, it had to be purchased. A ritual drama re-enacted this business and aggressive Aryan history by showing the buyer snatching back the calf, which was paid for the soma plant, after the transaction occurs. The soma plant was then placed in a cart and welcomed as an honored guest and king at the sacrifice. Animals were slain and cut up in the rites before their meat was eaten. After various offerings and other ceremonies the soma juice is poured and toasted to different gods, and finally the text lists the sacrificial fees, usually goats, cows, gold, clothes, and food.

Coronation ceremonies supported the inauguration of kings. The priests tried to keep themselves above the warrior caste though by praising soma as king of the Brahmins. Waters were drawn from various rivers to sprinkle on the king and indicate the area of his kingdom, and he strode in each direction to signify his sovereignty. The king was anointed by the royal priest, giving some water to his son, the designated prince, and ritually enacting a raid against a kinsman's cattle, once again affirming their history of conquest. The booty was taken and divided into three parts for the priest, those who drank, and the original owner. A ritual dice game was played, which the king was allowed to win. The king then rode out in his chariot and was publicly worshiped as a divine ruler.

Agricultural rites were common and regular, and chariot races were no doubt popular at some of the festivals. The Purusha (person) sacrifice symbolized human sacrifice, which may refer back to the time when a hunting and pastoral people did not allow their enemies to live because of the shortage of food. However, in an agricultural society more labor was needed and could produce surplus food. The Purusha sacrifice recognized 184 professional crafts and guilds.

Finally the highest sacrifice was considered to be the Sarvamedha in which the sacrificer offered all of his possessions as the fee at the end of the ceremony. The last chapter of the *Yajur Veda* is actually the *Isha Upanishad,* expressing the mystical view that the supreme spirit pervades everything.

This society was highly patriarchal, and the status of women declined, especially as men often married non-Aryan women. Women did not attend public assemblies and could not inherit property on their own. Polyandry was discouraged, but polygamy, adultery, and prostitution were generally accepted except during certain rituals. A sacrificer was not allowed to seek a prostitute on the first day of the sacrificial fire, nor the wife of another on the second day, nor his own wife on the third day.

The priests placed themselves at the top of the caste system as they supervised a religion most of the people could not understand without them. After the *Atharva Veda* was accepted, each sacrifice required at least four priests, one on each side of the fire using the *Rig*, *Sama*, *Yajur*, and *Atharva Vedas*, plus their assistants. After the wars of conquest were completed and the warrior caste settled down to rule, the priests were needed to sustain social stability. Yet in these times the caste system was much more flexible, as it is indicated that one should not ask about the caste of a learned man. The Brahmins, as the priest caste was called, had three obligations or debts to pay back in life: they paid back the seers by studying the *Vedas*, the gods by offering sacrifices, and their fathers by raising a family.

Like their European ancestors, the Aryan warriors considered themselves above laboring for food and so organized society that food would be provided for them. One ethical duty later found in the epics was that of taking care of refugees, probably because as marauding raiders they had often been refugees themselves. The priests assured their livelihood by making sure that penance through religious ritual was a prime social value.

ATHARVA VEDA

The latest and fourth *Veda* is in a different category. For a long time many referred to only three *Vedas*, by which complete ceremonies could be conducted with the *Rig hotr* reciting, the *Sama udgatri* singing, and the *Yajur adhvaryu* performing the ritual. Even later the *Atharvan* Brahmin's part was often performed unaccompanied by the other three priests. Also much of it draws from the customs and beliefs of pre-Aryan or pre-Vedic India. The *Atharva Veda* is much longer than the *Sama* and *Yajur* and only about a sixth of it is from the *Rig Veda*.

The *Atharva Veda* is primarily magical spells and incantations. The line between prayer and magic and between white and black magic is usually drawn by ethical considerations. The *bheshajani* are for healing and cures using herbs to treat fever, leprosy, jaundice, dropsy, and other diseases. The Aryans looked down on doctors and medicine, probably because the natives were more skilled in these than they. Other more positive spells were for successful childbirth, romance, fecundity, virility, etc.

The negative or bewitching spells were called *abhichara* and attempted to cause diseases or harm to enemies; often they were aimed at serpents and demons. The sorcery is ascribed to one of the authors, Angiras, whose name is related to Agni (Latin *ignis)*, the divine messenger and possibly a distant cognate of the Greek word for messenger, angel. Another author, Atharvan, derives from the old Iranian root, *atar*, meaning fire. The third author, Bhrigu, was the name of a tribe which opposed Sudas in the battle of ten kings in the *Rig Veda*, and his name has also been related to a Greek word for fire. The fourth author is Brahmin, the name which was given to the *Atharvan* priest, which eventually became so sacred that it was used as a name not only for the priestly caste but even for God the Creator.

In addition to physicians the Vedic Aryans also held in contempt *Atharvan* astrologers as well as magic, but from this came not only astrology but also the beginning of Ayurvedic medicine. Like most ancient peoples, they also believed that the main cause of disease was evil spirits, possession, or what we would call psychological factors. The magical elements, particularly the *abhicara*, and the subjects of healing, herbs, and cooking, which were mostly in the woman's domain, made the *Atharva Veda* obnoxious to many Vedic priests. However, these rituals were very popular, and the Brahmin priest's share of the fees soon became equal to the other three priests' combined. Eventually this shamanic tradition had to be incorporated into the Vedic religion, especially later when it faced the new challenges of Jainism and Buddhism.

The Brahmin caste became even stronger, and their wealth can be seen by the belief that the cow by right belonged exclusively to them. Taxes were collected probably by the warrior Kshatriya caste from the Vaisya artisans, farmers, and merchants. The Sudra workers were too poor to be taxed, and the Brahmins were exempt. One verse (*Atharva Veda* 3:29:3) describes heaven as "where a tax is not paid by a weak man for a stronger."

Marriage ceremonies are included. Here is a brief example:

I am he; you are she.

I am song; you are verse.

I am heaven; you are earth.

Let us two dwell together here;
let us generate children.

According to the *Atharva Veda* (5:17:8-9), a Brahmin could take a wife from the husband of any other caste simply by seizing her hand. Book 18 contains only funeral verses. There are coronation rites for kings, though the prayer is that the people will choose the king, usually already selected by heredity or the council. Philosophy and abstraction are creeping in, as there are two hymns to the deity of time, and *kama* (love, desire, pleasure) is praised as "the first seed of the mind" that generated heaven. (*Atharva Veda* 19:52)

Let us conclude this section on the *Atharva Veda* with some selections from its beautiful hymn to the Earth as a sample of the more positive expression of the *Vedas*:

High Truth, unyielding Order, Consecration,

Ardor and Prayer and Holy Ritual uphold the Earth, may she, the ruling Mistress of what has been and what will come to be, for us spread wide a limitless domain.

Untrammeled in the midst of men, the Earth, adorned with heights and gentle slopes and plains, bears plants and herbs of various healing powers.

May she spread wide for us, afford us joy!

On whom are ocean, river, and all waters, on whom have sprung up food and plowman's crops, on whom moves all that breathes and stirs abroad -

Earth, may she grant to us the long first draught!

To Earth belong the four directions of space.

On her grows food; on her the plowman toils.

She carries likewise all that breathes and stirs.

Earth, may she grant us cattle and food in plenty!

On whom the men of olden days roamed far, on whom the conquering Gods smote the demons, the home of cattle, horses, and of birds, may Earth vouchsafe to us good fortune and glory!

Bearer of all things, hoard of treasures rare, sustaining mother, Earth the golden-breasted who bears the Sacred Universal Fire, whose spouse is Indra - may she grant us wealth!

Limitless Earth, whom the Gods, never sleeping, protect forever with unflagging care, may she exude for us the well-loved honey, shed upon us her splendor copiously!

Earth, who of yore was Water in the oceans, discerned by the Sages' secret powers, whose immortal heart, enwrapped in Truth, abides aloft in the highest firmament, may she procure for us splendor and power, according to her highest royal state!

On whom the flowing Waters, ever the same, course without cease or failure night and day, may she yield milk, this Earth of many streams, and shed on us her splendor copiously!

May Earth, whose measurements the Asvins marked, over whose breadth the foot of Vishnu strode, whom Indra, Lord of power, freed from foes, stream milk for me, as a mother for her son!

Your hills, O Earth, your snow-clad mountain peaks, your forests, may they show us kindliness!

Brown, black, red, multifarious in hue and solid is this vast Earth, guarded by Indra.

Invincible, unconquered, and unharmed,

I have on her established my abode.

Impart to us those vitalizing forces that come, O Earth, from deep within your body, your central point, your navel, purify us wholly.

The Earth is mother; I am son of Earth.

The Rain-giver is my father; may he shower on us blessings!

The Earth on which they circumscribe the altar, on which a band of workmen prepare the oblation, on which the tall bright sacrificial posts are fixed before the start of the oblation - may Earth, herself increasing, grant us increase!

That man, O Earth, who wills us harm, who fights us, who by his thoughts or deadly arms opposes, deliver him to us, forestalling action.

All creatures, born from you, move round upon you.

You carry all that has two legs, three, or four.

To you, O Earth, belong the five human races, those mortals upon whom the rising sun sheds the immortal splendor of his rays.

May the creatures of earth, united together, let flow for me the honey of speech!

Grant to me this boon, O Earth.

Mother of plants and begetter of all things, firm far-flung Earth, sustained by Heavenly Law, kindly and pleasant is she. May we ever dwell on her bosom, passing to and fro!...

Do not thrust us aside from in front or behind, from above or below! Be gracious, O Earth.

Let us not encounter robbers on our path.

Restrain the deadly weapons!

As wide a vista of you as my eye may scan, O Earth, with the kindly help of Sun, so widely may my sight be never dimmed in all the long parade of years to come!

Whether, when I repose on you, O Earth,

I turn upon my Right *side or my left, or whether, extended flat upon my back,*

I meet your pressure from head to foot, be gentle, Earth! You are the couch of all!

Whatever I dig up of you, O Earth, may you of that have quick replenishment!

O purifying One, may my thrust never reach Right *into your vital points, your heart!*

Your circling seasons, nights succeeding days, your summer, O Earth, your splashing rains, your autumn, your winter and frosty season yielding to spring—may each and all produce for us their milk!...

From your numberless tracks by which mankind may travel, your roads on which move both chariots and wagons your paths which are used by the good and the bad, may we choose a way free from foes and robbers!

May you grant us the blessing of all that is wholesome!

She carries in her lap the foolish and also the wise.

She bears the death of the wicked as well as the good.

She lives in friendly collaboration with the boar, offering herself as sanctuary to the wild pig....

Peaceful and fragrant, gracious to the touch, may Earth, swollen with milk, her breasts overflowing, grant me her blessing together with her milk!

The Maker of the world sought her with oblations when she was shrouded in the depth of the ocean.

A vessel of gladness, long cherished in secret, the earth was revealed to mankind for their joy.

Primeval Mother, disperser of men, you, far-flung Earth, fulfill all our desires.

Whatever you lack, may the Lord of creatures, the First-born of Right, supply to you fully!

May your dwellings, O Earth, free from sickness and wasting, flourish for us! Through a long life, watchful, may we always offer to you our tribute!

O Earth, O Mother, dispose my lot in gracious fashion that I be at ease.

In harmony with all the powers of Heaven set me, O Poet, in grace and good fortune!

Brahmanas

Between about 900 and 700 BC the *Brahmanas* were written in prose as sacerdotal commentaries on the four *Vedas* to guide the practices of the sacrifices and give explanations often mythical and fanciful for these customs. However, their limited focus of justifying the priestly actions in the sacrifices restricted the themes of these first attempts at imaginative literature. Nevertheless they do give us information about the social customs of this period and serve as a transition from the *Vedas* to the *Aranyakas* and the mystical *Upanishads*.

The caste system based on color *(varna)* was now established, though not as rigidly as it became later. The essential difference was between the light-skinned Aryans, who made up the top three castes of the priestly Brahmins, warrior Kshatriyas, and artisan Vaishyas, and the dark-skinned Dasas, who were the servant Sudras. Sudras, like women, could not own property, and only rarely did they rise above service positions. The Vaishyas were the basis of the economic system of trade, crafts, and farming. The Vaishyas were considered inferior by the Brahmins and Kshatriyas, and a female was generally not allowed to marry below her caste, though it was common for a male to do so. Even a Brahmin's daughter was not supposed to marry a Kshatriya.

The rivalry for prestige and power was between the Brahmins and the Kshatriyas or *rajanyas*. Brahmins often held debates on Brahman and other religious issues. Janaka, a *rajanya* gained knowledge and defeated some Brahmins in discussion. So some Brahmins suggested a symposium on Brahman to prove who was superior, but since Brahmins were expected to be superior on these issues, Yajnavalkya prudently replied, "We are Brahmins; he is a *rajanya*. If we win, whom shall we say that we have defeated? But if he defeats us, they will say a *rajanya* has defeated Brahmins; so let us not convene this symposium."

Kings were consecrated by Vedic rites and ruled with the help of the assembly *(sabha)* that met in a hall to administer justice; women were excluded. Ordeals were used, such as making a suspected thief touch a hot ax to see if his hand burned, which might be the origin of the saying, "being caught red-handed." Politics and legislation took place in a larger council *(samiti)*. Taxes were collected to support these institutions and the army. Each village was administered by a Gramani, a Vaisya who functioned like a mayor with civil rather than military authority. The Gramani and the royal charioteer *(Suta)* were considered the kingmakers. This latter privileged position was not merely the driver of the king but also his chief advisor and perhaps storyteller as well. The royal priest or *Purohito* was also supposed to advise the king in peace and protect him in war. The season of dew after the monsoons ended was considered the time for "sacking cities," as ambitious kings came into conflict with each other in wars.

In addition to the discussions of sacerdotal matters, the *Brahmanas* do contain some stories meant to explain or rationalize their religious practices. Some of these are quite imaginative, though the usual pattern is for the hero to discover a rite to perform or a chant to intone which miraculously solves whatever problem is pressing to give a happy ending.

Wendy O'Flaherty has translated some stories from the *Jaiminiya Brahmana*, illustrating how they dealt with the fears of death, God, the father, wives, and demonic women; many of these stories are sexually explicit, indicating that these people were not afraid of discussing their sexuality. However, since the usual way of handling these fears was to use a sacrificial ritual, the solutions probably had only limited social and psychological value.

The most famous of these stories, and the best in my opinion, is the tale of Bhrigu's journey in the other world. Bhrigu was the son of Varuna and devoted to learning, and he thought that he was better than the other Brahmins and even better than the gods and his own father. So Varuna decided to teach him something by stopping his life breaths, causing Bhrigu to enter the world beyond, where he saw someone cut another man to pieces and eat him, a second man eating another who was screaming, a third eating a man who was silently screaming, another world where two women were guarding a treasure, a fifth where a stream of blood was guarded by a naked black man with a club and a stream of butter provided all the desires of golden men in golden bowls, and a sixth world where flowed five rivers of blue and white lotuses and flowing honey with wonderful music, celestial nymphs dancing and singing, and a fragrant odor.

When Bhrigu returned, his father Varuna explained to him that the first man represented people who in ignorance destroy trees, which in turn eat them; the second are those who cook animals that cry out and in the other world are eaten by them in return; the third are those who ignorantly cook rice and barley, which scream silently and also eat them in return; the two women are Faith and non-Faith; the river of blood represents those who squeeze the blood out of a Brahmin, and the naked black man guarding is Anger; but the true sacrificers are the golden men, who get the river of butter and the paradise of the five rivers.

To me this myth is a clear warning against the harmful actions of deforestation and meat-eating, and even the eating of living vegetables is to be done in silent respect. It shows an intuitive understanding of the principle of karma or the consequences of action as well as the growing importance of the concept of faith in addition to the usual theme of the sacrifice.

The power of the word is increasing, as the sacrifices were glorified and given power even over the Vedic gods. *Japa* or the practice of chanting a *mantram* like *Aum* practiced ascetically with the sacrifices was believed to produce all one's desires. At the same time knowledge was beginning to be valued. In one exchange mind says that speech merely imitates it, but speech emphasizes the importance of expression and communication; however, Prajapati decides that mind is more important even than the word. This new god, Prajapati, is said to have given birth to both the gods and the demons. The ethical principle of truth appears as the gods are described as being truthful and the demons as being false. However, realizing the ways of the world, many complain that the demons grew strong and rich, just as cattle like salty soil; but by performing the sacrifice the gods attained the whole truth and triumph, as, analogically I might add, people will eventually realize that cattle as well as salt ruins the land.

Prajapati not only was the first to sacrifice but was considered the sacrifice itself. He practiced *tapas* to create by the heat of his own effort, and this heat was also related to cosmic fire and light as well as the warmth of the body and breath. Another concept of energy associated with the breath was *prana*; it also was identified with goodness, as the texts imply that as the life force it cannot be impure or bad. Prajapati not only created but entered into things as form and name, giving them order. Eventually Prajapati would be replaced by Brahman, who was identified with truth and would become the Creator God in the trinity that would include Vishnu, a sun-god who becomes the Preserver, and Shiva, who is derived from the indigenous Rudra, the Destroyer. With all the mental activity going on analyzing the rites and their explanation, abstractions were increasing in the religion.

A judgment after death using a scale to weigh good against evil is described in the *Satapatha Brahmana*, an idea which may have been transported from Egypt by merchants. This text recommends that the one who knows this will balance one's deeds in this world so that in the next the good deeds will rise, not the evil ones. Belief in repeated lives through reincarnation is indicated in several passages in the *Brahmanas*. A beef-eater is punished by being born into a strange and sinful creature. As knowledge rivaled the value of ritual, this new problem of how to escape from an endless cycle of rebirth presented itself.

Aranyakas

The larger body of Vedic literature is divided into two parts with the four *Rig, Sama, Yajur*, and *Atharva Samhitas* and their *Brahmanas* making up the Karmakanda on the work of the sacrifices and the *Aranyakas* and the *Upanishads* the section on knowledge called the Jnanakanda. The *Aranyakas* and the *Upanishads* were tacked on to the end of *Brahmanas*, and the only three *Aranyakas* extant share the names of the *Brahmanas* they followed and the *Upanishads* they preceded: *Aitareya, Kausitaki*, and the *Taittiriya*; the first two are associated with the *Rig Veda*, the last with the *Yajur Veda*.

The *Aranyakas* are called the forest texts, because ascetics retreated into the forest to study the spiritual doctrines with their students, leading to less emphasis on the sacrificial rites that were still performed in the towns. They were transitional between the *Brahmanas* and the *Upanishads* in that they still discuss rites and have magical content, dull lists of formulas and some hymns from the *Vedas* as well as the early speculations and intellectual discussions that flowered in the *Upanishads*. The sages who took in students in their forest hermitages were not as wealthy as the Brahmins in the towns who served royalty and other wealthy patrons.

The *Taittiriya Aranyaka* tells how when the Vataramsa sages were first approached by other sages, they retreated; but when the sages came back with faith and *tapas* (ardor), they instructed them how to expiate the sin of abortion. Prayers were offered for pregnant women whether they were married or not, even if the father was unknown because of promiscuity. Yet the double standard against women for unchastity was in effect, unless a student seduced the teacher's wife. Truth was the highest value; through truth the right to heaven was retained. Debtors were in fear of punishment in hell, probably because the social punishments in this world were severe—torture and perhaps even death.

The emphasis now was on knowledge, even on wisdom, as they prayed for intelligence. The concept of *prana* as the life energy of the breath is exalted as that which establishes the entire soul. *Prana* is found in trees, animals, and people in ascending order. Human immortality is identified with the soul *(atman)*, not the body. Hell is still feared, but by practicing austerity *(tapas)* to gain knowledge individuals hope to be born into a better world after death or be liberated from rebirth. Non-attachment *(vairagya)* also purifies the body and overcomes death. The essence of the Vedic person was considered Brahman, and the knower or inner person was known as the soul *(atman)*. The guardians of the spiritual treasures of the community were called Brahmavadins (those who discuss Brahman). A son approached his father and asked what was supreme. The father replied, "Truth, *tapas*, self-control, charity, *dharma* (duty), and progeny."

EARLY UPANISHADS

The term *Upanishad* means literally "those who sit near" and implies listening closely to the secret doctrines of a spiritual teacher. Although there are over two hundred *Upanishads*, only fifteen are mentioned by the philosophic commentator Shankara (788-820 CE). These fifteen and the *Maitri* are considered Vedic and the principal *Upanishads*; the rest were written later and are related to the Puranic worship of Shiva, Shakti, and Vishnu. The oldest and longest of the *Upanishads* are the *Brihad-Aranyaka* and the *Chandogya* from about the seventh century BC.

The *Brihad-Aranyaka* has three *Aranyaka* chapters followed by six *Upanishad* chapters. The first chapter of the *Brihad-Aranyaka* Upanishad describes the world as represented by the horse-sacrifice. The primordial battle between the gods and the devils accounts for the evil found in the senses, mind, and speech, but by striking off the evil the divinities were carried beyond death. The priest chants for profound aspiration, one of the most famous verses from the *Upanishads*:

From the unreal lead me to the real!

From darkness lead me to light!

From death lead me to immortality!

The primary message of the *Upanishads* is that this can be done by meditating with the awareness that one's soul *(atman)* is one with all things. Thus whoever knows that one is Brahman (God) becomes this all; even the gods cannot prevent this, since that one becomes their soul *(atman)*. Therefore whoever worships another divinity, thinking it is other than oneself, does not know.

Out of God *(Brahman)* came the Brahmin caste of priests and teachers and the Kshatriyas to rule, development through the Vaishyas and the Sudras. However, a principle was created as justice *(dharma)*, than which nothing is higher, so that a weak person may control one stronger, as if by a king. They say that those who speak the truth speak justice and vice versa, because they are the same. By meditating on the soul *(atman)* alone, one does not perish and can create whatever one wants. Whatever suffering occurs remains with the creatures; only the good goes to the soul, because evil does not go to the gods. The soul is identified with the real, the immortal, and the life-breath *(prana)*, which is veiled by name and form (individuality). By restraining the senses and the mind, one may rest in the space within the heart and become a great Brahmin and like a king may move around within one's body as one pleases. The world of name and form is real, but the soul is the truth or reality of the real. Immortality cannot be obtained through wealth, and all persons and things in the world are dear not for love of them (husband, wife, sons, wealth, gods, etc.); but for the love of the soul, all these are dear. The soul is the overlord of all things, as the spokes of the wheel are held together by the hub.

The principle of action *(karma)* is explained as "one becomes good by good action, bad by bad action." How can one get beyond the duality of seeing, smelling, hearing, speaking to, thinking of, and understanding another? Can one see the seer, smell the smeller, hear the hearer, think the thinker, and understand the understander? It is the soul which is in all things; everything else is wretched. By passing beyond hunger and thirst, sorrow and delusion, old age and death, by overcoming desire for sons, wealth, and worlds, let a Brahmin become disgusted with learning and live as a child; disgusted with that, let one become an ascetic until one transcends both the non-ascetic and the ascetic states. Thus is indicated a spiritual path of learning and discipline that ultimately transcends even learning and discipline in the soul, the inner controller, the immortal, the one dwelling in the mind, whom the mind does not know, who controls the mind from within.

The one departing this world without knowing the imperishable is pitiable, but the one knowing it is a Brahmin. The following refrain is repeated often:

That soul is not this, not that.

It is incomprehensible, for it is not comprehended.

It is indestructible, for it is never destroyed.

It is unattached, for it does not attach itself.

It is unfettered; it does not suffer; it is not injured.

The soul is considered intelligent, dear, true, endless, blissful, and stable. As a king prepares a chariot or ship when going on a journey, one should prepare one's soul with the mystic doctrines of the *Upanishads*. The knowledge that is the light in the heart enables one to transcend this world and death while appearing asleep. The evils that are obtained with a body at birth are left behind upon departing at death. One dreams by projecting from oneself, not by sensing actual objects. In sleep the immortal may leave one's nest and go wherever one pleases. In addition to being free from desire the ethical admonition of being without crookedness or sin is also indicated. At death the soul goes out first, then the life, and finally the breaths go out.

The soul is made of everything; as one acts, one becomes. The doer of good becomes good; the doer of evil becomes evil. As is one's desire, such is one's resolve; as is the resolve, such is the action, which one attains for oneself. When one's mind is attached, the inner self goes into the action. Obtaining the consequences of one's actions, whatever one does in this world comes again from the other world to this world of action *(karma)*.

By releasing the desires in one's heart, one may be liberated in immortality, reaching *Brahman* (God). One is the creator of all, one with the world. Whoever knows this becomes immortal, but others go only to sorrow. The knowing is sought through the spiritual practices of repeating the *Vedas*, sacrifices, offerings, penance, and fasting. Eventually one sees everything, as the soul overcomes both the thoughts of having done wrong and having done right. The evil does not burn one; rather one burns the evil. In the soul's being the world-all is known. The student should practice self-restraint, giving, and compassion.

The *Chandogya Upanishad* belongs to the *Sama Veda* and is the last eight chapters of the ten-chapter *Chandogya Brahmana*. The first two chapters of the *Brahmana* discuss sacrifices and other forms of worship. As part of the *Sama Veda*, which is the chants, the *Chandogya Upanishad* emphasizes the importance of chanting the sacred *Aum*. The chanting of *Aum* is associated with the life breath *(prana)*, which is so powerful that when the devils struck it, they fell to pieces. The religious life recommended in the *Chandogya Upanishad* has three parts. The first is sacrifice, study of the

Vedas, and giving alms; the second is austerity; and the third is studying the sacred knowledge while living in the house of a teacher. One liberal giver, who had many rest-houses built and provided with food, said, "Everywhere people will be eating of my food."

The soul in the heart is identified with *Brahman* (God), and it is the same as the light which shines higher than in heaven. Knowing and reverencing the sacrificial fire is believed to repel evil-doing from oneself. To the one who knows the soul, evil action does not adhere, just as water does not adhere to the leaf of the lotus flower. To know the soul as divine is called the "Loveliness-uniter" because all lovely things come to such.

The doctrine of reincarnation is clearly implied in the *Chandogya Upanishad* as it declares that those whose conduct is pleasant here will enter a pleasant womb of a Brahmin, Kshatriya, or Vaisya; but those of stinking conduct will enter a stinking womb of a dog, swine, or outcast. Thus reincarnation is explained as an ethical consequence of one's actions *(karma)*.

At death the voice goes into the mind, the mind into the breath, the breath into heat, and heat into the highest divinity, the finest essence of truth and soul. Speaking to Svetaketu, the teacher explains that a tree may be struck at the root, the middle, or the top, but it will continue to live if pervaded by the living soul. Yet if the life leaves one branch of it, it dries up; and if it leaves the whole of it, the whole dries up. Then the teacher explains how the soul is the essence of life and does not die, concluding with the repeated refrain that his student thus ought to identify with the soul.

Truly, indeed, when the living soul leaves it,
this body dies; the living soul does not die.
That which is the subtle essence
this whole world has for its soul.
That is reality (truth). That is the soul.
That you are, Svetaketu.

Then the teacher placed salt in water and asked his student to taste different parts of the water. Just so is Being hidden in all of reality, but it is not always perceived. Just as the thief burns his hand on the hot ax when tested, the one who did not steal and is true does not burn his hand, so the whole world has that truth in its soul.

Speech is to be valued, because it makes known right and wrong, true and false, good and bad, pleasant and unpleasant. Mind is revered, because it enables one to do sacred works. Will is valued, because heaven and earth and all things were formed by being willed. Thought is important, because it is better not to be thoughtless. Meditation is revered, because one attains greatness by meditating. Understanding is valued, because by it we can understand everything. Strength maintains everything. Food, water, heat, and space each have their values. Finally also memory, hope, and life *(prana)* are to be revered.

Those, who take delight in the soul, have intercourse with it and find pleasure and bliss in it and freedom; but those, who do not, have perishable worlds and no freedom. The seer does not find death nor sickness nor any distress but sees the all and obtains the all entirely. The soul is free of evil, ageless, deathless, sorrowless, hungerless, and thirstless. For those, who go from here having found the soul here, there is freedom in all worlds. No evil can go into the Brahma-world.

The chaste life of the student of sacred knowledge is the essence of austerity, fasting, and the hermit life, for in that way one finds the reality of the soul. The soul must be searched out and understood. The *Chandogya Upanishad* concludes with the advice that one should learn the *Veda* from the family of a teacher while working for the teacher, then study in one's own home producing sons and pupils, concentrate one's senses upon the soul, be harmless toward all living things except in the sacrifices (The religion has not yet purified itself of animal sacrifices.), so that one may attain the Brahma-world and not return here again. The implication is that one may become free of the cycle of reincarnation.

The *Taittiriya* and *Aitareya Upanishads* were associated with *Aranyakas* of the same name. In the *Taittiriya Upanishad* once again *Aum* is emphasized, as is peace of soul. Prayers often end with *Aum* and the chanting of peace *(shanti)* three times. This may be preceded by the noble sentiment, "May we never hate."17 One teacher says truth is first, another austerity, and a third claims that study and teaching of the *Veda* is first, because it includes austerity and discipline.

The highest goal is to know *Brahman*, for that is truth, knowledge, infinite and found hidden in the heart of being and in the highest heaven, where one may abide with the eternal and intelligent Spirit *(Brahman)*. Words turn away from it, and the mind is baffled by the delight of the eternal; the one who knows this shall not fear anything now or hereafter. Creation becomes a thing of bliss, for who could labor to draw in breath or have the strength to breathe it out if there were not this bliss in the heaven of one's heart?

The *Aitareya Upanishad* begins with the one Spirit creating the universe out of its being. As guardians for the worlds, Spirit made the *Purusha* (person). Out of the cosmic egg came speech, breath, eyes and sight, ears and hearing, skin, hair, and herbs; from the navel and outbreath came death, and from the organ of pleasure seed and waters were born.

In the concluding chapter of this short *Upanishad* the author asked who is this Spirit by whom one sees and hears and smells and speaks and knows? The answer is the following:

> *That which is heart, this mind—that is,*
> *consciousness, perception, discernment, intelligence,*
> *wisdom, insight, persistence, thought, thoughtfulness,*
> *impulse, memory, conception, purpose, life, desire, will*
> *are all names of intelligence.*

All things are guided by and based on this intelligence of Spirit *(Brahman)*. Ascending from this world with the intelligent soul, one obtains all desires in the heavenly world, even immortality.

The *Kaushitaki Upanishad* begins by asking if there is an end to the cycle of reincarnation. The teacher answers that one is born again according to one's actions *(karma)*. Ultimately the one who knows Spirit *(Brahman)* transcends even good and evil deeds and all pairs of opposites as a chariot-driver looks down upon two chariot wheels.

A ceremony is described whereby a dying father bequeaths all he has to his son. If he recovers, it is recommended that he live under the lordship of his son or wander as a religious mendicant. This practice of spiritual seeking as a beggar became one of the distinctive characteristics of Indian culture.

A story is told of Pratardana, who by fighting and virility arrives at the beloved home of Indra, who grants him a gift. Pratardana asks Indra to choose for him what would be most beneficial to humanity, but Indra replies that a superior does not choose for an inferior. Pratardana responds that then it is not a gift. After bragging of many violent deeds and saying that anyone who understands him is not injured even after committing the worst crimes such as murdering a parent, Indra identifies himself with the breathing spirit *(prana)* of the intelligent soul *(prajnatman)*. This breathing spirit is the essence of life and thus immortal. It is by intelligence *(prajna)* that one is able to master all of the senses and faculties of the soul. All these faculties are fixed in the intelligence, which is fixed in the breathing spirit, which is in truth the blissful, ageless, immortal soul. One does not become greater by good action nor less by bad action. One's own self *(atman)* causes one to lead up from these worlds by good action or is led downward by bad action. The soul itself *(atman)* is the world-protector and the sovereign of the world. Thus ultimately the soul is responsible for everything it experiences.

It is mentioned in the *Kaushitaki Upanishad* that it is contrary to nature for a Kshatriya to receive a Brahmin as a student. However, the *Upanishads* represent a time when the Kshatriya caste began to compete with Brahmins in spiritual endeavors. Though the Brahmins had control of the formal religion in the villages where the Kshatriyas controlled the government, by tutoring their sons and others in the forest the Kshatriyas developed a less ritualistic and traditional spirituality that is recorded in the mystical *Upanishads*.

Kena, Katha, Isha, and Mundaka

The *Kena Upanishad* consists of an older prose section and some more recent verse with which it begins. The word *Kena* means "by whom" and is the first word in a series of questions asking by whom is the mind projected, by whom does breathing go forth, by whom is speech impelled? What god is behind the eye and ear? The answer to these questions points to a mystical self that is beyond the mind and senses but is that God by which the mind and senses operate.

Those, who think they know it well, know it only slightly. What relates to oneself and the gods needs to be investigated. Beyond thought it is not known by those who think they know it. Beyond understanding it is not known by those who think they understand it, but by those who realize they do not understand it. It is correctly known by an awakening, for the one who knows it finds immortality. It can only be known by the soul. If one does not know it, it is a great loss. The wise see it in all beings and upon leaving this world become immortal.

In the prose section this mystical Spirit *(Brahman)* is shown to transcend the Vedic gods of fire (Agni), wind (Vayu), and even powerful Indra, who being above the other gods at least came nearest to it, realizing that it was Brahman. In summary the *Kena Upanishad* concludes that austerity, restraint, and work are the foundation of the mystical doctrine; the *Vedas* are its limbs, and truth is its home. The one who knows it strikes off evil and becomes established in the most excellent, infinite, heavenly world.

The *Katha Upanishad* utilizes an ancient story from the *Rig Veda* about a father who gives his son Nachiketas to death (Yama) but brings in some of the highest teachings of mystical spirituality, helping us to realize why the *Upanishads* are referred to as the "end of the *Vedas*" in the double sense of completing the Vedic scripture and in explaining the ultimate goals.

When Vajashrava was sacrificing all his possessions, faith entered into Nachiketas, his son, who asked his father three times to whom would he give him. Losing patience with these pestering questions, the father finally said, "I give you to Death (Yama)." Nachiketas knew that he was not the first to go to death, nor would he be the last, and like grain one is born again anyway. When he arrived at the house of Death, Yama was not there and only returned after three days. Because Nachiketas had not received the traditional hospitality for three days, Yama granted him three gifts. His first request was that his father would greet him cheerfully when he returned. The second was that he be taught about the sacrificial fire. These were easily granted.

The third request of Nachiketas was that the mystery of what death is be explained to him, for even the gods have had doubts about this. Death tries to make him ask for something else, such as wealth or long life with many pleasures, but Nachiketas firmly insists on his original request, knowing that these other gifts will soon pass away.

So Death begins by explaining that the good is much better than the pleasant, which Nachiketas has just proved that he understands. He wisely wants knowledge not ignorance, and Death describes how those, who think themselves learned but who are ignorant, run around deluded and are like the blind leading the blind. Those, who think this world is the only one, continually come under the control of Death. Death explains that this knowledge cannot be known by reasoning or thought, but it must be declared by another. I interpret this to mean that it must be learned by direct experience or from one who has had the experience.

Death tells how the truth is hard to see, but one must enter into the hidden, secret place in the depth of the heart. By considering this as God, one through *yoga* (union) wisely leaves joy and sorrow behind. One must transcend what is right and not right, what has been done and will be done. The sacred word *Aum* is declared to be the imperishable Spirit *(Brahman)*. The wise realize that they are not born nor die but are unborn, constant, eternal, primeval; this is not slain when the body is slain.

Smaller than the small, greater than the great, the soul is in the heart of every creature here. The one who is not impulsive sees it and is free of sorrow. Through the grace of the creator one sees the greatness of the soul. While sitting one may travel far; while lying down one may go everywhere. Who else but oneself can know the god of joy and sorrow, who is bodiless among bodies and stable among the unstable?

This soul is not obtained by instruction nor by intellect nor by much learning, but is obtained by the one chosen by this; to such the soul reveals itself. However, it is not revealed to those who have not ceased from bad conduct nor to those who are not peaceful. Those, who drink of justice, enter the secret place in the highest heaven. Thus correct ethics is a requirement, and one must also become peaceful.

Psychology is explained in the *Katha Upanishad* by using the analogy of a chariot. The soul is the lord of the chariot, which is the body. The intuition *(buddhi)* is the chariot-driver, the mind the reins, the senses the horses, and the objects of the senses the paths. Those, who do not understand and whose minds are undisciplined with senses out of control, are like the wild horses of a chariot that never reaches its goals; these go on to reincarnate. The wise reach their goal with Vishnu and are not born again. The hierarchy, starting from the bottom, consists of the objects of sense, the senses, the mind, the intuition, the soul, the unmanifest, and the person *(Purusha).*

Though hidden, the soul may be seen by subtle seers with superior intellect. The intelligent restrain speech with the mind, the mind with the knowing soul, the knowing soul with the intuitive soul, and the intuitive soul with the peaceful soul. Yet the spiritual path is as difficult as crossing on the sharpened edge of a razor. By discerning what has no sound nor touch nor form nor decay nor taste nor beginning nor end, one is liberated from the mouth of death.

A wise person, seeking immortality, looked within and saw the soul. The childish go after outward pleasures and walk into the net of widespread death. The wise do not seek stability among the unstable things here. Knowing the experiencer, the living soul is the lord of what has been and what will be. This is the ancient one born from discipline standing in the secret place. This is the truth that all things are one, but those, who see a difference here, go from death to death like water runs to waste among the hills. The soul goes into embodiment according to its actions and according to its knowledge.

The inner soul is in all things yet outside also; it is the one controller which when perceived gives eternal happiness and peace. Its light is greater than the sun, moon, stars, lightning, and fire which do not shine in the world illuminated by this presence. The metaphor of an upside down tree is used to show that heaven is the true root of all life.

The senses may be controlled by the mind, and the mind by the greater self. Through yoga the senses are held back so that one becomes undistracted even by the stirring of the intuition. Thus is found the origin and the end. When all the desires of the heart are cut like knots, then a mortal becomes immortal. There is a channel from the heart to the crown of the head by which one goes up into immortality, but the other channels go in various directions. One should draw out from one's body the inner soul, like an arrow from a reed, to know the pure, the immortal. The *Katha Upanishad* concludes that with this knowledge learned from Death with the entire rule of yoga, Nachiketas attained Brahman and became free from passion and death, and so may any other who knows this concerning the soul.

Greatly respected, the short *Isha Upanishad* is often put at the beginning of the *Upanishads*. *Isha* means "Lord" and marks the trend toward monotheism in the *Upanishads*. The Lord encloses all that moves in the world. The author recommends that enjoyment be found by renouncing the world and not coveting the possessions of others. The One pervades and transcends everything in the world.

> *Whoever sees all beings in the soul and the soul in all beings does not shrink away from this.*
>
> *In whom all beings have become one with the knowing soul what delusion or sorrow is there for the one who sees unity?*
>
> *It is radiant, incorporeal, invulnerable, without tendons, pure, untouched by evil.*
>
> *Wise, intelligent, encompassing, self-existent, it organizes objects throughout eternity.*

The One transcends ignorance and knowledge, non-becoming and becoming. Those, who know these pairs of opposites, pass over death and win immortality. The *Isha*

Upanishad concludes with a prayer to the sun and to Agni. The *Mundaka Upanishad* declares Brahman the first of the gods, the creator of all and the protector of the world. Connected to the *Atharva Veda* the *Mundaka Upanishad* has Brahman teaching his eldest son Atharvan. Yet the lower knowledge of the four *Vedas* and the six *Vedangas* (phonetics, ritual, grammar, definition, metrics, and astrology) is differentiated from the higher knowledge of the imperishable source of all things. The ceremonial sacrifices are to be observed; but they are now considered "unsafe boats," and fools, who approve them as better, go again to old age and death.

Like the *Katha*, the *Mundaka Upanishad* warns against the ignorance of thinking oneself learned and going around deluded like the blind leading the blind. Those, who work *(karma)* without understanding because of attachment, when their rewards are exhausted, sink down wretched. "Thinking sacrifices and works of merit are most important, the deluded know nothing better." After enjoying the results of their good works, they enter this world again or even a lower one. The *Mundaka Upanishad* recommends a more mystical path:

> *Those who practice discipline and faith in the forest, the peaceful knowers who live on charity, depart without attachment through the door of the sun, to where lives the immortal Spirit, the imperishable soul.*
>
> *Having tested the worlds won by works, let the seeker of God arrive at detachment.*
>
> *What is not made is not attained by what is done.*

To gain this knowledge the seeker is to go with fuel in hand to a teacher who is learned in the scriptures and established in God. Approaching properly, calming the mind and attaining peace, the knowledge of God may be taught in the truth of reality by which one knows the imperishable Spirit.

The formless that is higher than the imperishable and is the source and goal of all beings may be found in the secret of the heart. The reality of immortal life may be known by using the weapons of the *Upanishads* as a bow, placing an arrow on it sharpened by meditation, stretching it with thought directed to that, and knowing the imperishable as the target. *Aum* is the bow; the soul is the arrow; and God is the target. Thus meditating on the soul and finding peace in the heart, the wise perceive the light of blissful immortality. The knot of the heart is loosened, all doubts vanish, and one's works *(karma)* cease when it is seen. Radiant is the light of lights that illuminates the whole world. God truly is this immortal, in front, behind, to the right and left, below and above; God is all this great universe.

By seeing the brilliant creator, the God-source, being a knower, the seer shakes off good and evil, reaching the supreme identity of life that shines in all beings. Enjoying the soul, doing holy works, such is the best knower of God. The soul can be attained by truth, discipline, correct knowledge, and by studying God. Truth conquers and opens the path to the gods by which sages, whose desires are satisfied, ascend to the supreme home. Vast, divine, subtler than the subtle, it shines out far and close by, resting in the secret place seen by those with vision. It is not grasped by sight nor speech nor angels nor austerity nor work but by the grace of wisdom and the mental purity of meditation which sees the indivisible.

Whatever world a person of pure heart holds clearly in mind is obtained. Yet whoever entertains desires, dwelling on them, is born here and there on account of those desires; but for the one whose desire is satisfied, whose soul is perfected, all desires here on earth vanish away. This soul is not attained by instruction nor intellect nor much learning but by the one whom it chooses, who enters into the all itself. Ascetics with natures purified by renunciation enter the God-worlds and transcend death. As rivers flow into the ocean, the liberated knower reaches the divine Spirit. Whoever knows that supreme God becomes God.

Later Upanishads

These *Upanishads* are being discussed in this chapter in their estimated chronological order. The previous group is from about the sixth century BC, and thus some of them are probably contemporary with the life of the Buddha (563-483 BC). This next group is almost certainly after the time of the Buddha, but it is difficult to tell how old they are. The *Prashna Upanishad* is also associated with the *Atharva Veda* and discusses six questions; *Prashna* means question. Six men approached the teacher Pippalada with sacrificial fuel in hands and questions in their minds. Pippalada agreed to answer their questions if they would live with him another year in austerity, chastity, and faith.

The first question is, "From where are all these creatures born?" The answer is that the Creator (Prajapati) wanted them, but two paths are indicated that lead to reincarnation and immortality. The second question is how many angels support and illumine a creature and which is supreme? The answer is space, air, fire, water, earth, speech, mind, sight, and hearing, but the life-breath *(prana)* is supreme. The third question seeks to know the relationship between this life-breath and the soul. The short answer is, "This life is born from the soul *(atman).*"

The fourth question concerns sleep, waking, and dreams. During sleep the mind re-experiences what it has seen and heard, felt and thought and known. When one is overcome by light, the god dreams no longer; then all the elements return to the soul in happiness. The fifth question asks about the result of meditating on the word Aum. When someone meditates on all three letters, then the supreme may be attained. The sixth question asks about the Spirit with sixteen parts. The sixteen parts of the Spirit are life, faith, space, air, light, water, earth, senses, mind, food, virility, discipline, affirmations *(mantra)*, action, world, and naming (individuality). All the parts are like spokes of a wheel, the hub of which is the Spirit.

In the *Shvetashvatara Upanishad* monotheism takes the form of worshipping Rudra (Shiva). The later quality of this *Upanishad* is also indicated by its use of terms from the Samkhya school of philosophy. The person *(Purusha)* is distinguished from nature *(Prakriti)*, which is conceived of as illusion *(maya)*. The method of devotion *(bhakti)* is presented, and the refrain "By knowing God one is released from all fetters" is often repeated. Nevertheless the Upanishadic methods of discipline and meditation are recommended to realize the soul by controlling the mind and thoughts. Breathing techniques are also mentioned as is yoga. The qualities *(gunas)* that come with action *(karma)* and its consequences are to be transcended. Liberation is still found in the unity of God (Brahman) by discrimination *(samkhya)* and union *(yoga)*. By the highest devotion *(bhakti)* for God and the spiritual teacher *(guru)* all this may be manifested to the great soul *(mahatma)*.

The short *Mandukya Upanishad* is associated with the *Atharva Veda* and delineates four levels of consciousness: waking, dreaming, deep sleep, and a fourth mystical state of being one with the soul. These are associated with the three elements of the sacred chant *Aum* (a, u, and m) and the silence at its cessation. Thus this sacred chant may be used to experience the soul itself.

The thirteenth and last of what are considered the principal *Upanishads* is the *Maitri Upanishad*. It begins by recommending meditation upon the soul and life *(prana)*. It tells of a king, Brihadratha, who established his son as king and, realizing that his body is not eternal, became detached from the world and went into the forest to practice austerity. After a thousand days Shakayanya, a knower of the soul, appeared to teach him. The king sought liberation from reincarnating existence. The teacher assures him that he will become a knower of the soul. The serene one, who rising up out of the body reaches the highest light in one's own form, is the soul, immortal and fearless.

The body is like a cart without intelligence, but it is driven by a supersensuous, intelligent being, who is pure, clean, void, tranquil, breathless, selfless, endless, undecaying, steadfast, eternal, unborn, and independent. The reins are the five organs of perception; the steeds are the organs of action; and the charioteer is the mind. The soul is unmanifest, subtle, imperceptible, incomprehensible, selfless, pure, steadfast, stainless, unagitated, desireless, fixed like a spectator, and self-abiding.

How then does the soul, overcome by the bright and dark fruits of action *(karma)*, enter good or evil wombs? The elemental self is overcome by these actions and pairs of opposites, the qualities *(gunas)* of nature *(prakriti)* and does not see the blessed one, who causes action standing within oneself. Bewildered, full of desire, distracted, this self-conceit binds oneself by thinking "This is I," and "That is mine." So as a bird is caught in a snare, it enters into a good or evil womb.

Yet the cause of these actions is the inner person. The elemental self is overcome by its attachment to qualities. The characteristics of the dark quality *(tamas)* are delusion, fear, despondency, sleepiness, weariness, neglect, old age, sorrow, hunger, thirst, wretchedness, anger, atheism, ignorance, jealousy, cruelty, stupidity, shamelessness, meanness, and rashness. The characteristics of the passionate quality *(rajas)* are desire, affection, emotion, coveting, malice, lust, hatred, secretiveness, envy, greed, fickleness, distraction, ambition, favoritism, pride, aversion, attachment, and gluttony.

How then may this elemental self on leaving this body come into complete union with the soul? Like the waves of great rivers or the ocean tide, it is hard to keep back the consequences of one's actions or the approach of death. Like the lame bound with the fetters made of the fruit of good and evil, like the prisoner lacking independence, like the dead beset by fear, the intoxicated by delusions, like one rushing around are those possessed by an evil spirit; like one bitten by a snake are those bitten by objects of sense; like the gross darkness of passion, the juggling of illusion, like a falsely apparent dream, like an actor in temporary dress or a painted scene falsely delighting the mind, all these attachments prevent the self from remembering the highest place.

The antidote is to study the *Veda*, to pursue one's duty in each stage of the religious life, and to practice the proper discipline, which results in the pure qualities *(sattva)* that lead to understanding and the soul. By knowledge, discipline, and meditation God is apprehended, and one attains undecaying and immeasurable happiness in complete union with the soul. The soul is identical with the various gods and powers.

> *Having bid peace to all creatures and gone to the forest, then having put aside objects of sense, from out of one's own body one should perceive this, who has all forms, the golden one, all-knowing, the final goal, the only light."*

The means of attaining the unity of the One is the sixfold yoga of breath control *(pranayama)*, withdrawal of the senses *(pratyahara)*, attention *(dhyana)*, concentration *(dharana)*, contemplation *(tarka)*, and meditation *(samadhi)*.

> *When one sees the brilliant maker, lord, person, the God-source, then, being a knower, shaking off good and evil, the sage makes everything one in the supreme imperishable.*

When the mind is suppressed, one sees the brilliant soul, which is more subtle than the subtle; having seen the soul oneself, one becomes selfless and is regarded as immeasurable, without origin - the mark of liberation *(moksha)*. By serenity of thought one destroys good and evil action *(karma)*. In selflessness one attains absolute unity.

The sound *Aum* may be used. Meditation is directed to the highest principle within and also outer objects, qualifying the unqualified understanding; but when the mind has been dissolved, there is the bliss witnessed by the soul that is the pure and immortal Spirit. But if one is borne along by the stream of the qualities, unsteady, wavering, bewildered, full of desire, and distracted one goes into self-conceit. Standing free from dependence, conception, and self-conceit is the mark of liberation.

The influence of Buddhism can be seen in the description of liberation from one's own thoughts. As fire destitute of fuel goes out, so thought losing activity becomes extinct in its source. What is one's thought, that one becomes; this is the eternal mystery. By the serenity of thought one destroys good and bad karma; focused on the soul, one enjoys eternal delight. The mind is the means of bondage and release. Though the sacrificial fire is still important, meditation has become the primary means of liberation. The *Mahanarayana Upanishad* is a long hymn to various forms of God with prayers for everything from wealth to liberation. At one point the author identifies with the divine light:

> *I am that supreme light of Brahman which shines as the inmost essence of all that exists.*

In reality I am the same infinite Brahman even when I am experiencing myself as a finite self owing to ignorance.

Now by the onset of knowledge I am really that Brahman which is my eternal nature.

Therefore I realize this identity by making myself, the finite self, an oblation into the fire of the infinite Brahman which I am always.

May this oblation be well made.

The *Jabala Upanishad*, which is quoted by Shankara, gives a description of the four stages of religious life for a pious Hindu. Yajnavalkya suggests that after completing the life of a student, a householder, and a forest dweller, let one renounce, though one may renounce while a student or householder if one has the spirit of renunciation. Suicide apparently was not forbidden, for to the one who is weary of the world but is not yet fit to become a recluse, Yajnavalkya recommends a hero's death (in battle), fasting to death, throwing oneself into water or fire, or taking a final journey (to exhaustion). The wandering ascetic though wearing an orange robe, with a shaven head, practicing non-possession, purity, nonviolence, and living on charity obtains the state of Brahman.

The *Vajrasuchika Upanishad* claims to blast ignorance and exalts those endowed with knowledge. It raises the question who is of the Brahmin class. Is it the individual soul, the body, based on birth, knowledge, work, or performing the rites? It is not the individual soul *(jiva)*, because the same soul passes through many bodies.

It is not the body, because all bodies are composed of the same elements even though Brahmins tend to be white, Kshatriyas red, Vaishyas tawny, and Sudras dark in complexion. It is not birth, because many sages are of diverse origin. It is not knowledge, because many Kshatriyas have attained wisdom and seen the highest reality. It is not work, because good men perform works based on their past karma. It is not performing the rites, because many Kshatriyas and others have given away gold as an act of religious duty.

The true Brahmin directly perceives the soul, which functions as the indwelling spirit of all beings, blissful, indivisible, immeasurable, realizable only through one's experience. Manifesting oneself directly through the fulfillment of nature becomes rid of the faults of desire, attachment, spite, greed, expectation, bewilderment, ostentation, and so on and is endowed with tranquillity. Only one possessed of these qualities is a Brahmin. This flexible viewpoint indicates that the caste system may not yet have been as rigid as it was later to become.

Although as the major teachings passed down orally from the century before the Buddha, the *Upanishads* don't tell us too much about the worldly society of India, they do express a widespread mysticism and spiritual life-style that was to prepare the way for the new religions of Jainism and Buddhism as well as the deepened spirituality and mystical philosophies of Hinduism. The values of the teachers and ascetics of this culture that has been likened to the New Thought movement of the recent New Age philosophy were spiritual and other worldly, but if they did not do much to improve the whole society, at least they did not do the harm of the conquering Aryans.

A personal educational system of spiritual tutoring for adults developed, and individuals were encouraged to improve themselves spiritually as they gave and received charity. (When renouncing they gave to charity; then they accepted charity for basic sustenance.) The rituals of animal sacrifices were de-emphasized, and knowledge became greatly valued, especially self-knowledge. The doctrine of reincarnation made the sacrifices for a better life now or in the future eventually give way to the higher spiritual goal of liberation from the entire cycle of rebirth. Thus austerity and meditation became the primary methods of spiritual realization.

3
The Aryan Invasion

The Aryan Invasion theory was first propounded when linguistic similarities between Sanskrit and the major European languages were discovered by European scholars during the colonial era. In an atmosphere of raging eurocentricism, it was inevitable that any explanation of this seemingly inexplicable discovery would taken on racial and ideological overtones.

COLONIAL EXPOSITIONS OF THE ARYAN INVASION THEORY

British intellectuals were particularly nonplussed by this apparent link between the languages of the conquerors and the conquered. In the earliest phases of British rule in India, the East India Company proceeded largely unconsciously - without moral dilemmas and without overt recourse to ideological or racial superiority. But as the rule of the East India Company expanded, and battles became more hard fought and the resistance to British occupation in India grew, the ideology of European racial superiority became almost essential in justifying British presence in India - not only to assuage British conscience, but also to convince the Indian people that the British were not mere colonial conquerors but a superior race on a noble civilizational mission.

After 1857, the British education system in India had been deliberately designed to assist in the development of a narrow but influential class of deeply indoctrinated and predominantly loyal agents of British colonial rule in India. British elaborations of the Aryan invasion theory became powerful and convenient ideological tools in generating legitimacy for British rule. In its most classical and colonially tinged incarnation, it portrayed the Aryans as a highly advanced and culturally superior race in the ancient world, locating their original home in Northern Europe. It then went on to suggest that some time in antiquity, the Aryans migrated from their original home in Europe and brought with them their language and their superior culture and transcendental philosophy to civilize the primitive and materially backward Dravidian people of the subcontinent. All the greatness of Indian civilization was ascribed to the Aryans, thus implying that if India were to ever achieve greatness again, a return to Aryan rule was imperative.

And by claiming a cultural continuity between this noble race of ancient times and themselves, the British could become inheritors of the grand Aryan tradition and assert their "legitimate" civilizational right to rule over the people of the subcontinent - not to exploit them, but so as to "reinvigorate" Indian civilization by reintroducing Aryan rule that had been disfigured and corrupted by the violent and barbaric incursions of the Muslims. Preposterous and distorted as it was, this absurdly racist proposition was made palatable to a self-doubting and repressed class of upper-caste Hindus who were told that they were descendants of the Aryans, and could identify with the manifold and globally encompassing achievements of the Aryan people by accepting British authority so as to participate in this great Aryan renaissance in India.

The theory gained rapid currency amongst upper-caste Hindus who had legitimate gripes against the Muslim nobility for having been denied equal access to power in the Muslim courts, but were too enfeebled to put up a fight on their own, and were too alienated from the mass of artisans and peasants to join in popular rebellions against the feudal dispensation. The British rulers offered the opportunity of gaining petty privileges in exchange for acquiescence to colonial rule, and the Aryan invasion theory provided the ideological justification for betraying the rest of ones nation. By placing the ancestral home of the Aryans far off in Northern Europe, the British were putting the idea in the heads of such upper-caste Hindus that they were far removed from the Indian masses and had no good reason to identify with them. Wittingly or unwittingly, the Aryan invasion theory thus became the emotional bait for a section of the Indian population who were to aid and abet the colonial project in India. Although some of these Indians ultimately did develop national feelings, and forged a national identity that eventually came into conflict with the continuation of colonial rule, the theory continued to play an important role in confusing the psyche of the post-independence Indian intelligentsia.

Since the Aryan invasion refers to a period of considerable antiquity, and there is little physical evidence to support any authoritative conclusion, theories affirming (or opposing) the invasion hypothesis can vary from being wildly speculative at worst, to being reasonably plausible at best. Even the most diligent and objective of historians can at best come up with informed conjectures, leaving open the possibility for uncertainty, and ideologically-driven diversionary postulations. The absence of concrete data and the ambiguity involved in interpreting surviving texts from the Aryan period makes the task of combating history-writing that has been colored by colonially influenced analysis doubly difficult. Nevertheless, it is possible to construct the contours of what may be more plausible, and at least eliminate what is obviously fiction or fantasy.

ARGUMENTS FOR AND AGAINST THE INVASION THEORY

Opponents of the invasion theory make a somewhat plausible case that the sacrificial rites and rituals described in some of the Vedic texts bear a resemblance to practices that may have been common during the Harappan period. The similiarity of Harappan and Vedic altars is indeed intriguing. This would bolster the argument that Brahmins of the Vedic age emerged from the Harappan priesthood, and not from any Aryan invasion. But a link between the Harappan priesthood and Vedic Brahminism does not preclude the possibility of an invasion or foreign migration since North Western India attracted a constant stream of migrants and invaders.

However, the mere possibility of what may have happened cannot be the basis of an all-encomapssing theory such as the

"Aryan Invasion Theory". It must be grounded on more solid evidence to withstand critics who might describe such assertions as racially-tarred speculations.

Philological Analysis

Proponents of an invasion (or migration) theory feel quite strongly that the Indo-European linguistic commonality cannot be explained in any other way, and cite philological studies that appear to bolster their case.

However, some opponents of the invasion theory argue that the observed commonality of the Indo-European group of languages could have been achieved without an Aryan invasion. They observe that the Harappan civilization had extensive trade and commercial ties with Babylon as well as with civilizations to the further West. There is a remarkable similarity in seals and cultural artifacts found in Harappan India, Babylon and even the early civilizations of the Mediterranean such as Crete. Hence, they argue that a linguistic commonality may have developed quite early through trade and cultural contacts and that this common linguistic structure may have subsequently moved from South to North. Since Mediterranean Europe and the Middle Eastern civilizations developed well before the civilizations of Northern Europe, such a possibility is not altogether inconceivable.

But such a hypothesis does not preclude the possibility that invading or migrating clans may have also introduced non-Indian words into the existing Indian languages - leading to a composite language stream that incorporated both Indo-European and indigenous features. (Urdu is an example of a language that was introduced as a result of a series of invasions, adding a large body of foreign words while maintaining the syntactical structure and vocabulary base of the previous language.)

Since much of the Indo-European linguistic commonality appears to correspond to the basic vocabulary of a pastoral nomadic population, intrusions by patriarchal warrior clans from Central Asia cannot be ruled out. Authors such as Gimbutas *(The Civilization of the Goddess, the World of Old Europe)* present a reasonably convincing model of how the older matriarchal order in Europe was gradually broken down by migrants/conquerors who spoke a language that might account for certain common elements of the Indo-European group of languages. However, it would be inappropriate to mechanically apply the same conclusions to India, (nothwithstanding some of the linguistic and philological arguments in favor of such a theory) because other explanations for the linguistic similarities are now being illuminated through very recent DNA studies.

It must be emphasized that while there are both similarities and differences amongst the various Indo-European languages, our essay on Indian Languages shows quite convincingly that the differences outnumber the similarities. The essay shows how the primary and dominant motive force for the development of Indian languages, (including the so-called Indo-European languages of the North) especially during the written period was indigenous. Far too often, historians (and philologists) have tended to downplay (or ignore) the contributions of the Adivasi and Tamil language streams in the development of the Indic languages. A more objective and balanced philological analysis of the Indian languages points to rather limited Indo-European links, but to a considerably greater degree of independent indigenous development. Moreover, just as South Indian languages have absorbed Sanskrit words, North Indian languages have also absorbed words from Tamil and languages related to it.

Another criticism of the invasion theory lies in the interpretation of the word "Arya" to mean race, nationality or even linguistic group. Critics suggest that the word Arya as used in the Rig Veda and other texts is better translated as one who was noble in character (or noble in deed) or perhaps hailing from a noble (or royal) background. Hence, to use the term "Aryan" to describe the racial or national characteristics of an invading clan or clans would naturally be erroneous.

THE HORSE AND CHARIOT THEORIES

Notably, historians favoring the invasion theory have based many of their arguments on postulates connecting the introduction of the horse and chariot in India to invading (or migrating) "Aryans". They also point to the balladic character of some of the verses in the Rig Veda with references to armed cattle raids and warriors on horse-driven chariots who appear to portray a race or a group of clans of pastoral nomadic warriors. The imagery fits particularly well with artifacts found in Babylon and Ancient Persia (and other regions near the Caspian Sea) that depict warriors riding on horse-driven chariots. Other literary evidence from the Rig Veda also appears to connect the authors of these Rig Veda verses to the "Aryan" identified civilization of ancient Persia.

However such historians have failed to notice that there are drawings of horse and horse-drawn vehicles (*tangas*) in the caves of Bhimbhetka and other sites that counter the notion that the horse was unknown in India till an "Aryan Invasion/ Migration". This would then suggest that the chariots described in the Rig Veda could have simply been an evolution of the Indian *tanga*. And while there is little tangible evidence of warrior clans in the numerous urban settlements that comprise the Harappan civilization, it is not unlikely that as settled civilization developed in India, and as urbanization spread to new areas, warrior clans may have emerged entirely due to indigenous processes.

Commonalities of Vedic Gods with the Middle East

Other evidence to bolster the "Aryan Invasion Theory" lies in certain common names/references and features of some Vedic Gods that appear to be pan-West Asian. While this might suggest a certain ancient link between the North Indian nobility and the nobility of Persia and Western Asia, it does not substantiate the claim that the "Aryans" were Europeans or Caucasians. Moreover, there are many different ways in which such commonalities may have developed.

Since there are references in the *Manusmriti* to ruling clans who were clearly of non-Indian origin, there is no doubt that various foreign tribes/clans must have entered India as migrants or invaders. There are references to Greeks, Persians as well as to Chinese amongst India's ruling "Aryan" families. But there are also references to South Indian or "Dravidian" "Aryan" clans. To conflate these royals "Aryans" exclusively with European invaders would be clearly inappropriate. Moreover, to identify the timing of such an invasion with the period of the Rig Veda would also be entirely speculative.

This is not to say that India could have never been invaded by Caucasian or other clans, but rather that even if such invasions may have taken place, these invasions would have been neither unique nor decisive in shaping Indian history.

While it is not inconceivable that some of the ruling clans described in the Rig Veda may have entered India as invaders, the notion that the "Aryans" were exclusively outsiders, and that too European, and brought with them the entire text of the Vedas, and hence, laid the foundations of Indian civilization is what is most untenable, and is easily exposed if developments in Indian culture and philosophy are adequately studied in depth and with unbiased eyes.

As Indian critics of the Aryan invasion theory have demonstrated, (apart from the few common gods that are also referenced outside India) much of the imagery of the Vedas is indigenous. To many Indians - the references to plants and animals, and the climactic and geographical descriptions suggest a connection to Indian soil. Some of the spiritual values (and cultural mores and traditions) that emerge from the Rig Ved seem to have a distinctly Indian sources that many Indians can identify with intuitively and instinctively.

LINKS BETWEEN HARAPPAN AND VEDIC CIVILIZATION

In fact, there is some compelling circumstantial evidence linking the settlers of the Gangetic plain to earlier Harappan settlements. For instance, emerging geological evidence pointing to ancient river systems drying up and changing course, and the excavation of numerous settlements along the banks of these ancient river systems (such as the Saraswati basin that ran in parallel to the Indus) lends credence to the argument that the settlers of the Gangetic plain must have been predominantly domestic migrants.

Finds of *Shatranj* (chess) pieces, dice and terracotta animal and goddess figurines also point to connections between Harappan and later civilizations. It is also quite remarkable how the ornamentation of some temples in Rajasthan and Western Madhya Pradesh appears to derive from some of the excavated jewelry from Harappan sites in Northern India. And remarkably, there are no parallels to such motifs outside India.

Some scholars also see a continuity between the *Sulva Sutras* and the Harappan civilization which owing to its material advance must have very likely developed a level of arithmetic and ritual and abstract philosophy concomitant with it's achievements in urban planning and agricultural management. The evidence for decimal weights and measures in the Harappan civilization, and the later perfection of a decimal numeral system in India lends further substance to such claims.

Relevance of the Aryans

All this suggests that there is a much greater degree of continuity in Indian civilization than previously realized, and further examination of the Indian historical record will demonstrate that the numerous developments in philosophy and culture that have taken place in India cannot be attributed to "Aryan" invaders. In fact, the main significance of the invasion theory lies not in the determination of whether such an invasion took place or not, but rather in how much of a debt Indian civilization might owe to such an invasion.

For instance, prior to the series of Islamic invasions, and long after the "Aryan" period of Indian history, there have been numerous other invasions that had an impact on the subcontinent. Yet it is only the "Aryan" invasion that attracts popular and scholarly attention. This is primarily because of the importance ascribed to the "Aryan" invasion by British colonial historians.

Before the invention of the "exalted" Aryan (of European origin) by British (and other European and Western) ideologues, few Indians had any conscious memory of an "Aryan" warrior past since later ruling families in India had long since expanded and diversified from what may have been the ruling "Aryan" clans of the time of the Mahabharatha or even the Manusmriti. Not only had the "Kshatriya" caste expanded to accomodate several new clans, many of India's most illustrious Northern rulers (such as the Nandas, the Mauryas and the Guptas) were non-Kshatriyas.

Prior to any supposed "Aryan" invasion, India already had a relatively advanced settled-agriculture based urban civilization. And within a few centuries after their possible "imported" introduction in India, some of the "Aryan"-identified gods described in the Rig Veda ceased to be worshipped and gradually faded from mainstream Indian consciousness. Brahmin *gotra* (clan) names mentioned in the Rig Veda also lost their import and the vast majority of Brahmin *gotra* (clan) names that came into common use could not have had any "Aryan"-invasion connection. As Kosambi convincingly points out in his *Introduction to Indian History*, many of India's Brahmins rose from 'Hinduised' tribes that earlier practised animism or totem worship, or prayed to various fertility gods and/or goddesses, or revered fertility symbols such as the *linga* (phallus) or the *yoni (*vagina*)*. A majority of these Hinduised tribes retained many elements of their older forms of worship, and several Brahmin *gotra* (clan) names are derived from non-Aryan clan totems and other tribal associations.

For instance, one of the most popular gods in the Indian pantheon - *Shiva* - appears to have no connection with any possible "Aryan" invasion, and may in fact have its prototype in the fertility god of the Harappans. Similiarly, *Hanuman, Ganesh, Kali or Durga,* or Maharashtra's *Vithoba* - none could have any external "Aryan" connection, since they don't even find any mention in the Rig Veda. Whether in matters of popular religion or in matters of high philosophy, there is little contribution of note that can be traced directly to a supposed "Aryan invasion".

Uniquely Indian Aspects of Vedic Literature

As noted earlier, much of the Vedic literature - both in the style and substance of its verses, appears to be uniquely Indian, and it is not impossible that at least some of the verses may have Harappan origin. Many of the philosophical themes that are explored and developed in the *Vedic* literature have insightful naturalist references that are consistent with Indian geography. In addition, there are certain philosophical aspects of the Vedic literature that don't appear to be replicated in quite the same way in any other civilization that was contemporaneous to the Vedic civilization.

The best of the Vedic *Shlokas* refer to a common life-spirit that links all living creatures, to human social-interconnectedness, to the notion of unity in diversity and how different sections of society might have different prayers and different wishes. Whereas some verses point to god as being a source for wish-fulfillment, in other verses, there are doubts and queries about the nature of god, whether a god really exists, and whether such questions can every be really answered. These aspects of Vedic thought were elaborated upon by later schools of Indian philosophy, and recur frequently in Indian literature and philosophy. But such verses appear to have no direct parallel in civilizations to India's West.

Already in the Vedic period, there is an amorphous quality to spiritual beliefs that included atheistic, agnostic and soul-based (as opposed to god-based) philosphical assertions and queries that gave Indian spiritual practice and organization its own and somewhat unique flavor.

While some of India's rational schools developed in parallel with the Vedas, and are included as appendices to the Vedic texts, others developed practically independently of the *Vedas,* or even in opposition - as polemics to the *Vedas* (such as those of the Jains and the Buddhists). The *Upanishads,* the *Sankhya*, and the *Nyaya-Vaisheshika* schools, the numerous treatises on medicine, ethics, scientific method, logic and mathematics clearly developed on Indian soil as a result of Indian experiences and intellectual efforts.

India's great surviving temples and Stupas with their rich carvings and sculpture were all created with aesthetic principles and formulations that developed centuries after any invading or migrating "Aryans" would have completely melted into Indian society. And though it is not impossible that these foreign "Aryans" may have introduced certain technological innovations and inventions, knowledge of brick-making, textile production, tool-making, pottery and metallurgy was already available to the Harappans and residents of the Indo-Saraswati civilization.

The grammar of Sanskrit and its highly systematized alphabet also had little to do with any "Aryan" invasion. Sanskrit is a highly structured and methodical language, optimized for engaging in rational debates and expressing mathematical formulas. Its skillfully organized alphabet bears little resemblance to the rather random and arbitrary alphabet of its European "cousins". Much of its vocabulary and syntax developed long after any supposed invasion, and although the oral structure of Tamil may differ from those of the North in some respects, the majority of India's languages (both Northern and Southern) share a large base of a common Sanskrit-derived vocabulary. Besides, words travelled from South to North and from Adivasis to non-Adivasis as well.

In addition, what is especially significant is how the North Indian scripts share so much in common with the scripts of Southern India. The phonetic organization of consonants and vowels, phonetic spelling, and the many other commonalities that bind all of India's syllabic scripts weakens the entire linguistic premise of the Aryan invasion theory. In fact, when it comes to scripts, consonant and vowel sounds, all Indian languages are closely related, and their closest relatives are to be found in South East Asia, Ethiopia (and even Korea and Mongolia to some degree) but not in Europe.

While the Aryans of the *Vedas* may be credited with laying the foundations of "Hindu" civilization in the Gangetic plain, the essence of Hindu civilization emerged gradually, taking several centuries to crystallize. Undergoing both internal reform and fusion with pre-existing tribal and matriarchal cultures, the Hinduism of both the rulers and the masses kept evolving. Even as it retained certain philosophical elements from Vedic literature, it also broadened and in some ways diverged completely from the Vedas.

Beyond the Northern (Yamuna/Gangetic) plains, the influence of Aryan-identified Vedic civilization was generally more limited. Vedic influences on the civilizations in Bengal, Assam and Orissa were initially almost minimal, and these Eastern civilizations largely followed their own (and somewhat unique trajectories), as did the civilizations of South India -

absorbing Vedic philosophical concepts gradually and only partially. Throughout India, Buddhism and Jainism also found converts, and in Kashmir, the North West, and in the East - Buddhism had a particularly profound influence, while in Western India (such as in Rajasthan, Gujarat, Western Madhya Pradesh and Karnataka) Jainism was very influential. In Jharkhand, Chhatisgarh, West Bengal and Orissa, Tantric influences were important.

In essence, Indian civilization whether Hindu, Buddhist or Jain, or any other, developed primarily from the unique (and varied) conditions of Indian geography and the human exertion that went into modifying those conditions to advance agriculture and settled civilization. Taken in the general context of say three or four thousand years of Indian history, it is hard to ascribe to an "Aryan" invasion/s the sort of paramountcy assigned by the British. While British motives in magnifying the "Aryan" character of Indian civilization are only too apparent, this contemporary obsession with the "Aryan" question that appears to have gripped large sections of the Indian intelligentsia suggests that the ideological confusion created by the British has not yet been fully sorted out.

One consequence of this is that the debate on the Aryan question has been highly contentious, with historians adopting strident and extreme positions, not seeing that there can be both continuities and discontinuities in the development of Indian civilization. It has also diverted many of India's historians from equally (or more) important tasks - such as describing and integrating those periods of Indian history where considerable new archeological material is now available and needs to be incorporated into the presently known and documented view of Indian history.

Key aspects of Indian history remain poorly researched and documented. Many Sanskrit and vernacular texts have not been studied and assimilated by English speaking historians. Regional variations in Indian history have not been studied enough. A deeper understanding of some of the lesser known kingdoms all across India is required to correct false generalizations about Indian history. Much more effort is required in understanding social movements, gender and caste equations. Simplifications and generalizations based on antiquated documents like the *Manusmriti* (which was mainly resurrected by British historians) provide a very incomplete and distorted picture of actual social relations and practice in India. The *Manusmriti* also offers little in terms of understanding local and regional peculiarities in matters of social relations.

Considerable work is also required in unifying haphazard and scattered studies in the area of India's economic history and the history of philosophy, science, technology and manufacturing. It is also important that the vast body of work that has been published since independence in English be translated into the nation's many languages and regional dialects. It is tragic that so much of the best research done in Indian history is available only to English speakers. These are just some of the tasks that need greater attention from the community of Indian historians.

Intriguing as the "Aryan"-origin debate may be, it is in the end only one facet of Indian history, and merits further attention only if historians and archeologists can offer fresh and new insights on this subject and relate them to the broad dynamics of Indian civilization.

4

The Laws of Manu

1. The great sages approached Manu, who was seated with a collected mind, and, having duly worshipped him, spoke as follows:

2. 'Deign, divine one, to declare to us precisely and in due order the sacred laws of each of the (four chief) castes (varna) and of the intermediate ones.

3. 'For thou, O Lord, alone knowest the purport, (i.e.) the rites, and the knowledge of the soul, (taught) in this whole ordinance of the Self-existent (Svayambhu), which is unknowable and unfathomable.'

4. He, whose power is measureless, being thus asked by the high-minded great sages, duly honoured them, and answered, 'Listen!'

5. This (universe) existed in the shape of Darkness, unperceived, destitute of distinctive marks, unattainable by reasoning, unknowable, wholly immersed, as it were, in deep sleep.

6. Then the divine Self-existent (Svayambhu, himself) indiscernible, (but) making (all) this, the great elements and the rest, discernible, appeared with irresistible (creative) power, dispelling the darkness.

7. He who can be perceived by the internal organ (alone), who is subtile, indiscernible, and eternal, who contains all created beings and is inconceivable, shone forth of his own (will).

8. He, desiring to produce beings of many kinds from his own body, first with a thought created the waters, and placed his seed in them.

9. That (seed) became a golden egg, in brilliancy equal to the sun; in that (egg) he himself was born as Brahman, the progenitor of the whole world.

10. The waters are called narah, (for) the waters are, indeed, the offspring of Nara; as they were his first residence (ayana), he thence is named Narayana.

11. From that (first) cause, which is indiscernible, eternal, and both real and unreal, was produced that male (Purusha), who is famed in this world (under the appellation of) Brahman.

12. The divine one resided in that egg during a whole year, then he himself by his thought (alone) divided it into two halves;

13. And out of those two halves he formed heaven and earth, between them the middle sphere, the eight points of the horizon, and the eternal abode of the waters.

14. From himself (atmanah) he also drew forth the mind, which is both real and unreal, likewise from the mind egoism, which possesses the function of self-consciousness (and is) lordly;

15. Moreover, the great one, the soul, and all (products) affected by the three qualities, and, in their order, the five organs which perceive the objects of sensation.

16. But, joining minute particles even of those six, which possess measureless power, with particles of himself, he created all beings.

17. Because those six (kinds of) minute particles, which form the (creator's) frame, enter (a-sri) these (creatures), therefore the wise call his frame sarira, (the body.)

18. That the great elements enter, together with their functions and the mind, through its minute parts the framer of all beings, the imperishable one.

19. But from minute body (-framing) particles of these seven very powerful Purushas springs this (world), the perishable from the imperishable.

20. Among them each succeeding (element) acquires the quality of the preceding one, and whatever place (in the sequence) each of them occupies, even so many qualities it is declared to possess.

21. But in the beginning he assigned their several names, actions, and conditions to all (created beings), even according to the words of the Veda.

22. He, the Lord, also created the class of the gods, who are endowed with life, and whose nature is action; and the subtile class of the Sadhyas, and the eternal sacrifice.

23. But from fire, wind, and the sun he drew forth the threefold eternal Veda, called Rik, Yagus, and Saman, for the due performance of the sacrifice.

24. Time and the divisions of time, the lunar mansions and the planets, the rivers, the oceans, the mountains, plains, and uneven ground.

25. Austerity, speech, pleasure, desire, and anger, this whole creation he likewise produced, as he desired to call these beings into existence.

26. Moreover, in order to distinguish actions, he separated merit from demerit, and he caused the creatures to be affected by the pairs (of opposites), such as pain and pleasure.

27. But with the minute perishable particles of the five (elements) which have been mentioned, this whole (world) is framed in due order.

28. But to whatever course of action the Lord at first appointed each (kind of beings), that alone it has spontaneously adopted in each succeeding creation.

29. Whatever he assigned to each at the (first) creation, noxiousness or harmlessness, gentleness or ferocity, virtue or sin, truth or falsehood, that clung (afterwards) spontaneously to it.

30. As at the change of the seasons each season of its own accord assumes its distinctive marks, even so corporeal beings (resume in new births) their (appointed) course of action.

31. But for the sake of the prosperity of the worlds he caused the Brahmana, the Kshatriya, the Vaisya, and the Sudra to proceed from his mouth, his arms, his thighs, and his feet.

32. Dividing his own body, the Lord became half male and half female; with that (female) he produced Virag.

33. But know me, O most holy among the twice-born, to be the creator of this whole (world), whom that male, Virag, himself produced, having performed austerities.

34. Then I, desiring to produce created beings, performed very difficult austerities, and (thereby) called into existence ten great sages, lords of created beings,

35. Mariki, Atri, Angiras, Pulastya, Pulaha, Kratu, Praketas, Vasishtha, Bhrigu, and Narada.

36. They created seven other Manus possessing great brilliancy, gods and classes of gods and great sages of measureless power,

37. Yakshas (the servants of Kubera, the demons called) Rakshasas and Pisakas, Gandharvas (or musicians of the gods), Apsarases (the dancers of the gods), Asuras, (the snake-deities called) Nagas and Sarpas, (the bird-deities called) Suparnas and the several classes of the manes,

38. Lightnings, thunderbolts and clouds, imperfect (rohita) and perfect rainbows, falling meteors, supernatural noises, comets, and heavenly lights of many kinds,

39 (Horse-faced) Kinnaras, monkeys, fishes, birds of many kinds, cattle, deer, men, and carnivorous beasts with two rows of teeth,

40. Small and large worms and beetles, moths, lice, flies, bugs, all stinging and biting insects and the several kinds of immovable things.

41. Thus was this whole (creation), both the immovable and the movable, produced by those high-minded ones by means of austerities and at my command, (each being) according to (the results of) its actions.

42. But whatever act is stated (to belong) to (each of) those creatures here below, that I will truly declare to you, as well as their order in respect to birth.

43. Cattle, deer, carnivorous beasts with two rows of teeth, Rakshasas, Pisakas, and men are born from the womb.

44. From eggs are born birds, snakes, crocodiles, fishes, tortoises, as well as similar terrestrial and aquatic (animals).

45. From hot moisture spring stinging and biting insects, lice, flies, bugs, and all other (creatures) of that kind which are produced by heat.

46. All plants, propagated by seed or by slips, grow from shoots; annual plants (are those) which, bearing many flowers and fruits, perish after the ripening of their fruit;

47. (Those trees) which bear fruit without flowers are called vanaspati (lords of the forest); but those which bear both flowers and fruit are called vriksha.

48. But the various plants with many stalks, growing from one or several roots, the different kinds of grasses, the climbing plants and the creepers spring all from seed or from slips.

49. These (plants) which are surrounded by multiform Darkness, the result of their acts (in former existences), possess internal consciousness and experience pleasure and pain.

50. The (various) conditions in this always terrible and constantly changing circle of births and deaths to which created beings are subject, are stated to begin with (that of) Brahman, and to end with (that of) these (just mentioned immovable creatures).

51. When he whose power is incomprehensible, had thus produced the universe and men, he disappeared in himself, repeatedly suppressing one period by means of the other.

52. When that divine one wakes, then this world stirs; when he slumbers tranquilly, then the universe sinks to sleep.

53. But when he reposes in calm sleep, the corporeal beings whose nature is action, desist from their actions and mind becomes inert.

54. When they are absorbed all at once in that great soul, then he who is the soul of all beings sweetly slumbers, free from all care and occupation.

55. When this (soul) has entered darkness, it remains for a long time united with the organs (of sensation), but performs not its functions; it then leaves the corporeal frame.

56. When, being clothed with minute particles (only), it enters into vegetable or animal seed, it then assumes, united (with the fine body), a (new) corporeal frame.

57. Thus he, the imperishable one, by (alternately) waking and slumbering, incessantly revivifies and destroys this whole movable and immovable (creation).

58. But he having composed these Institutes (of the sacred law), himself taught them, according to the rule, to me alone in the beginning; next I (taught them) to Mariki and the other sages.

59. Bhrigu, here, will fully recite to you these Institutes; for that sage learned the whole in its entirety from me.

60. Then that great sage Bhrigu, being thus addressed by Manu, spoke, pleased in his heart, to all the sages, 'Listen!'

61. Six other high-minded, very powerful Manus, who belong to the race of this Manu, the descendant of the Self-existent (Svayambhu), and who have severally produced created beings,

62. (Are) Svarokisha, Auttami, Tamasa, Raivata, Kakshusha, possessing great lustre, and the son of Vivasvat.

63. These seven very glorious Manus, the first among whom is Svayambhuva, produced and protected this whole movable and immovable (creation), each during the period (allotted to him).

64. Eighteen nimeshas (twinklings of the eye, are one kashtha), thirty kashthas one kala, thirty kalas one muhurta, and as many (muhurtas) one day and night.

65. The sun divides days and nights, both human and divine, the night (being intended) for the repose of created beings and the day for exertion.

66. A month is a day and a night of the manes, but the division is according to fortnights. The dark (fortnight) is their day for active exertion, the bright (fortnight) their night for sleep.

67. A year is a day and a night of the gods; their division is (as follows): the half year during which the sun progresses

to the north will be the day, that during which it goes southwards the night.

68. But hear now the brief (description of) the duration of a night and a day of Brahman and of the several ages (of the world, yuga) according to their order.

69. They declare that the Krita age (consists of) four thousand years (of the gods); the twilight preceding it consists of as many hundreds, and the twilight following it of the same number.

70. In the other three ages with their twilights preceding and following, the thousands and hundreds are diminished by one (in each).

71. These twelve thousand (years) which thus have been just mentioned as the total of four (human) ages, are called one age of the gods.

72. But know that the sum of one thousand ages of the gods (makes) one day of Brahman, and that his night has the same length.

73. Those (only, who) know that the holy day of Brahman, indeed, ends after (the completion of) one thousand ages (of the gods) and that his night lasts as long, (are really) men acquainted with (the length of) days and nights.

74. At the end of that day and night he who was asleep, awakes and, after awaking, creates mind, which is both real and unreal.

75. Mind, impelled by (Brahman's) desire to create, performs the work of creation by modifying itself, thence ether is produced; they declare that sound is the quality of the latter.

76. But from ether, modifying itself, springs the pure, powerful wind, the vehicle of all perfumes; that is held to possess the quality of touch.

77. Next from wind modifying itself, proceeds the brilliant light, which illuminates and dispels darkness; that is declared to possess the quality of colour;

78. And from light, modifying itself, (is produced) water, possessing the quality of taste, from water earth which has the quality of smell; such is the creation in the beginning.

79. The before-mentioned age of the gods, (or) twelve thousand (of their years), being multiplied by seventy-one, (constitutes what) is here named the period of a Manu (Manvantara).

80. The Manvantaras, the creations and destructions (of the world, are) numberless; sporting, as it were, Brahman repeats this again and again.

81. In the Krita age Dharma is four-footed and entire, and (so is) Truth; nor does any gain accrue, to men by unrighteousness.

82. In the other (three ages), by reason of (unjust) gains (agama), Dharma is deprived successively of one foot, and through (the prevalence of) theft, falsehood, and fraud the merit (gained by men) is diminished by one fourth (in each).

83. (Men are) free from disease, accomplish all their aims, and live four hundred years in the Krita age, but in the Treta and (in each of) the succeeding (ages) their life is lessened by one quarter.

84. The life of mortals, mentioned in the Veda, the desired results of sacrificial rites and the (supernatural) power of embodied (spirits) are fruits proportioned among men according to (the character of) the age.

85. One set of duties (is prescribed) for men in the Krita age, different ones in the Treta and in the Dvapara, and (again) another (set) in the Kali, in a proportion as (those) ages decrease in length.

86. In the Krita age the chief (virtue) is declared to be (the performance of) austerities, in the Treta (divine) knowledge, in the Dvapara (the performance of) sacrifices, in the Kali liberality alone.

87. But in order to protect this universe He, the most resplendent one, assigned separate (duties and) occupations to those who sprang from his mouth, arms, thighs, and feet.

88. To Brahmanas he assigned teaching and studying (the Veda), sacrificing for their own benefit and for others, giving and accepting (of alms).

89. The Kshatriya he commanded to protect the people, to bestow gifts, to offer sacrifices, to study (the Veda), and to abstain from attaching himself to sensual pleasures;

90. The Vaisya to tend cattle, to bestow gifts, to offer sacrifices, to study (the Veda), to trade, to lend money, and to cultivate land.

91. One occupation only the lord prescribed to the Sudra, to serve meekly even these (other) three castes.

92. Man is stated to be purer above the navel (than below); hence the Self-existent (Svayambhu) has declared the purest (part) of him (to be) his mouth.

93. As the Brahmana sprang from (Brahman's) mouth, as he was the first-born, and as he possesses the Veda, he is by right the lord of this whole creation.

94. For the Self-existent (Svayambhu), having performed austerities, produced him first from his own mouth, in order that the offerings might be conveyed to the gods and manes and that this universe might be preserved.

95. What created being can surpass him, through whose mouth the gods continually consume the sacrificial viands and the manes the offerings to the dead?

96. Of created beings the most excellent are said to be those which are animated; of the animated, those which subsist by intelligence; of the intelligent, mankind; and of men, the Brahmanas;

97. Of Brahmanas, those learned (in the Veda); of the learned, those who recognise (the necessity and the manner of performing the prescribed duties); of those who possess this knowledge, those who perform them; of the performers, those who know the Brahman.

98. The very birth of a Brahmana is an eternal incarnation of the sacred law; for he is born to (fulfil) the sacred law, and becomes one with Brahman.

99. A Brahmana, coming into existence, is born as the highest on earth, the lord of all created beings, for the protection of the treasury of the law.

100. Whatever exists in the world is, the property of the Brahmana; on account of the excellence of his origin The Brahmana is, indeed, entitled to all.

101. The Brahmana eats but his own food, wears but his own apparel, bestows but his own in alms; other mortals subsist through the benevolence of the Brahmana.

102. In order to clearly settle his duties those of the other (castes) according to their order, wise Manu sprung from the Self-existent, composed these Institutes (of the sacred Law).

103. A learned Brahmana must carefully study them, and he must duly instruct his pupils in them, but nobody else (shall do it).

104. A Brahmana who studies these Institutes (and) faithfully fulfils the duties (prescribed therein), is never tainted by sins, arising from thoughts, words, or deeds.

105. He sanctifies any company (which he may enter), seven ancestors and seven descendants, and he alone deserves (to possess) this whole earth.

106. (To study) this (work) is the best means of securing welfare, it increases understanding, it procures fame and long life, it (leads to) supreme bliss.

107. In this (work) the sacred law has been fully stated as well as the good and bad qualities of (human) actions and the immemorial rule of conduct, (to be followed) by all the four castes (varna).

108. The rule of conduct is transcendent law, whether it be taught in the revealed texts or in the sacred tradition; hence a twice-born man who possesses regard for himself, should be always careful to (follow) it.

109. A Brahmana who departs from the rule of conduct, does not reap the fruit of the Veda, but he who duly follows it, will obtain the full reward.

110. The sages who saw that the sacred law is thus grounded on the rule of conduct, have taken good conduct to be the most excellent root of all austerity.

111. The creation of the universe, the rule of the sacraments, the ordinances of studentship, and the respectful behaviour

(towards Gurus), the most excellent rule of bathing (on return from the teacher's house),

112. (The law of) marriage and the description of the (various) marriage-rites, the regulations for the great sacrifices and the eternal rule of the funeral sacrifices,

113. The description of the modes of (gaining) subsistence and the duties of a Snataka, (the rules regarding) lawful and forbidden food, the purification of men and of things,

114. The laws concerning women, (the law) of hermits, (the manner of gaining) final emancipation and (of) renouncing the world, the whole duty of a king and the manner of deciding lawsuits,

115. The rules for the examination of witnesses, the laws concerning husband and wife, the law of (inheritance and) division, (the law concerning) gambling and the removal of (men nocuous like) thorns,

116. (The law concerning) the behaviour of Vaisyas and Sudras, the origin of the mixed castes, the law for all castes in times of distress and the law of penances,

117. The threefold course of transmigrations, the result of (good or bad) actions, (the manner of attaining) supreme bliss and the examination of the good and bad qualities of actions,

118. The primeval laws of countries, of castes (gati), of families, and the rules concerning heretics and companies (of traders and the like)- (all that) Manu has declared in these Institutes.

119. As Manu, in reply to my questions, formerly promulgated these Institutes, even so learn ye also the (whole work) from me.

1. Learn that sacred law which is followed by men learned (in the Veda) and assented to in their hearts by the virtuous, who are ever exempt from hatred and inordinate affection.

2. To act solely from a desire for rewards is not laudable, yet an exemption from that desire is not (to be found) in this (world): for on (that) desire is grounded the study of the Veda and the performance of the actions, prescribed by the Veda.

3. The desire (for rewards), indeed, has its root in the conception that an act can yield them, and in consequence of (that) conception sacrifices are performed; vows and the laws prescribing restraints are all stated to be kept through the idea that they will bear fruit.

4. Not a single act here (below) appears ever to be done by a man free from desire; for whatever (man) does, it is (the result of) the impulse of desire.

5. He who persists in discharging these (prescribed duties) in the right manner, reaches the deathless state and even in this (life) obtains (the fulfilment of) all the desires that he may have conceived.

6. The whole Veda is the (first) source of the sacred law, next the tradition and the virtuous conduct of those who know the (Veda further), also the customs of holy men, and (finally) self-satisfaction.

7. Whatever law has been ordained for any (person) by Manu, that has been fully declared in the Veda: for that (sage was) omniscient.

8. But a learned man after fully scrutinising all this with the eye of knowledge, should, in accordance with the authority of the revealed texts, be intent on (the performance of) his duties.

9. For that man who obeys the law prescribed in the revealed texts and in the sacred tradition, gains fame in this (world) and after death unsurpassable bliss.

10. But by Sruti (revelation) is meant the Veda, and by Smriti (tradition) the Institutes of the sacred law: those two must not be called into question in any matter, since from those two the sacred law shone forth.

11. Every twice-born man, who, relying on the Institutes of dialectics, treats with contempt those two sources (of the law), must be cast out by the virtuous, as an atheist and a scorner of the Veda.

12. The Veda, the sacred tradition, the customs of virtuous men, and one's own pleasure, they declare to be visibly the fourfold means of defining the sacred law.

13. The knowledge of the sacred law is prescribed for those who are not given to the acquisition of wealth and to the gratification of their desires; to those who seek the knowledge of the sacred law the supreme authority is the revelation (Sruti).

14. But when two sacred texts (Sruti) are conflicting, both are held to be law; for both are pronounced by the wise (to be) valid law.

15. (Thus) the (Agnihotra) sacrifice may be (optionally) performed, at any time after the sun has risen, before he has risen, or when neither sun nor stars are visible; that (is declared) by Vedic texts.

16. Know that he for whom (the performance of) the ceremonies beginning with the rite of impregnation (Garbhadhana) and ending with the funeral rite (Antyeshti) is prescribed, while sacred formulas are being recited, is entitled (to study) these Institutes, but no other man whatsoever.

17. That land, created by the gods, which lies between the two divine rivers Sarasvati and Drishadvati, the (sages) call Brahmavarta.

18. The custom handed down in regular succession (since time immemorial) among the (four chief) castes (varna) and the mixed (races) of that country, is called the conduct of virtuous men.

19. The plain of the Kurus, the (country of the) Matsyas, Pankalas, and Surasenakas, these (form), indeed, the country of the Brahmarshis (Brahmanical sages, which ranks) immediately after Brahmavarta.

20. From a Brahmana, born in that country, let all men on earth learn their several usages.

21. That (country) which (lies) between the Himavat and the Vindhya (mountains) to the east of Prayaga and to the west of Vinasana (the place where the river Sarasvati disappears) is called Madhyadesa (the central region).

22. But (the tract) between those two mountains (just mentioned), which (extends) as far as the eastern and the western oceans, the wise call Aryavarta (the country of the Aryans).

23. That land where the black antelope naturally roams, one must know to be fit for the performance of sacrifices; (the tract) different from that (is) the country of the Mlekkhas (barbarians).

24. Let twice-born men seek to dwell in those (above-mentioned countries); but a Sudra, distressed for subsistence, may reside anywhere.

25. Thus has the origin of the sacred law been succinctly described to you and the origin of this universe; learn (now) the duties of the castes (varna).

26. With holy rites, prescribed by the Veda, must the ceremony on conception and other sacraments be performed for twice-born men, which sanctify the body and purify (from sin) in this (life) and after death.

27. By burnt oblations during (the mother's) pregnancy, by the Gatakarman (the ceremony after birth), the Kauda (tonsure), and the Maungibandhana (the tying of the sacred girdle of Munga grass) is the taint, derived from both parents, removed from twice-born men.

28. By the study of the Veda, by vows, by burnt oblations, by (the recitation of) sacred texts, by the (acquisition of the) threefold sacred science, by offering (to the gods, Rishis, and manes), by (the procreation of) sons, by the great sacrifices, and by (Srauta) rites this (human) body is made fit for (union with) Brahman.

29. Before the navel-string is cut, the Gatakarman (birth-rite) must be performed for a male (child); and while sacred formulas are being recited, he must be fed with gold, honey, and butter.

30. But let (the father perform or) cause to be performed the Namadheya (the rite of naming the child), on the tenth or twelfth (day after birth), or on a lucky lunar day, in a lucky muhurta, under an auspicious constellation.

31. Let (the first part of) a Brahmana's name (denote something) auspicious, a Kshatriya's be connected with power, and a Vaisya's with wealth, but a Sudra's (express something) contemptible.

32. (The second part of) a Brahmana's (name) shall be (a word) implying happiness, of a Kshatriya's (a word) implying protection, of a Vaisya's (a term) expressive of thriving, and of a Sudra's (an expression) denoting service.

33. The names of women should be easy to pronounce, not imply anything dreadful, possess a plain meaning, be pleasing and auspicious, end in long vowels, and contain a word of benediction.

34. In the fourth month the Nishkramana (the first leaving of the house) of the child should be performed, in the sixth month the Annaprasana (first feeding with rice), and optionally (any other) auspicious ceremony required by (the custom of) the family.

35. According to the teaching of the revealed texts, the Kudakarman (tonsure) must be performed, for the sake of spiritual merit, by all twice-born men in the first or third year.

36. In the eighth year after conception, one should perform the initiation (upanayana) of a Brahmana, in the eleventh after conception (that) of a Kshatriya, but in the twelfth that of a Vaisya.

37. (The initiation) of a Brahmana who desires proficiency in sacred learning should take place in the fifth (year after conception), (that) of a Kshatriya who wishes to become powerful in the sixth, (and that) of a Vaisya who longs for (success in his) business in the eighth.

38. The (time for the) Savitri (initiation) of a Brahmana does not pass until the completion of the sixteenth year (after conception), of a Kshatriya until the completion of the twenty-second, and of a Vaisya until the completion of the twenty-fourth.

39. After those (periods men of) these three (castes) who have not received the sacrament at the proper time, become Vratyas (outcasts), excluded from the Savitri (initiation) and despised by the Aryans.

40. With such men, if they have not been purified according to the rule, let no Brahmana ever, even in times of distress, form a connexion either through the Veda or by marriage.

41. Let students, according to the order (of their castes), wear (as upper dresses) the skins of black antelopes, spotted deer, and he-goats, and (lower garments) made of hemp, flax or wool.

42. The girdle of a Brahmana shall consist of a of a triple cord of Munga grass, smooth and soft; (that) of a Kshatriya, of a bowstring, made of Murva fibres; (that) of a Vaisya, of hempen threads.

43. If Munga grass (and so forth) be not procurable, (the girdles) may be made of Kusa, Asmantaka, and Balbaga (fibres), with a single threefold knot, or with three or five (knots according to the custom of the family).

44. The sacrificial string of a Brahmana shall be made of cotton, (shall be) twisted to the right, (and consist) of three threads, that of a Kshatriya of hempen threads, (and) that of a Vaisya of woollen threads.

45. A Brahmana shall (carry), according to the sacred law, a staff of Bilva or Palasa; a Kshatriya, of Vata or Khadira; (and) a Vaisya, of Pilu or Udumbara.

46. The staff of a Brahmana shall be made of such length as to reach the end of his hair; that of a Kshatriya, to reach his forehead; (and) that of a Vaisya, to reach (the tip of his) nose.

47. Let all the staves be straight, without a blemish, handsome to look at, not likely to terrify men, with their bark perfect, unhurt by fire.

48. Having taken a staff according to his choice, having worshipped the sun and walked round the fire, turning his right hand towards it, (the student) should beg alms according to the prescribed rule.

49. An initiated Brahmana should beg, beginning (his request with the word) lady (bhavati); a Kshatriya, placing (the word) lady in the middle, but a Vaisya, placing it at the end (of the formula).

50. Let him first beg food of his mother, or of his sister, or of his own maternal aunt, or of (some other) female who will not disgrace him (by a refusal).

51. Having collected as much food as is required (from several persons), and having announced it without guile to his teacher, let him eat, turning his face towards the east, and having purified himself by sipping water.

52. (His meal will procure) long life, if he eats facing the east; fame, if he turns to the south; prosperity, if he turns to the west; truthfulness, if he faces the east.

53. Let a twice-born man always eat his food with concentrated mind, after performing an ablution; and after he has eaten, let him duly cleanse himself with water and sprinkle the cavities (of his head).

54. Let him always worship his food, and eat it without contempt; when he sees it, let him rejoice, show a pleased face, and pray that he may always obtain it.

55. Food, that is always worshipped, gives strength and manly vigour; but eaten irreverently, it destroys them both.

56. Let him not give to any man what he leaves, and beware of eating between (the two meal-times); let him not over-eat himself, nor go anywhere without having purified himself (after his meal).

57. Excessive eating is prejudicial to health, to fame, and to (bliss in) heaven; it prevents (the acquisition of) spiritual merit, and is odious among men; one ought, for these reasons, to avoid it carefully.

58. Let a Brahmana always sip water out of the part of the hand (tirtha) sacred to Brahman, or out of that sacred to Ka (Pragapati), or out of (that) sacred to the gods, never out of that sacred to the manes.

59. They call (the part) at the root of the thumb the tirtha sacred to Brahman, that at the root of the (little) finger (the tirtha) sacred to Ka (Pragapati), (that) at the tips (of the fingers, the tirtha) sacred to the gods, and that below (between the index and the thumb, the tirtha) sacred to the manes.

60. Let him first sip water thrice; next twice wipe his mouth; and, lastly, touch with water the cavities (of the head), (the seat of) the soul and the head.

61. He who knows the sacred law and seeks purity shall always perform the rite of sipping with water neither hot nor frothy, with the (prescribed) tirtha, in a lonely place, and turning to the east or to the north.

62. A Brahmana is purified by water that reaches his heart, a Kshatriya by water reaching his throat, a Vaisya by water taken into his mouth, (and) a Sudra by water touched with the extremity (of his lips).

63. A twice-born man is called upavitin when his right arm is raised (and the sacrificial string or the dress, passed under it, rests on the left shoulder); (when his) left (arm) is raised (and the string, or the dress, passed under it, rests on the right shoulder, he is called) prakinavitin; and nivitin when it hangs down (straight) from the neck.

64. His girdle, the skin (which serves as his upper garment), his staff, his sacrificial thread, (and) his water-pot he must throw into water, when they have been damaged, and take others, reciting sacred formulas.

65. (The ceremony called) Kesanta (clipping the hair) is ordained for a Brahmana in the sixteenth year (from conception); for a Kshatriya, in the twenty-second; and for a Vaisya, two (years) later than that.

66. This whole series (of ceremonies) must be performed for females (also), in order to sanctify the body, at the proper time and in the proper order, but without (the recitation of) sacred texts.

67. The nuptial ceremony is stated to be the Vedic sacrament for women (and to be equal to the initiation), serving the husband (equivalent to) the residence in (the house of the) teacher, and the household duties (the same) as the (daily) worship of the sacred fire.

68. Thus has been described the rule for the initiation of the twice-born, which indicates a (new) birth, and sanctifies; learn (now) to what duties they must afterwards apply themselves.

69. Having performed the (rite of) initiation, the teacher must first instruct the (pupil) in (the rules of) personal

purification, of conduct, of the fire-worship, and of the twilight devotions.

70. But (a student) who is about to begin the Study (of the Veda), shall receive instruction, after he has sipped water in accordance with the Institutes (of the sacred law), has made the Brahmangali, (has put on) a clean dress, and has brought his organs under due control.

71. At the beginning and at the end of (a lesson in the) Veda he must always clasp both the feet of his teacher, (and) he must study, joining his hands; that is called the Brahmangali (joining the palms for the sake of the Veda).

72. With crossed hands he must clasp (the feet) of the teacher, and touch the left (foot) with his left (hand), the right (foot) with his right (hand).

73. But to him who is about to begin studying, the teacher always unwearied, must say: Ho, recite! He shall leave off (when the teacher says): Let a stoppage take place!

74. Let him always pronounce the syllable Om at the beginning and at the end of (a lesson in) the Veda; (for) unless the syllable Om precede (the lesson) will slip away (from him), and unless it follow it will fade away.

75. Seated on (blades of Kusa grass) with their points to the east, purified by Pavitras (blades of Kusa grass), and sanctified by three suppressions of the breath (Pranayama), he is worthy (to pronounce) the syllable Om.

76. Pragapati (the lord of creatures) milked out (as it were) from the three Vedas the sounds A, U, and M, and (the Vyahritis) Bhuh, Bhuvah, Svah.

77. Moreover from the three Vedas Pragapati, who dwells in the highest heaven (Parameshthin), milked out (as it were) that Rik-verse, sacred to Savitri (Savitri), which begins with the word tad, one foot from each.

78. A Brahmana, learned in the Veda, who recites during both twilights that syllable and that (verse), preceded by the Vyahritis, gains the (whole) merit which (the recitation of) the Vedas confers.

79. A twice-born man who (daily) repeats those three one thousand times outside (the village), will be freed after a month even from great guilt, as a snake from its slough.

80. The Brahmana, the Kshatriya, and the Vaisya who neglect (the recitation of) that Rik-verse and the timely (performance of the) rites (prescribed for) them, will be blamed among virtuous men.

81. Know that the three imperishable Mahavyahritis, preceded by the syllable Om, and (followed) by the three-footed Savitri are the portal of the Veda and the gate leading (to union with) Brahman.

82. He who daily recites that (verse), untired, during three years, will enter (after death) the highest Brahman, move as free as air, and assume an ethereal form.

83. The monosyllable (Om) is the highest Brahman, (three) suppressions of the breath are the best (form of) austerity, but nothing surpasses the Savitri truthfulness is better than silence.

84. All rites ordained in the Veda, burnt oblations and (other) sacrifices, pass away; but know that the syllable (Om) is imperishable, and (it is) Brahman, (and) the Lord of creatures (Pragapati).

85. An offering, consisting of muttered prayers, is ten times more efficacious than a sacrifice performed according to the rules (of the Veda); a (prayer) which is inaudible (to others) surpasses it a hundred times, and the mental (recitation of sacred texts) a thousand times.

86. The four Pakayagnas and those sacrifices which are enjoined by the rules (of the Veda) are all together not equal in value to a sixteenth part of the sacrifice consisting of muttered prayers.

87. But, undoubtedly, a Brahmana reaches the highest goal by muttering prayers only; (whether) he perform other (rites) or neglect them, he who befriends (all creatures) is declared (to be) a (true) Brahmana.

88. A wise man should strive to restrain his organs which run wild among alluring sensual objects, like a charioteer his horses.

89. Those eleven organs which former sages have named, I will properly (and) precisely enumerate in due order,

90. (Viz.) the ear, the skin, the eyes, the tongue, and the nose as the fifth, the anus, the organ of generation, hands and feet, and the (organ of) speech, named as the tenth.

91. Five of them, the ear and the rest according to their order, they call organs of sense, and five of them, the anus and the rest, organs of action.

92. Know that the internal organ (manas) is the eleventh, which by its quality belongs to both (sets); when that has been subdued, both those sets of five have been conquered.

93. Through the attachment of his organs (to sensual pleasure) a man doubtlessly will incur guilt; but if he keep them under complete control, he will obtain success (in gaining all his aims).

94. Desire is never extinguished by the enjoyment of desired objects; it only grows stronger like a fire (fed) with clarified butter.

95. If one man should obtain all those (sensual enjoyments) and another should renounce them all, the renunciation of all pleasure is far better than the attainment of them.

96. Those (organs) which are strongly attached to sensual pleasures, cannot so effectually be restrained by abstinence (from enjoyments) as by a constant (pursuit of true) knowledge.

97. Neither (the study of) the Vedas, nor liberality, nor sacrifices, nor any (self-imposed) restraint, nor austerities, ever procure the attainment (of rewards) to a man whose heart is contaminated (by sensuality).

98. That man may be considered to have (really) subdued his organs, who on hearing and touching and seeing, on tasting and smelling (anything) neither rejoices nor repines.

99. But when one among all the organs slips away (from control), thereby (man's) wisdom slips away from him, even as the water (flows) through the one (open) foot of a (water-carrier's) skin.

100. If he keeps all the (ten) organs as well as the mind in subjection, he may gain all his aims, without reducing his body by (the practice) of Yoga.

101. Let him stand during the morning twilight, muttering the Savitri until the sun appears, but (let him recite it), seated, in the evening until the constellations can be seen distinctly.

102. He who stands during the morning twilight muttering (the Savitri), removes the guilt contracted during the (previous) night; but he who (recites it), seated, in the evening, destroys the sin he committed during the day.

103. But he who does not (worship) standing in the morning, nor sitting in the evening, shall be excluded, just like a Sudra, from all the duties and rights of an Aryan.

104. He who (desires to) perform the ceremony (of the) daily (recitation), may even recite the Savitri near water, retiring into the forest, controlling his organs and concentrating his mind.

105. Both when (one studies) the supplementary treatises of the Veda, and when (one recites) the daily portion of the Veda, no regard need be paid to forbidden days, likewise when (one repeats) the sacred texts required for a burnt oblation.

106. There are no forbidden days for the daily recitation, since that is declared to be a Brahmasattra (an everlasting sacrifice offered to Brahman); at that the Veda takes the place of the burnt oblations, and it is meritorious (even), when (natural phenomena; requiring) a cessation of the Veda-study, take the place of the exclamation Vashat.

107. For him who, being pure and controlling his organs, during a year daily recites the Veda according to the rule, that (daily recitation) will ever cause sweet and sour milk, clarified butter and honey to flow.

108. Let an Aryan who has been initiated, (daily) offer fuel in the sacred fire, beg food, sleep on the ground and do what is beneficial to this teacher, until (he performs the ceremony of) Samavartana (on returning home).

109. According to the sacred law the (following) ten (persons, viz.) the teacher's son, one who desires to do service, one who

imparts knowledge, one who is intent on fulfilling the law, one who is pure, a person connected by marriage or friendship, one who possesses (mental) ability, one who makes presents of money, one who is honest, and a relative, may be instructed (in the Veda).

110. Unless one be asked, one must not explain (anything) to anybody, nor (must one answer) a person who asks improperly; let a wise man, though he knows (the answer), behave among men as (if he were) an idiot.

111. Of the two persons, him who illegally explains (anything), and him who illegally asks (a question), one (or both) will die or incur (the other's) enmity.

112. Where merit and wealth are not (obtained by teaching) nor (at least) due obedience, in such (soil) sacred knowledge must not be sown, just as good seed (must) not (be thrown) on barren land.

113. Even in times of dire distress a teacher of the Veda should rather die with his knowledge than sow it in barren soil.

114. Sacred Learning approached a Brahmana and said to him: 'I am thy treasure, preserve me, deliver me not to a scorner; so (preserved) I shall become supremely strong.'

115. 'But deliver me, as to the keeper of thy treasure, to a Brahmana whom thou shalt know to be pure, of subdued senses, chaste and attentive.'

116. But he who acquires without permission the Veda from one who recites it, incurs the guilt of stealing the Veda, and shall sink into hell.

117. (A student) shall first reverentially salute that (teacher) from whom he receives (knowledge), referring to worldly affairs, to the Veda, or to the Brahman.

118. A Brahmana who completely governs himself, though he know the Savitri only, is better than he who knows the three Vedas, (but) does not control himself, eats all (sorts of) food, and sells all (sorts of goods).

119. One must not sit down on a couch or seat which a superior occupies; and he who occupies a couch or seat shall rise to meet a (superior), and (afterwards) salute him.

120. For the vital airs of a young man mount upwards to leave his body when an elder approaches; but by rising to meet him and saluting he recovers them.

121. He who habitually salutes and constantly pays reverence to the aged obtains an increase of four (things), (viz.) length of life, knowledge, fame, (and) strength.

122. After the (word of) salutation, a Brahmana who greets an elder must pronounce his name, saying, 'I am N. N.'

123. To those (persons) who, when a name is pronounced, do not understand (the meaning of) the salutation, a wise man should say, 'It is I;' and (he should address) in the same manner all women.

124. In saluting he should pronounce after his name the word bhoh; for the sages have declared that the nature of bhoh is the same as that of (all proper) names.

125. A Brahmana should thus be saluted in return, 'May'st thou be long-lived, O gentle one!' and the vowel 'a' must be added at the end of the name (of the person addressed), the syllable preceding it being drawn out to the length of three moras.

126. A Brahmana who does not know the form of returning a salutation, must not be saluted by a learned man; as a Sudra, even so is he.

127. Let him ask a Brahmana, on meeting him, after (his health, with the word) kusala, a Kshatriya (with the word) anamaya, a Vaisya (with the word) kshema, and a Sudra (with the word) anarogya.

128. He who has been initiated (to perform a Srauta sacrifice) must not be addressed by his name, even though he be a younger man; he who knows the sacred law must use in speaking to such (a man the particle) bhoh and (the pronoun) bhavat (your worship).

129. But to a female who is the wife of another man, and not a blood-relation, he must say, 'Lady' (bhavati) or 'Beloved sister!'

130. To his maternal and paternal uncles, fathers-in-law, officiating priests, (and other) venerable persons, he must say,

'I am N. N.,' and rise (to meet them), even though they be younger (than himself).

131. A maternal aunt, the wife of a maternal uncle, a mother-in-law, and a paternal aunt must be honoured like the wife of one's teacher; they are equal to the wife of one's teacher.

132. (The feet of the) wife of one's brother, if she be of the same caste (varna), must be clasped every day; but (the feet of) wives of (other) paternal and maternal relatives need only be embraced on one's return from a journey.

133. Towards a sister of one's father and of one's mother, and towards one's own elder sister, one must behave as towards one's mother; (but) the mother is more venerable than they.

134. Fellow-citizens are called friends (and equals though one be) ten years (older than the other), men practising (the same) fine art (though one be) five years (older than the other), Srotriyas (though) three years (intervene between their ages), but blood-relations only (if the) difference of age be very small.

135. Know that a Brahmana of ten years and Kshatriya of a hundred years stand to each other in the relation of father and son; but between those two the Brahmana is the father.

136. Wealth, kindred, age, (the due performance of) rites, and, fifthly, sacred learning are titles to respect; but each later-named (cause) is more weighty (than the preceding ones).

137. Whatever man of the three (highest) castes possesses most of those five, both in number and degree, that man is worthy of honour among them; and (so is) also a Sudra who has entered the tenth (decade of his life).

138. Way must be made for a man in a carriage, for one who is above ninety years old, for one diseased, for the carrier of a burden, for a woman, for a Snataka, for the king, and for a bridegroom.

139. Among all those, if they meet (at one time), a Snataka and the king must be (most) honoured; and if the king and a Snataka (meet), the latter receives respect from the king.

140. They call that Brahmana who initiates a pupil and teaches him the Veda together with the Kalpa and the Rahasyas, the teacher (akarya, of the latter).

141. But he who for his livelihood teaches a portion only of the Veda, or also the Angas of the Veda, is called the sub-teacher (upadhyaya).

142. That Brahmana, who performs in accordance with the rules (of the Veda) the rites, the Garbhadhana (conception-rite), and so forth, and gives food (to the child), is called the Guru (the venerable one).

143. He who, being (duly) chosen (for the purpose), performs the Agnyadheya, the Pakayagnas, (and) the (Srauta) sacrifices, such as the Agnishtoma (for another man), is called (his) officiating priest.

144. That (man) who truthfully fills both his ears with the Veda, (the pupil) shall consider as his father and mother; he must never offend him.

145. The teacher (akarya) is ten times more venerable than a sub-teacher (upadhyaya), the father a hundred times more than the teacher, but the mother a thousand times more than the father.

146. Of him who gives natural birth and him who gives (the knowledge of) the Veda, the giver of the Veda is the more venerable father; for the birth for the sake of the Veda (ensures) eternal (rewards) both in this (life) and after death.

147. Let him consider that (he received) a (mere animal) existence, when his parents begat him through mutual affection, and when he was born from the womb (of his mother).

148. But that birth which a teacher acquainted with the whole Veda, in accordance with the law, procures for him through the Savitri, is real, exempt from age and death.

149. (The pupil) must know that that man also who benefits him by (instruction in) the Veda, be it little or much, is called in these (Institutes) his Guru, in consequence of that benefit (conferred by instruction in) the Veda.

150. That Brahmana who is the giver of the birth for the sake of the Veda and the teacher of the prescribed duties becomes by law the father of an aged man, even though he himself be a child.

151. Young Kavi, the son of Angiras, taught his (relatives who were old enough to be) fathers, and, as he excelled them in (sacred) knowledge, he called them 'Little sons.'

152. They, moved with resentment, asked the gods concerning that matter, and the gods, having assembled, answered, 'The child has addressed you properly.'

153. 'For (a man) destitute of (sacred) knowledge is indeed a child, and he who teaches him the Veda is his father; for (the sages) have always said "child" to an ignorant man, and "father" to a teacher of the Veda.'

154. Neither through years, nor through white (hairs), nor through wealth, nor through (powerful) kinsmen (comes greatness). The sages have made this law, 'He who has learnt the Veda together with the Angas (Anukana) is (considered) great by us.'

155. The seniority of Brahmanas is from (sacred) knowledge, that of Kshatriyas from valour, that of Vaisyas from wealth in grain (and other goods), but that of Sudras alone from age.

156. A man is not therefore (considered) venerable because his head is gray; him who, though young, has learned the Veda, the gods consider to be venerable.

157. As an elephant made of wood, as an antelope made of leather, such is an unlearned Brahmana; those three have nothing but the names (of their kind).

158. As a eunuch is unproductive with women, as a cow with a cow is unprolific, and as a gift made to an ignorant man yields no reward, even so is a Brahmana useless, who (does) not (know) the Rikas.

159. Created beings must be instructed in (what concerns) their welfare without giving them pain, and sweet and gentle speech must be used by (a teacher) who desires (to abide by) the sacred law.

160. He, forsooth, whose speech and thoughts are pure and ever perfectly guarded, gains the whole reward which is conferred by the Vedanta.

161. Let him not, even though in pain, (speak words) cutting (others) to the quick; let him not injure others in thought

or deed; let him not utter speeches which make (others) afraid of him, since that will prevent him from gaining heaven.

162. A Brahmana should always fear homage as if it were poison; and constantly desire (to suffer) scorn as (he would long for) nectar.

163. For he who is scorned (nevertheless may) sleep with an easy mind, awake with an easy mind, and with an easy mind walk here among men; but the scorner utterly perishes.

164. A twice-born man who has been sanctified by the (employment of) the means, (described above) in due order, shall gradually and cumulatively perform the various austerities prescribed for (those who) study the Veda.

165. An Aryan must study the whole Veda together with the Rahasyas, performing at the same time various kinds of austerities and the vows prescribed by the rules (of the Veda).

166. Let a Brahmana who desires to perform austerities, constantly repeat the Veda; for the study of the Veda is declared (to be) in this world the highest austerity for a Brahmana.

167. Verily, that twice-born man performs the highest austerity up to the extremities of his nails, who, though wearing a garland, daily recites the Veda in private to the utmost of his ability.

168. A twice-born man who, not having studied the Veda, applies himself to other (and worldly study), soon falls, even while living, to the condition of a Sudra and his descendants (after him).

169. According to the injunction of the revealed texts the first birth of an Aryan is from (his natural) mother, the second (happens) on the tying of the girdle of Munga grass, and the third on the initiation to (the performance of) a (Srauta) sacrifice.

170. Among those (three) the birth which is symbolised by the investiture with the girdle of Munga grass, is his birth for the sake of the Veda; they declare that in that (birth) the Sivitri (verse) is his mother and the teacher his father.

171. They call the teacher (the pupil's) father because he gives the Veda; for nobody can perform a (sacred) rite before the investiture with the girdle of Munga grass.

172. (He who has not been initiated) should not pronounce (any) Vedic text excepting (those required for) the performance of funeral rites, since he is on a level with a Sudra before his birth from the Veda.

173. The (student) who has been initiated must be instructed in the performance of the vows, and gradually learn the Veda, observing the prescribed rules.

174. Whatever dress of skin, sacred thread, girdle, staff, and lower garment are prescribed for a (student at the initiation), the like (must again be used) at the (performance of the) vows.

175. But a student who resides with his teacher must observe the following restrictive rules, duly controlling all his organs, in order to increase his spiritual merit.

176. Every day, having bathed, and being purified, he must offer libations of water to the gods, sages and manes, worship (the images of) the gods, and place fuel on (the sacred fire).

177. Let him abstain from honey, meat, perfumes, garlands, substances (used for) flavouring (food), women, all substances turned acid, and from doing injury to living creatures.

178. From anointing (his body), applying collyrium to his eyes, from the use of shoes and of an umbrella (or parasol), from (sensual) desire, anger, covetousness, dancing, singing, and playing (musical instruments),

179. From gambling, idle disputes, backbiting, and lying, from looking at and touching women, and from hurting others.

180. Let him always sleep alone, let him never waste his manhood; for he who voluntarily wastes his manhood, breaks his vow.

181. A twice-born student, who has involuntarily wasted his manly strength during sleep, must bathe, worship the sun, and afterwards thrice mutter the Rik-verse (which begins), 'Again let my strength return to me.'

182. Let him fetch a pot full of water, flowers, cowdung, earth, and Kusa grass, as much as may be required (by his teacher), and daily go to beg food.

183. A student, being pure, shall daily bring food from the houses of men who are not deficient in (the knowledge of) the Veda and in (performing) sacrifices, and who are famous for (following their lawful) occupations.

184. Let him not beg from the relatives of his teacher, nor from his own or his mother's blood-relations; but if there are no houses belonging to strangers, let him go to one of those named above, taking the last-named first;

185. Or, if there are no (virtuous men of the kind) mentioned above, he may go to each (house in the) village, being pure and remaining silent; but let him avoid Abhisastas (those accused of mortal sin).

186. Having brought sacred fuel from a distance, let him place it anywhere but on the ground, and let him, unwearied, make with it burnt oblations to the sacred fire, both evening and morning.

187. He who, without being sick, neglects during seven (successive) days to go out begging, and to offer fuel in the sacred fire, shall perform the penance of an Avakirnin (one who has broken his vow).

188. He who performs the vow (of studentship) shall constantly subsist on alms, (but) not eat the food of one (person only); the subsistence of a student on begged food is declared to be equal (in merit) to fasting.

189. At his pleasure he may eat, when invited, the food of one man at (a rite) in honour of the gods, observing (however the conditions on his vow, or at a (funeral meal) in honor of the manes, behaving (however) like a hermit.

190. This duty is prescribed by the wise for a Brahmana only; but no such duty is ordained for a Kshatriya and a Vaisya.

191. Both when ordered by his teacher, and without a (special) command, (a student) shall always exert himself in studying (the Veda), and in doing what is serviceable to his teacher.

192. Controlling his body, his speech, his organs (of sense), and his mind, let him stand with joined hands, looking at the face of his teacher.

193. Let him always keep his right arm uncovered, behave decently and keep his body well covered, and when he is addressed (with the words), 'Be seated,' he shall sit down, facing his teacher.

194. In the presence of his teacher let him always eat less, wear a less valuable dress and ornaments (than the former), and let him rise earlier (from his bed), and go to rest later.

195. Let him not answer or converse with (his teacher), reclining on a bed, nor sitting, nor eating, nor standing, nor with an averted face.

196. Let him do (that), standing up, if (his teacher) is seated, advancing towards him when he stands, going to meet him if he advances, and running after him when he runs;

197. Going (round) to face (the teacher), if his face is averted, approaching him if he stands at a distance, but bending towards him if he lies on a bed, and if he stands in a lower place.

198. When his teacher is nigh, let his bed or seat be low; but within sight of his teacher he shall not sit carelessly at ease.

199. Let him not pronounce the mere name of his teacher (without adding an honorific title) behind his back even, and let him not mimic his gait, speech, and deportment.

200. Wherever (people) justly censure or falsely defame his teacher, there he must cover his ears or depart thence to another place.

201. By censuring (his teacher), though justly, he will become (in his next birth) an ass, by falsely defaming him, a dog; he who lives on his teacher's substance, will become a worm, and he who is envious (of his merit), a (larger) insect.

202. He must not serve the (teacher by the intervention of another) while he himself stands aloof, nor when he (himself) is angry, nor when a woman is near; if he is seated in a carriage or on a (raised) seat, he must descend and afterwards salute his (teacher).

203. Let him not sit with his teacher, to the leeward or to the windward (of him); nor let him say anything which his teacher cannot hear.

204. He may sit with his teacher in a carriage drawn by oxen, horses, or camels, on a terrace, on a bed of grass or leaves, on a mat, on a rock, on a wooden bench, or in a boat.

205. If his teacher's teacher is near, let him behave (towards him) as towards his own teacher; but let him, unless he has received permission from his teacher, not salute venerable persons of his own (family).

206. This is likewise (ordained as) his constant behaviour towards (other) instructors in science, towards his relatives (to whom honour is due), towards all who may restrain him from sin, or may give him salutary advice.

207. Towards his betters let him always behave as towards his teacher, likewise towards sons of his teacher, born by wives of equal caste, and towards the teacher's relatives both on the side of the father and of the mother.

208. The son of the teacher who imparts instruction (in his father's stead), whether younger or of equal age, or a student of (the science of) sacrifices (or of other Angas), deserves the same honour as the teacher.

209. (A student) must not shampoo the limbs of his teacher's son, nor assist him in bathing, nor eat the fragments of his food, nor wash his feet.

210. The wives of the teacher, who belong to the same caste, must be treated as respectfully as the teacher; but those who belong to a different caste, must be honoured by rising and salutation.

211. Let him not perform for a wife of his teacher (the offices of) anointing her, assisting her in the bath, shampooing her limbs, or arranging her hair.

212. (A pupil) who is full twenty years old, and knows what is becoming and unbecoming, shall not salute a young wife of his teacher (by clasping) her feet.

213. It is the nature of women to seduce men in this (world); for that reason the wise are never unguarded in (the company of) females.

214. For women are able to lead astray in (this) world not only a fool, but even a learned man, and (to make) him a slave of desire and anger.

215. One should not sit in a lonely place with one's mother, sister, or daughter; for the senses are powerful, and master even a learned man.

216. But at his pleasure a young student may prostrate himself on the ground before the young wife of a teacher, in accordance with the rule, and say, 'I, N. N., (worship thee, O lady).'

217. On returning from a journey he must clasp the feet of his teacher's wife and daily salute her (in the manner just mentioned), remembering the duty of the virtuous.

218. As the man who digs with a spade (into the ground) obtains water, even so an obedient (pupil) obtains the knowledge which lies (hidden) in his teacher.

219. A (student) may either shave his head, or wear his hair in braids, or braid one lock on the crown of his head; the sun must never set or rise while he (lies asleep) in the village.

220. If the sun should rise or set while he is sleeping, be it (that he offended) intentionally or unintentionally, he shall fast during the (next) day, muttering (the Savitri).

221. For he who lies (sleeping), while the sun sets or rises, and does not perform (that) penance, is tainted by great guilt.

222. Purified by sipping water, he shall daily worship during both twilights with a concentrated mind in a pure place, muttering the prescribed text according to the rule.

223. If a woman or a man of low caste perform anything (leading to) happiness, let him diligently practise it, as well as (any other permitted act) in which his heart finds pleasure.

224. (Some declare that) the chief good consists in (the acquisition of) spiritual merit and wealth, (others place it) in (the gratification of) desire and (the acquisition of) wealth, (others) in (the acquisition of) spiritual merit alone, and (others say that the acquisition of) wealth alone is the chief good here (below); but the (correct) decision is that it consists of the aggregate of (those) three.

225. The teacher, the father, the mother, and an elder brother must not be treated with disrespect, especially by a Brahmana, though one be grievously offended (by them).

226. The teacher is the image of Brahman, the father the image of Pragipati (the lord of created beings), the mother the image of the earth, and an (elder) full brother the image of oneself.

227. That trouble (and pain) which the parents undergo on the birth of (their) children, cannot be compensated even in a hundred years.

228. Let him always do what is agreeable to those (two) and always (what may please) his teacher; when those three are pleased, he obtains all (those rewards which) austerities (yield).

229. Obedience towards those three is declared to be the best (form of) austerity; let him not perform other meritorious acts without their permission.

230. For they are declared to be the three worlds, they the three (principal) orders, they the three Vedas, and they the three sacred fires.

231. The father, forsooth, is stated to be the Garhapatya fire, the mother the Dakshinagni, but the teacher the Ahavaniya fire; this triad of fires is most venerable.

232. He who neglects not those three, (even after he has become) a householder, will conquer the three worlds and, radiant in body like a god, he will enjoy bliss in heaven.

233. By honouring his mother he gains this (nether) world, by honouring his father the middle sphere, but by obedience to his teacher the world of Brahman.

234. All duties have been fulfilled by him who honours those three; but to him who honours them not, all rites remain fruitless.

235. As long as those three live, so long let him not (independently) perform any other (meritorious acts); let him always serve them, rejoicing (to do what is) agreeable and beneficial (to them).

236. He shall inform them of everything that with their consent he may perform in thought, word, or deed for the sake of the next world.

237. By (honouring) these three all that ought to be done by man, is accomplished; that is clearly the highest duty, every other (act) is a subordinate duty.

238. He who possesses faith may receive pure learning even from a man of lower caste, the highest law even from the lowest, and an excellent wife even from a base family.

239. Even from poison nectar may be taken, even from a child good advice, even from a foe (a lesson in) good conduct, and even from an impure (substance) gold.

240. Excellent wives, learning, (the knowledge of) the law, (the rules of) purity, good advice, and various arts may be acquired from anybody.

241. It is prescribed that in times of distress (a student) may learn (the Veda) from one who is not a Brahmana; and that he shall walk behind and serve (such a) teacher, as long as the instruction lasts.

242. He who desires incomparable bliss (in heaven) shall not dwell during his whole life in (the house of) a non-Brahmanical teacher, nor with a Brahmana who does not know the whole Veda and the Angas.

243. But if (a student) desires to pass his whole life in the teacher's house, he must diligently serve him, until he is freed from this body.

244. A Brahmana who serves his teacher till the dissolution of his body, reaches forthwith the eternal mansion of Brahman.

245. He who knows the sacred law must not present any gift to his teacher before (the Samavartana); but when, with the permission of his teacher, he is about to take the (final) bath, let him procure (a present) for the venerable man according to his ability,

246. (Viz.) a field, gold, a cow, a horse, a parasol and shoes, a seat, grain, (even) vegetables, (and thus) give pleasure to his teacher.

247. (A perpetual student) must, if his teacher dies, serve his son (provided he be) endowed with good qualities, or his widow, or his Sapinda, in the same manner as the teacher.

248. Should none of these be alive, he must serve the sacred fire, standing (by day) and sitting (during the night), and thus finish his life.

249. A Brahmana who thus passes his life as a student without breaking his vow, reaches (after death) the highest abode and will not be born again in this world.

1. The vow (of studying) the three Vedas under a teacher must be kept for thirty-six years, or for half that time, or for a quarter, or until the (student) has perfectly learnt them.

2. (A student) who has studied in due order the three Vedas, or two, or even one only, without breaking the (rules of) studentship, shall enter the order of householders.

3. He who is famous for (the strict performance of) his duties and has received his heritage, the Veda, from his father, shall be honoured, sitting on a couch and adorned with a garland, with (the present of) a cow (and the honey-mixture).

4. Having bathed, with the permission of his teacher, and performed according to the rule the Samavartana (the rite on returning home), a twice-born man shall marry a wife of equal caste who is endowed with auspicious (bodily) marks.

5. A damsel who is neither a Sapinda on the mother's side, nor belongs to the same family on the father's side, is recommended to twice-born men for wedlock and conjugal union.

6. In connecting himself with a wife, let him carefully avoid the ten following families, be they ever so great, or rich in kine, horses, sheep, grain, or (other) property,

7. (Viz.) one which neglects the sacred rites, one in which no male children (are born), one in which the Veda is not studied, one (the members of) which have thick hair on the body, those which are subject to hemorrhoids, phthisis, weakness of digestion, epilepsy, or white or black leprosy.

8. Let him not marry a maiden (with) reddish (hair), nor one who has a redundant member, nor one who is sickly, nor

one either with no hair (on the body) or too much, nor one who is garrulous or has red (eyes),

9. Nor one named after a constellation, a tree, or a river, nor one bearing the name of a low caste, or of a mountain, nor one named after a bird, a snake, or a slave, nor one whose name inspires terror.

10. Let him wed a female free from bodily defects, who has an agreeable name, the (graceful) gait of a Hamsa or of an elephant, a moderate (quantity of) hair on the body and on the head, small teeth, and soft limbs.

11. But a prudent man should not marry (a maiden) who has no brother, nor one whose father is not known, through fear lest (in the former case she be made) an appointed daughter (and in the latter) lest (he should commit) sin.

12. For the first marriage of twice-born men (wives) of equal caste are recommended; but for those who through desire proceed (to marry again) the following females, (chosen) according to the (direct) order (of the castes), are most approved.

13. It is declared that a Sudra woman alone (can be) the wife of a Sudra, she and one of his own caste (the wives) of a Vaisya, those two and one of his own caste (the wives) of a Kshatriya, those three and one of his own caste (the wives) of a Brahmana.

14. A Sudra woman is not mentioned even in any (ancient) story as the (first) wife of a Brahmana or of a Kshatriya, though they lived in the (greatest) distress.

15. Twice-born men who, in their folly, wed wives of the low (Sudra) caste, soon degrade their families and their children to the state of Sudras.

16. According to Atri and to (Gautama) the son of Utathya, he who weds a Sudra woman becomes an outcast, according to Saunaka on the birth of a son, and according to Bhrigu he who has (male) offspring from a (Sudra female, alone).

17. A Brahmana who takes a Sudra wife to his bed, will (after death) sink into hell; if he begets a child by her, he will lose the rank of a Brahmana.

18. The manes and the gods will not eat the (offerings) of that man who performs the rites in honour of the gods, of the manes, and of guests chiefly with a (Sudra wife's) assistance, and such (a man) will not go to heaven.

19. For him who drinks the moisture of a Sudra's lips, who is tainted by her breath, and who begets a son on her, no expiation is prescribed.

20. Now listen to (the) brief (description of) the following eight marriage-rites used by the four castes (varna) which partly secure benefits and partly produce evil both in this life and after death.

21. (They are) the rite of Brahman (Brahma), that of the gods (Daiva), that of the Rishis (Arsha), that of Pragapati (Pragapatya), that of the Asuras (Asura), that of the Gandharvas (Gandharva), that of the Rhashasas (Rakshasa), and that of the Pisakas (Paisaka).

22. Which is lawful for each caste (varna) and which are the virtues or faults of each (rite), all this I will declare to you, as well as their good and evil results with respect to the offspring.

23. One may know that the first six according to the order (followed above) are lawful for a Brahmana, the four last for a Kshatriya, and the same four, excepting the Rakshasa rite, for a Vaisya and a Sudra.

24. The sages state that the first four are approved (in the case) of a Brahmana, one, the Rakshasa (rite in the case) of a Kshatriya, and the Asura (marriage in that) of a Vaisya and of a Sudra.

25. But in these (Institutes of the sacred law) three of the five (last) are declared to be lawful and two unlawful; the Paisaka and the Asura (rites) must never be used.

26. For Kshatriyas those before-mentioned two rites, the Gandharva and the Rakshasa, whether separate or mixed, are permitted by the sacred tradition.

27. The gift of a daughter, after decking her (with costly garments) and honouring (her by presents of jewels), to a man learned in the Veda and of good conduct, whom (the father) himself invites, is called the Brahma rite.

28. The gift of a daughter who has been decked with ornaments, to a priest who duly officiates at a sacrifice, during the course of its performance, they call the Daiva rite.

29. When (the father) gives away his daughter according to the rule, after receiving from the bridegroom, for (the fulfilment of) the sacred law, a cow and a bull or two pairs, that is named the Arsha rite.

30. The gift of a daughter (by her father) after he has addressed (the couple) with the text, 'May both of you perform together your duties,' and has shown honour (to the bridegroom), is called in the Smriti the Pragapatya rite.

31. When (the bridegroom) receives a maiden, after having given as much wealth as he can afford, to the kinsmen and to the bride herself, according to his own will, that is called the Asura rite.

32. The voluntary union of a maiden and her lover one must know (to be) the Gandharva rite, which springs from desire and has sexual intercourse for its purpose.

33. The forcible abduction of a maiden from her home, while she cries out and weeps, after (her kinsmen) have been slain or wounded and (their houses) broken open, is called the Rakshasa rite.

34. When (a man) by stealth seduces a girl who is sleeping, intoxicated, or disordered in intellect, that is the eighth, the most base and sinful rite of the Pisakas.

35. The gift of daughters among Brahmanas is most approved, (if it is preceded) by (a libation of) water; but in the case of other castes (it may be performed) by (the expression of) mutual consent.

36. Listen now to me, ye Brahmanas, while I fully declare what quality has been ascribed by Manu to each of these marriage-rites.

37. The son of a wife wedded according to the Brahma rite, if he performs meritorious acts, liberates from sin ten ancestors, ten descendants and himself as the twenty-first.

38. The son born of a wife, wedded according to the Daiva rite, likewise (saves) seven ancestors and seven descendants,

the son of a wife married by the Arsha rite three (in the ascending and descending lines), and the son of a wife married by the rite of Ka (Pragapati) six (in either line).

39. From the four marriages, (enumerated) successively, which begin with the Brahma rite spring sons, radiant with knowledge of the Veda and honoured by the Sishtas (good men).

40. Endowded with the qualities of beauty and goodness, possessing wealth and fame, obtaining as many enjoyments as they desire and being most righteous, they will live a hundred years.

41. But from the remaining (four) blamable marriages spring sons who are cruel and speakers of untruth, who hate the Veda and the sacred law.

42. In the blameless marriages blameless children are born to men, in blamable (marriages) blamable (offspring); one should therefore avoid the blamable (forms of marriage).

43. The ceremony of joining the hands is prescribed for (marriages with) women of equal caste (varna); know that the following rule (applies) to weddings with females of a different caste (varna).

44. On marrying a man of a higher caste a Kshatriya bride must take hold of an arrow, a Vaisya bride of a goad, and a Sudra female of the hem of the (bridegroom's) garment.

45. Let (the husband) approach his wife in due season, being constantly satisfied with her (alone); he may also, being intent on pleasing her, approach her with a desire for conjugal union (on any day) excepting the Parvans.

46. Sixteen (days and) nights (in each month), including four days which differ from the rest and are censured by the virtuous, (are called) the natural season of women.

47. But among these the first four, the eleventh and the thirteenth are (declared to be) forbidden; the remaining nights are recommended.

48. On the even nights sons are conceived and daughters on the uneven ones; hence a man who desires to have sons should approach his wife in due season on the even (nights).

49. A male child is produced by a greater quantity of male seed, a female child by the prevalence of the female; if (both are) equal, a hermaphrodite or a boy and a girl; if (both are) weak or deficient in quantity, a failure of conception (results).

50. He who avoids women on the six forbidden nights and on eight others, is (equal in chastity to) a student, in whichever order he may live.

51. No father who knows (the law) must take even the smallest gratuity for his daughter; for a man who, through avarice, takes a gratuity, is a seller of his offspring.

52. But those (male) relations who, in their folly, live on the separate property of women, (e.g. appropriate) the beasts of burden, carriages, and clothes of women, commit sin and will sink into hell.

53. Some call the cow and the bull (given) at an Arsha wedding 'a gratuity;' (but) that is wrong, since (the acceptance of) a fee, be it small or great, is a sale (of the daughter).

54. When the relatives do not appropriate (for their use) the gratuity (given), it is not a sale; (in that case) the (gift) is only a token of respect and of kindness towards the maidens.

55. Women must be honoured and adorned by their fathers, brothers, husbands, and brothers-in-law, who desire (their own) welfare.

56. Where women are honoured, there the gods are pleased; but where they are not honoured, no sacred rite yields rewards.

57. Where the female relations live in grief, the family soon wholly perishes; but that family where they are not unhappy ever prospers.

58. The houses on which female relations, not being duly honoured, pronounce a curse, perish completely, as if destroyed by magic.

59. Hence men who seek (their own) welfare, should always honour women on holidays and festivals with (gifts of) ornaments, clothes, and (dainty) food.

60. In that family, where the husband is pleased with his wife and the wife with her husband, happiness will assuredly be lasting.

61. For if the wife is not radiant with beauty, she will not attract her husband; but if she has no attractions for him, no children will be born.

62. If the wife is radiant with beauty, the whole house is bright; but if she is destitute of beauty, all will appear dismal.

63. By low marriages, by omitting (the performance of) sacred rites, by neglecting the study of the Veda, and by irreverence towards Brahmanas, (great) families sink low.

64. By (practising) handicrafts, by pecuniary transactions, by (begetting) children on Sudra females only, by (trading in) cows, horses, and carriages, by (the pursuit of) agriculture and by taking service under a king,

65. By sacrificing for men unworthy to offer sacrifices and by denying (the future rewards for good) works, families, deficient in the (knowledge of the) Veda, quickly perish.

66. But families that are rich in the knowledge of the Veda, though possessing little wealth, are numbered among the great, and acquire great fame.

67. With the sacred fire, kindled at the wedding, a householder shall perform according to the law the domestic ceremonies and the five (great) sacrifices, and (with that) he shall daily cook his food.

68. A householder has five slaughter-houses (as it were, viz.) the hearth, the grinding-stone, the broom, the pestle and mortar, the water-vessel, by using which he is bound (with the fetters of sin).

69. In order to successively expiate (the offences committed by means) of all these (five) the great sages have prescribed for householders the daily (performance of the five) great sacrifices.

70. Teaching (and studying) is the sacrifice (offered) to Brahman, the (offerings of water and food called) Tarpana the sacrifice to the manes, the burnt oblation the sacrifice offered to the gods, the Bali offering that offered to the Bhutas, and the hospitable reception of guests the offering to men.

71. He who neglects not these five great sacrifices, while he is able (to perform them), is not tainted 'y the sins

(committed) in the five places of slaughter, though he constantly lives in the (order of) house (-holders).

72. But he who does not feed these five, the gods, his guests, those whom he is bound to maintain, the manes, and himself, lives not, though he breathes.

73. They call (these) five sacrifices also, Ahuta, Huta, Prahuta, Brahmya-huta, and Prasita.

74. Ahuta (not offered in the fire) is the muttering (of Vedic texts), Huta the burnt oblation (offered to the gods), Prahuta (offered by scattering it on the ground) the Bali offering given to the Bhutas, Brahmya-huta (offered in the digestive fire of Brahmanas), the respectful reception of Brahmana (guests), and Prasita (eaten) the (daily oblation to the manes, called) Tarpana.

75. Let (every man) in this (second order, at least) daily apply himself to the private recitation of the Veda, and also to the performance of the offering to the gods; for he who is diligent in the performance of sacrifices, supports both the movable and the immovable creation.

76. An oblation duly thrown into the fire, reaches the sun; from the sun comes rain, from rain food, therefrom the living creatures (derive their subsistence).

77. As all living creatures subsist by receiving support from air, even so (the members of) all orders subsist by receiving support from the householder.

78. Because men of the three (other) orders are daily supported by the householder with (gifts of) sacred knowledge and food, therefore (the order of) householders is the most excellent order.

79. (The duties of) this order, which cannot be practised by men with weak organs, must be carefully observed by him who desires imperishable (bliss in) heaven, and constant happiness in this (life).

80. The sages, the manes, the gods, the Bhutas, and guests ask the householders (for offerings and gifts); hence he who knows (the law), must give to them (what is due to each).

81. Let him worship, according to the rule, the sages by the private recitation of the Veda, the gods by burnt oblations, the manes by funeral offerings (Sraddha), men by (gifts of) food, and the Bhutas by the Bali offering.

82. Let him daily perform a funeral sacrifice with food, or with water, or also with milk, roots, and fruits, and (thus) please the manes.

83. Let him feed even one Brahmana in honour of the manes at (the Sraddha), which belongs to the five great sacrifices; but let him not feed on that (occasion) any Brahmana on account of the Vaisvadeva offering.

84. A Brahmana shall offer according to the rule (of his Grihya-sutra a portion) of the cooked food destined for the Vaisvadeva in the sacred domestic fire to the following deities:

85. First to Agni, and (next) to Soma, then to both these gods conjointly, further to all the gods (Visve Devah), and (then) to Dhanvantari,

86. Further to Kuhu (the goddess of the new-moon day), to Anumati (the goddess of the full-moon day), to Pragapati (the lord of creatures), to heaven and earth conjointly, and finally to Agni Svishtakrit (the fire which performs the sacrifice well).

87. After having thus duly offered the sacrificial food, let him throw Bali offerings in all directions of the compass, proceeding (from the east) to the south, to Indra, Yama, Varuna, and Soma, as well as to the servants (of these deities).

88. Saying, '(Adoration) to the Maruts,' he shall scatter (some food) near the door, and (some) in water, saying, '(Adoration to the waters;' he shall throw (some) on the pestle and the mortar, speaking thus, '(Adoration) to the trees.'

89. Near the head (of the bed) he shall make an offering to Sri (fortune), and near the foot (of his bed) to Bhadrakali; in the centre of the house let him place a Bali for Brahman and for Vastoshpati (the lord of the dwelling) conjointly.

90. Let him throw up into the air a Bali for all the gods, and (in the day-time one) for the goblins roaming about by day, (and in the evening one) for the goblins that walk at night.

91. In the upper story let him offer a Bali to Sarvatmabhuti; but let him throw what remains (from these offerings) in a southerly direction for the manes.

92. Let him gently place on the ground (some food) for dogs, outcasts, Kandalas (Svapak), those afflicted with diseases that are punishments of former sins, crows, and insects.

93. That Brahmana who thus daily honours all beings, goes, endowed with a resplendent body, by a straight road to the highest dwelling-place (i.e. Brahman).

94. Having performed this Bali offering, he shall first feed his guest and, according to the rule, give alms to an ascetic (and) to a student.

95. A twice-born householder gains, by giving alms, the same reward for his meritorious act which (a student) obtains for presenting, in accordance with the rule, a cow to his teacher.

96. Let him give, in accordance with the rule, to a Brahmana who knows the true meaning of the Veda, even (a small portion of food as) alms, or a pot full of water, having garnished (the food with seasoning, or the pot with flowers and fruit).

97. The oblations to gods and manes, made by men ignorant (of the law of gifts), are lost, if the givers in their folly present (shares of them) to Brahmanas who are mere ashes.

98. An offering made in the mouth-fire of Brahmanas rich in sacred learning and austerities, saves from misfortune and from great guilt.

99. But let him offer, in accordance with the rule, to a guest who has come (of his own accord) a seat and water, as well as food, garnished (with seasoning), according to his ability.

100. A Brahmana who stays unhonoured (in the house), takes away (with him) all the spiritual merit even of a man who subsists by gleaning ears of corn, or offers oblations in five fires.

101. Grass, room (for resting), water, and fourthly a kind word; these (things) never fail in the houses of good men.

102. But a Brahmana who stays one night only is declared to be a guest (atithi); for because he stays (sthita) not long (anityam), he is called atithi (a guest).

103. One must not consider as a guest a Brahmana who dwells in the same village, nor one who seeks his livelihood by social intercourse, even though he has come to a house where (there is) a wife, and where sacred fires (are kept).

104. Those foolish householders who constantly seek (to live on) the food of others, become, in consequence of that (baseness), after death the cattle of those who give them food.

105. A guest who is sent by the (setting) sun in the evening, must not be driven away by a householder; whether he have come at (supper-) time or at an inopportune moment, he must not stay in the house without entertainment.

106. Let him not eat any (dainty) food which he does not offer to his guest; the hospitable reception of guests procures wealth, fame, long life, and heavenly bliss.

107. Let him offer (to his guests) seats, rooms, beds, attendance on departure and honour (while they stay), to the most distinguished in the best form, to the lower ones in a lower form, to equals in an equal manner.

108. But if another guest comes after the Vaisvadeva offering has been finished, (the householder) must give him food according to his ability, (but) not repeat the Bali offering.

109. A Brahmana shall not name his family and (Vedic) gotra in order to obtain a meal; for he who boasts of them for the sake of a meal, is called by the wise a foul feeder (vantasin).

110. But a Kshatriya (who comes) to the house of a Brahmana is not called a guest (atithi), nor a Vaisya, nor a Sudra, nor a personal friend, nor a relative, nor the teacher.

111. But if a Kshatriya comes to the house of a Brahmana in the manner of a guest, (the house-holder) may feed him according to his desire, after the above-mentioned Brahmanas have eaten.

112. Even a Vaisya and a Sudra who have approached his house in the manner of guests, he may allow to eat with his servants, showing (thereby) his compassionate disposition.

113. Even to others, personal friends and so forth, who have come to his house out of affection, he may give food,

garnished (with seasoning) according to his ability, (at the same time) with his wife.

114. Without hesitation he may give food, even before his guests, to the following persons, (viz.) to newly-married women, to infants, to the sick, and to pregnant women.

115. But the foolish man who eats first without having given food to these (persons) does, while he crams, not know that (after death) he himself will be devoured by dogs and vultures.

116. After the Brahmanas, the kinsmen, and the servants have dined, the householder and his wife may afterwards eat what remains.

117. Having honoured the gods, the sages, men, the manes, and the guardian deities of the house, the householder shall eat afterwards what remains.

118. He who prepares food for himself (alone), eats nothing but sin; for it is ordained that the food which remains after (the performance of) the sacrifices shall be the meal of virtuous men.

119. Let him honour with the honey-mixture a king, an officiating priest, a Snataka, the teacher, a son-in-law, a father-in-law, and a maternal uncle, (if they come) again after a full year (has elapsed since their last visit).

120. A king and a Srotriya, who come on the performance of a sacrifice, must be honoured with the honey-mixture, but not if no sacrifice is being performed; that is a settled rule.

121. But the wife shall offer in the evening (a portion) of the dressed food as a Bali-oblation, without (the recitation of) sacred formulas; for that (rite which is called the) Vaisvadeva is prescribed both for the morning and the evening.

122. After performing the Pitriyagna, a Brahmana who keeps a sacred fire shall offer, month by month, on the new-moon day, the funeral sacrifice (Sraddha, called) Pindanvaharyaka.

123. The wise call the monthly funeral offering to the manes Anvaharya (to be offered after the cakes), and that must

be carefully performed with the approved (sorts of) flesh (mentioned below).

124. I will fully declare what and how many (Brahmanas) must be fed on that (occasion), who must be avoided, and on what kinds of food (they shall dine).

125. One must feed two (Brahmanas) at the offering to the gods, and three at the offering to the manes, or one only on either occasion; even a very wealthy man shall not be anxious (to entertain) a large company.

126. A large company destroys these five (advantages) the respectful treatment (of the invited, the propriety of) place and time, purity and (the selection of) virtuous Brahmana (guests); he therefore shall not seek (to entertain) a large company.

127. Famed is this rite for the dead, called (the sacrifice sacred to the manes (and performed) on the new-moon day; if a man is diligent in (performing) that, (the reward of) the rite for the dead, which is performed according to Smarta rules, reaches him constantly.

128. Oblations to the gods and manes must be presented by the givers to a Srotriya alone; what is given to such a most worthy Brahmana yields great reward.

129. Let him feed even one learned man at (the sacrifice) to the gods, and one at (the sacrifice) to the manes; (thus) he will gain a rich reward, not (if he entertains) many who are unacquainted with the Veda.

130. Let him make inquiries even regarding the remote (ancestors of) a Brahmana who has studied an entire (recension of the) Veda; (if descended from a virtuous race) such a man is a worthy recipient of gifts (consisting) of food offered to the gods or to the manes, he is declared (to procure as great rewards as) a guest (atithi).

131. Though a million of men, unaquainted with the Rikas, were to dine at a (funeral sacrifice), yet a single man, learned in the Veda, who is satisfied (with his entertainment), is worth them all as far as the (production of) spiritual merit (is concerned).

132. Food sacred to the manes or to the gods must be given to a man distinguished by sacred knowledge; for hands, smeared with blood, cannot be cleansed with blood.

133. As many mouthfuls as an ignorant man swallows at a sacrifice to the gods or to the manes, so many red-hot spikes, spears, and iron balls must (the giver of the repast) swallow after death.

134. Some Brahmanas are devoted to (the pursuit of) knowledge, and others to (the performance of) austerities; some to austerities and to the recitation of the Veda, and others to (the performance of) sacred rites.

135. Oblations to the manes ought to be carefully presented to those devoted to knowledge, but offerings to the gods, in accordance with the reason (of the sacred law), to (men of) all the four (above-mentioned classes).

136. If there is a father ignorant of the sacred texts whose son has learned one whole recension of the Veda and the Angas, and a son ignorant of the sacred texts whose father knows an entire recension of the Veda and the Angas,

137. Know that he whose father knows the Veda, is the more venerable one (of the two); yet the other one is worthy of honour, because respect is due to the Veda (which he has learned).

138. Let him not entertain a personal friend at a funeral sacrifice; he may gain his affection by (other) valuable gifts; let him feed at a Sraddha a Brahmana whom he considers neither as a foe nor as a friend.

139. He who performs funeral sacrifices and offerings to the gods chiefly for the sake of (gaining) friends, reaps after death no reward for Sraddhas and sacrifices.

140. That meanest among twice-born men who in his folly contracts friendships through a funeral sacrifice, loses heaven, because he performed a Sraddha for the sake of friendship.

141. A gift (of food) by twice-born men, consumed with (friends and relatives), is said to be offered to the Pisakas; it remains in this (world) alone like a blind cow in one stable.

142. As a husbandman reaps no harvest when he has sown the seed in barren soil, even so the giver of sacrificial food gains no reward if he presented it to a man unacquainted with the Rikas.

143. But a present made in accordance with the rules to a learned man, makes the giver and the recipient partakers of rewards both in this (life) and after death.

144. (If no learned Brahmana be at hand), he may rather honour a (virtuous) friend than an enemy, though the latter may be qualified (by learning and so forth); for sacrificial food, eaten by a foe, bears no reward after death.

145. Let him (take) pains (to) feed at a Sraddha an adherent of the Rig-veda who has studied one entire (recension of that) Veda, or a follower of the Yagur-veda who has finished one Sakha, or a singer of Samans who (likewise) has completed (the study of an entire recension).

146. If one of these three dines, duly honoured, at a funeral sacrifice, the ancestors of him (who gives the feast), as far as the seventh person, will be satisfied for a very long time.

147. This is the chief rule (to be followed) in offering sacrifices to the gods and manes; know that the virtuous always observe the following subsidiary rule.

148. One may also entertain (on such occasions) one's maternal grandfather, a maternal uncle, a sister's son, a father-in-law, one's teacher, a daughter's son, a daughter's husband, a cognate kinsman, one's own officiating priest or a man for whom one offers sacrifices.

149. For a rite sacred to the gods, he who knows the law will not make (too close) inquiries regarding an (invited) Brahmana; but when one performs a ceremony in honour of the manes, one must carefully examine (the qualities and parentage of the guest).

150. Manu has declared that those Brahmanas who are thieves, outcasts, eunuchs, or atheists are unworthy (to partake) of oblations to the gods and manes.

151. Let him not entertain at a Sraddha one who wears his hair in braids (a student), one who has not studied (the

Veda), one afflicted with a skin-disease, a gambler, nor those who sacrifice for a multitude (of sacrificers).

152. Physicians, temple-priests, sellers of meat, and those who subsist by shop-keeping must be avoided at sacrifices offered to the gods and to the manes.

153. A paid servant of a village or of a king, man with deformed nails or black teeth, one who opposes his teacher, one who has forsaken the sacred fire, and a usurer;

154. One suffering from consumption, one who subsists by tending cattle, a younger brother who marries or kindles the sacred fire before the elder, one who neglects the five great sacrifices, an enemy of the Brahmana race, an elder brother who marries or kindles the sacred fire after the younger, and one who belongs to a company or corporation,

155. An actor or singer, one who has broken the vow of studentship, one whose (only or first) wife is a Sudra female, the son of a remarried woman, a one-eyed man, and he in whose house a paramour of his wife (resides);

156. He who teaches for a stipulated fee and he who is taught on that condition, he who instructs Sudra pupils and he whose teacher is a Sudra, he who speaks rudely, the son of an adulteress, and the son of a widow,

157. He who forsakes his mother, his father, or a teacher without a (sufficient) reason, he who has contracted an alliance with outcasts either through the Veda or through a marriage,

158. An incendiary, a prisoner, he who eats the food given by the son of an adulteress, a seller of Soma, he who undertakes voyages by sea, a bard, an oil-man, a suborner to perjury,

159. He who wrangles or goes to law with his father, the keeper of a gambling-house, a drunkard, he who is afflicted with a disease (in punishment of former) crimes, he who is accused of a mortal sin, a hypocrite, a seller of substances used for flavouring food,

160. A maker of bows and of arrows, he who lasciviously dallies with a brother's widow, the betrayer of a friend, one who subsists by gambling, he who learns (the Veda) from his son,

161. An epileptic man, who suffers from scrofulous swellings of the glands, one afflicted with white leprosy, an informer, a madman, a blind man, and he who cavils at the Veda must (all) be avoided.

162. A trainer of elephants, oxen, horses, or camels, he who subsists by astrology, a bird-fancier, and he who teaches the use of arms,

163. He who diverts water-courses, and he who delights in obstructing them, an architect, a messenger, and he who plants trees (for money),

164. A breeder of sporting-dogs, a falconer, one who defiles maidens, he who delights in injuring living creatures, he who gains his subsistence from Sudras, and he who offers sacrifices to the Ganas,

165. He who does not follow the rule of conduct, a (man destitute of energy like a) eunuch, one who constantly asks (for favours), he who lives by agriculture, a club-footed man, and he who is censured by virtuous men,

166. A shepherd, a keeper of buffaloes, the husband of a remarried woman, and a carrier of dead bodies, (all these) must be carefully avoided.

167. A Brahmana who knows (the sacred law) should shun at (sacrifices) both (to the gods and to the manes) these lowest of twice-born men, whose conduct is reprehensible, and who are unworthy (to sit) in the company (at a repast).

168. As a fire of dry grass is (unable to consume the offerings and is quickly) extinguished, even so (is it with) an unlearned Brahmana; sacrificial food must not be given to him, since it (would be) offered in ashes.

169. I will fully declare what result the giver obtains after death, if he gives food, destined for the gods or manes, to a man who is unworthy to sit in the company.

170. The Rakshasas, indeed, consume (the food) eaten by Brahmanas who have not fulfilled the vow of studentship, by a Parivettri and so forth, and by other men not admissible into the company.

171. He must be considered as a Parivettri who marries or begins the performance of the Agnihotra before his elder brother, but the latter as a Parivitti.

172. The elder brother who marries after the younger, the younger brother who marries before the elder, the female with whom such a marriage is contracted, he who gives her away, and the sacrificing priest, as the fifth, all fall into hell.

173. He who lasciviously dallies with the widow of a deceased brother, though she be appointed (to bear a child by him) in accordance with the sacred law, must be known to be a Didhishupati.

174. Two (kinds of) sons, a Kunda and a Golaka, are born by wives of other men; (he who is born) while the husband lives, will be a Kunda, and (he who is begotten) after the husband's death, a Golaka.

175. But those two creatures, who are born of wives of other men, cause to the giver the loss (of the rewards), both in this life and after death, for the food sacred to gods or manes which has been given (to them).

176. The foolish giver (of a funeral repast) does not reap the reward for as many worthy guests as a man, inadmissible into company, can look on while they are feeding.

177. A blind man by his presence causes to the giver (of the feast) the loss of the reward for ninety (guests), a one-eyed man for sixty, one who suffers from white leprosy for a hundred, and one punished by a (terrible) disease for a thousand.

178. The giver (of a Sraddha) loses the reward, due for such a non-sacrificial gift, for as many Brahmanas as a (guest) who sacrifices for Sudras may touch (during the meal) with his limbs.

179. And if a Brahmana, though learned in the Veda, accepts through covetousness a gift from such (a man), he will quickly perish, like a vessel of unburnt clay in water.

180 (Food) given to a seller of Soma becomes ordure, (that given) to a physician pus and blood, but (that presented) to a temple-priest is lost, and (that given) to a usurer finds no place (in the world of the gods).

181. What has been given to a Brahmana who lives by trade that is not (useful) in this world and the next, and (a present) to a Brahmana born of a remarried woman (resembles) an oblation thrown into ashes.

182. But the wise declare that the food which (is offered) to other unholy, inadmissible men, enumerated above, (is turned into) adipose secretions, blood, flesh, marrow, and bone.

183. Now hear by what chief of twice-born men a company defiled by (the presence of) unworthy (guests) is purified, and the full (description of) the Brahmanas who sanctify a company.

184. Those men must be considered as the sanctifiers of a company who are most learned in all the Vedas and in all the Angas, and who are the descendants of Srotriyas.

185. A Trinakiketa, one who keeps five sacred fires, a Trisuparna, one who is versed in the six Angas, the son of a woman married according to the Brahma rite, one who sings the Gyeshthasaman,

186. One who knows the meaning of the Veda, and he who expounds it, a student, one who has given a thousand (cows), and a centenarian must be considered as Brahmanas who sanctify a company.

187. On the day before the Sraddha-rite is performed, or on the day when it takes place, let him invite with due respect at least three Brahmanas, such as have been mentioned above.

188. A Brahmana who has been invited to a (rite) in honour of the manes shall always control himself and not recite the Veda, and he who performs the Sraddha (must act in the same manner).

189. For the manes attend the invited Brahmanas, follow them (when they walk) like the wind, and sit near them when they are seated.

190. But a Brahmana who, being duly invited to a rite in honour of the gods or of the manes, in any way breaks (the appointment), becomes guilty (of a crime), and (in his next birth) a hog.

191. But he who, being invited to a Sraddha, dallies with a Sudra woman, takes upon himself all the sins which the giver (of the feast) committed.

192. The manes are primeval deities, free from anger, careful of purity, ever chaste, averse from strife, and endowed with great virtues.

193. Now learn fully from whom all these (manes derive) their origin, and with what ceremonies they ought to be worshipped.

194. The (various) classes of the manes are declared to be the sons of all those sages, Mariki and the rest, who are children of Manu, the son of Hiranyagarbha.

195. The Somasads, the sons of Virag, are stated to be the manes of the Sadhyas, and the Agnishvattas, the children of Mariki, are famous in the world (as the manes) of the gods.

196. The Barhishads, born of Atri, are recorded to be (the manes) of the Daityas, Danavas, Yakshas, Gandharvas, Snake-deities, Rakshasas, Suparnas, and a Kimnaras.

197. The Somapas those of the Brahmanas, the Havirbhugs those of the Kshatriyas, the Agyapas those of the Vaisyas, but the Sukalins those of the Sudras.

198. The Somapas are the sons of Kavi (Bhrigu), the Havishmats the children of Angiras, the Agyapas the offspring of Pulastya, but the Sukalins (the issue) of Vasishtha.

199. One should know that (other classes), the Agnidagdhas, the Anagnidagdhas, the Kavyas, the Barhishads, the Agnishvattas, and the Saumyas, are (the manes) of the Brahmanas alone.

200. But know also that there exist in this (world) countless sons and grandsons of those chief classes of manes which have been enumerated.

201. From the sages sprang the manes, from the manes the gods and the Danavas, but from the gods the whole world, both the movable and the immovable in due order.

202. Even water offered with faith (to the manes) in vessels made of silver or adorned with silver, produces endless (bliss).

203. For twice-born men the rite in honour of the manes is more important than the rite in honour of the gods; for the offering to the gods which precedes (the Sraddhas), has been declared to be a means of fortifying (the latter).

204. Let him first invite a (Brahmana) in honour of the gods as a protection for the (offering to the manes); for the Rakshasas destroy a funeral sacrifice which is left without such a protection.

205. Let him make (the Sraddha) begin and end with (a rite) in honour of the gods; it shall not begin and end with a (rite) to the manes; for he who makes it begin and end with a (rite) in honour of the manes, soon perishes together with his progeny.

206. Let him smear a pure and secluded place with cowdung, and carefully make it sloping towards the south.

207. The manes are always pleased with offerings made in open, naturally pure places, on the banks of rivers, and in secluded spots.

208. The (sacrificer) shall make the (invited) Brahmanas, who have duly performed their ablutions, sit down on separate, prepared seats, on which blades of Kusa grass have been placed.

209. Having placed those blameless Brahmanas on their seats, he shall honour them with fragrant garlands and perfumes, beginning with (those who are invited in honour of) the gods.

210. Having presented to them water, sesamum grains, and blades of Kusa grass, the Brahmana (sacrificer) shall offer (oblations) in the sacred fire, after having received permission (to do so) from (all) the Brahmana (guests) conjointly.

211. Having first, according to the rule, performed, as a means of protecting (the Sraddha), oblations to Agni, to Soma, and to Yama, let him afterwards satisfy the manes by a gift of sacrificial food.

212. But if no (sacred) fire (is available), he shall place (the offerings) into the hand of a Brahmana; for Brahmanas who know the sacred texts declare, 'What fire is, even such is a Brahmana.'

213. They (also) call those first of twice-born men the ancient deities of the funeral sacrifice, free from anger, easily pleased, employed in making men prosper.

214. After he has performed (the oblations) in the fire, (and) the whole series of ceremonies in such a manner that they end in the south, let him sprinkle water with his right hand on the spot (where the cakes are to be placed).

215. But having made three cakes out of the remainder of that sacrificial food, he must, concentrating his mind and turning towards the south, place them on (Kusa grass) exactly in the same manner in which (he poured out the libations of) water.

216. Having offered those cakes according to the (prescribed) rule, being pure, let him wipe the same hand with (the roots of) those blades of Kusa grass for the sake of the (three ancestors) who partake of the wipings (lepa).

217. Having (next) sipped water, turned round (towards the north), and thrice slowly suppressed his breath, (the sacrificer) who knows the sacred texts shall worship (the guardian deities of) the six seasons and the manes.

218. Let him gently pour out the remainder of the water near the cakes, and, with fixed attention, smell those cakes, in the order in which they were placed (on the ground).

219. But taking successively very small portions from the cakes, he shall make those seated Brahmana eat them, in accordance with the rule, before (their dinner).

220. But if the (sacrificer's) father is living, he must offer (the cakes) to three remoter (ancestors); or he may also feed his father at the funeral sacrifice as (one of the) Brahmana (guests).

221. But he whose father is dead, while his grandfather lives, shall, after pronouncing his father's name, mention (that of) his great-grandfather.

222. Manu has declared that either the grandfather may eat at that Sraddha (as a guest), or (the grandson) having received permission, may perform it, as he desires.

223. Having poured water mixed with sesamum, in which a blade of Kusa grass has been placed, into the hands of the (guests), he shall give (to each) that (above-mentioned) portion of the cake, saying, 'To those, Svadha!'

224. But carrying (the vessel) filled with food with both hands, the (sacrificer) himself shall gently place it before the Brahmanas, meditating on the manes.

225. The malevolent Asuras forcibly snatch away that food which is brought without being held with both hands.

226. Let him, being pure and attentive, carefully place on the ground the seasoning (for the rice), such as broths and pot herbs, sweet and sour milk, and honey,

227. (As well as) various (kinds of) hard food which require mastication, and of soft food, roots, fruits, savoury meat, and fragrant drinks.

228. All this he shall present (to his guests), being pure and attentive, successively invite them to partake of each (dish), proclaiming its qualities.

229. Let him on no account drop a tear, become angry or utter an untruth, nor let him touch the food with his foot nor violently shake it.

230. A tear sends the (food) to the Pretas, anger to his enemies, a falsehood to the dogs, contact with his foot to the Rakshasas, a shaking to the sinners.

231. Whatever may please the Brahmanas, let him give without grudging it; let him give riddles from the Veda, for that is agreeable to the manes.

232. At a (sacrifice in honour) of the manes, he must let (his guests) hear the Veda, the Institutes of the sacred law, legends, tales, Puranas, and Khilas.

233. Himself being delighted, let him give delight to the Brahmanas, cause them to partake gradually and slowly (of each dish), and repeatedly invite (them to eat) by (offering) the food and (praising) its qualities.

234. Let him eagerly entertain at a funeral sacrifice a daughter's son, though he be a student, and let him place a

Nepal blanket on the on the seat (of each guest), scattering sesamum grains on the ground.

235. There are three means of sanctification, (to be used) at a Sraddha, a daughter's son, a Nepal blanket, and sesamum grains; and they recommend three (other things) for it, cleanliness, suppression of anger, and absence of haste.

236. All the food must be very hot, and the (guests) shall eat in silence; (even though) asked by the giver (of the feast), the Brahmanas shall not proclaim the qualities of the sacrificial food.

237. As long as the food remains warm, as long as they eat in silence, as long as the qualities of the food are not proclaimed, so long the manes partake (of it).

238. What (a guest) eats, covering his head, what he eats with his face turned towards the south, what he eats with sandals on (his feet), that the Rakshasas consume.

239. A Kandala, a village pig, a cock, a dog, a menstruating woman, and a eunuch must not look at the Brahmanas while they eat.

240. What (any of) these sees at a burnt-oblation, at a (solemn) gift, at a dinner (given to Brahmanas), or at any rite in honour of the gods and manes, that produces not the intended result.

241. A boar makes (the rite) useless by inhaling the smell (of the offerings), a cock by the air of his wings, a dog by throwing his eye (on them), a low-caste man by touching (them).

242. If a lame man, a one-eyed man, one deficient in a limb, or one with a redundant limb, be even the servant of the performer (of the Sraddha), he must be removed from that place (where the Sraddha is held).

243. To a Brahmana (householder), or to an ascetic who comes for food, he may, with the permission of (his) Brahmana (guests), show honour according to his ability.

244. Let him mix all the kinds of food together, sprinkle them with water and put them, scattering them (on Kusa grass), down on the ground in front of (his guests), when they have finished their meal.

245. The remnant (in the dishes), and the portion scattered on Kusa grass, shall be the share of deceased (children) who received not the sacrament (of cremation) and of those who (unjustly) forsook noble wives.

246. They declare the fragments which have fallen on the ground at a (Sraddha) to the manes, to be the share of honest, dutiful servants.

247. But before the performance of the Sapindikarana, one must feed at the funeral sacrifice in honour of a (recently-) deceased Aryan (one Brahmana) without (making an offering) to the gods, and give one cake only.

248. But after the Sapindikarana of the (deceased father) has been performed according to the sacred law, the sons must offer the cakes with those ceremonies, (described above.)

249. The foolish man who, after having eaten a Sraddha (-dinner), gives the leavings to a Sudra, falls headlong into the Kalasutra hell.

250. If the partaker of a Sraddha (-dinner) enters on the same day the bed of a Sudra female, the manes of his (ancestors) will lie during that month in her ordure.

251. Having addressed the question, 'Have you dined well?' (to his guests), let him give water for sipping to them who are satisfied, and dismiss them, after they have sipped water, (with the words) 'Rest either (here or at home)!'

252. The Brahmana (guests) shall then answer him, 'Let there be Svadha;' for at all rites in honour of the manes the word Svadha is the highest benison.

253. Next let him inform (his guests) who have finished their meal, of the food which remains; with the permission of the Brahmanas let him dispose (of that), as they may direct.

254. At a (Sraddha) in honour of the manes one must use (in asking of the guests if they are satisfied, the word) svaditam; at a Goshthi-sraddha, (the word) susrutam; at a Vriddhi-sraddha, (the word) sampannam; and at (a rite) in honour of the gods, (the word) rukitam.

255. The afternoon, Kusa grass, the due preparation of the dwelling, sesamum grains, liberality, the careful preparation

of the food, and (the company of) distinguished Brahmanas are true riches at all funeral sacrifices.

256. Know that Kusa grass, purificatory (texts), the morning, sacrificial viands of all kinds, and those means of purification, mentioned above, are blessings at a sacrifice to the gods.

257. The food eaten by hermits in the forest, milk, Soma-juice, meat which is not prepared (with spices), and salt unprepared by art, are called, on account of their nature, sacrificial food.

258. Having dismissed the (invited) Brahmanas, let him, with a concentrated mind, silent and pure, look towards the south and ask these blessings of the manes:

259. 'May liberal men abound with us! May (our knowledge of) the Vedas and (our) progeny increase! May faith not forsake us! May we have much to give (to the needy)!'

260. Having thus offered (the cakes), let him, after (the prayer), cause a cow, a Brahmana, a goat, or the sacred fire to consume those cakes, or let him throw them into water.

261. Some make the offering of the cakes after (the dinner); some cause (them) to be eaten by birds or throw them into fire or into water.

262. The (sacrificer's) first wife, who is faithful and intent on the worship of the manes, may eat the middle-most cake, (if she be) desirous of bearing a son.

263. (Thus) she will bring forth a son who will be long-lived, famous, intelligent, rich, the father of numerous offspring, endowed with (the quality of) goodness, and righteous.

264. Having washed his hands and sipped water, let him prepare (food) for his paternal relations and, after giving it to them with due respect, let him feed his maternal relatives also.

265. But the remnants shall be left (where they lie) until the Brahmanas have been dismissed; afterwards he shall perform the (daily) domestic Bali-offering; that is a settled (rule of the) sacred law.

266. I will now fully declare what kind of sacrificial food, given to the manes according to the rule, will serve for a long time or for eternity.

267. The ancestors of men are satisfied for one month with sesamum grains, rice, barley, masha beans, water, roots, and fruits, which have been given according to the prescribed rule,

268. Two months with fish, three months with the meat of gazelles, four with mutton, and five indeed with the flesh of birds,

269. Six months with the flesh of kids, seven with that of spotted deer, eight with that of the black antelope, but nine with that of the (deer called) Ruru,

270. Ten months they are satisfied with the meat of boars and buffaloes, but eleven months indeed with that of hares and tortoises,

271. One year with cow-milk and milk-rice; from the flesh of a long-eared white he-goat their satisfaction endures twelve years.

272. The (vegetable called) Kalasaka, (the fish called) Mahasalka, the flesh of a rhinoceros and that of a red goat, and all kinds of food eaten by hermits in the forest serve for an endless time.

273. Whatever (food), mixed with honey, one gives on the thirteenth lunar day in the rainy season under the asterism of Maghah, that also procures endless (satisfaction).

274. 'May such a man (the manes say) be born in our family who will give us milk-rice, with honey and clarified butter, on the thirteenth lunar day (of the month of Bhadrapada) and (in the afternoon) when the shadow of an elephant falls towards the east.'

275. Whatever (a man), full of faith, duly gives according to the prescribed rule, that becomes in the other world a perpetual and imperishable (gratification) for the manes.

276. The days of the dark half of the month, beginning with the tenth, but excepting the fourteenth, are recommended for a funeral sacrifice; (it is) not thus (with) the others.

277. He who performs it on the even (lunar) days and under the even constellations, gains (the fulfilment of) all his wishes; he who honours the manes on odd (lunar days) and under odd (constellations), obtains distinguished offspring.

278. As the second half of the month is preferable to the first half, even so the afternoon is better for (the performance of) a funeral sacrifice than the forenoon.

279. Let him, untired, duly perform the (rites) in honour of the manes in accordance with the prescribed rule, passing the sacred thread over the right shoulder, proceeding from the left to the right (and) holding Kusa grass in his hands, up to the end (of the ceremony).

280. Let him not perform a funeral sacrifice at night, because the (night) is declared to belong to the Rakshasas, nor in the twilight, nor when the sun has just risen.

281. Let him offer here below a funeral sacrifice, according to the rule given above, (at least) thrice a year, in winter, in summer, and in the rainy season, but that which is included among the five great sacrifices, every day.

282. The burnt-oblation, offered at a sacrifice to the manes, must not be made in a common fire; a Brahmana who keeps a sacred fire (shall) not (perform) a funeral sacrifice except on the new-moon day.

283. Even when a Brahmana, after bathing, satisfies the manes with water, he obtains thereby the whole reward for the performance of the (daily) Sraddha.

284. They call (the manes of) fathers Vasus, (those of) grandfathers Rudras, and (those of) great-grandfathers Adityas; thus (speaks) the eternal Veda.

285. Let him daily partake of the vighasa and daily eat amrita (ambrosia); but vighasa is what remains from the meal (of Brahmana guests) and the remainder of a sacrifice (is called) amrita.

286. Thus all the ordinances relating to the five (daily great) sacrifices have been declared to you; hear now the law for the manner of living fit for Brahmanas.

CHAPTER IV.

1. Having dwelt with a teacher during the fourth part of (a man's) life, a Brahmana shall live during the second quarter (of his existence) in his house, after he has wedded a wife.

2. A Brahmana must seek a means of subsistence which either causes no, or at least little pain (to others), and live (by that) except in times of distress.

3. For the purpose of gaining bare subsistence, let him accumulate property by (following those) irreproachable occupations (which are prescribed for) his (caste), without (unduly) fatiguing his body.

4. He may subsist by Rita (truth), and Amrita (ambrosia), or by Mrita (death) and by Pramrita (what causes many deaths); or even by (the mode) called Satyanrita (a mixture of truth and falsehood), but never by Svavritti (a dog's mode of life).

5. By Rita shall be understood the gleaning of corn; by Amrita, what is given unasked; by Mrita, food obtained by begging and agriculture is declared to be Pramrita.

6. But trade and (money-lending) are Satyanrita, even by that one may subsist. Service is called Svavritti; therefore one should avoid it.

7. He may either possess enough to fill a granary, or a store filling a grain-jar; or he may collect what suffices for three days, or make no provision for the morrow.

8. Moreover, among these four Brahmana householders, each later-(named) must be considered more distinguished, and through his virtue to have conquered the world more completely.

9. One of these follows six occupations, another subsists by three, one by two, but the fourth lives by the Brahmasattra.

10. He who maintains himself by picking up grains and ears of corn, must be always intent on (the performance of) the Agnihotra, and constantly offer those Ishtis only, which are prescribed for the days of the conjunction and opposition (of the moon), and for the solstices.

11. Let him never, for the sake of subsistence, follow the ways of the world; let him live the pure, straightforward, honest life of a Brahmana.

12. He who desires happiness must strive after a perfectly contented disposition and control himself; for happiness has contentment for its root, the root of unhappiness is the contrary (disposition).

13. A Brahmana, who is a Snataka and subsists by one of the (above-mentioned) modes of life, must discharge the (following) duties which secure heavenly bliss, long life, and fame.

14. Let him, untired, perform daily the rites prescribed for him in the Veda; for he who performs those according to his ability, attains to the highest state.

15. Whether he be rich or even in distress, let him not seek wealth through pursuits to which men cleave, nor by forbidden occupations, nor (let him accept presents) from any (giver whosoever he may be).

16. Let him not, out of desire (for enjoyments), attach himself to any sensual pleasures, and let him carefully obviate an excessive attachment to them, by (reflecting on their worthlessness in) his heart.

17. Let him avoid all (means of acquiring) wealth which impede the study of the Veda; (let him maintain himself) anyhow, but study, because that (devotion to the Veda-study secures) the realisation of his aims.

18. Let him walk here (on earth), bringing his dress, speech, and thoughts to a conformity with his age, his occupation, his wealth, his sacred learning, and his race.

19. Let him daily pore over those Institutes of science which soon give increase of wisdom, those which teach the acquisition of wealth, those which are beneficial (for other worldly concerns), and likewise over the Nigamas which explain the Veda.

20. For the more a man completely studies the Institutes of science, the more he fully understands (them), and his great learning shines brightly.

21. Let him never, if he is able (to perform them), neglect the sacrifices to the sages, to the gods, to the Bhutas, to men, and to the manes.

22. Some men who know the ordinances for sacrificial rites, always offer these great sacrifices in their organs (of sensation), without any (external) effort.

23. Knowing that the (performance of the) sacrifice in their speech and their breath yields imperishable (rewards), some always offer their breath in their speech, and their speech in their breath.

24. Other Brahmanas, seeing with the eye of knowledge that the performance of those rites has knowledge for its root, always perform them through knowledge alone.

25. A Brahmana shall always offer the Agnihotra at the beginning or at the end of the day and of the night, and the Darsa and Paurnamasa (Ishtis) at the end of each half-month,

26. When the old grain has been consumed the (Agrayana) Ishti with new grain, at the end of the (three) seasons the (Katurmasya-) sacrifices, at the solstices an animal (sacrifice), at the end of the year Soma-offerings.

27. A Brahmana, who keeps sacred fires, shall, if he desires to live long, not eat new grain or meat, without having offered the (Agrayana) Ishti with new grain and an animal-(sacrifice).

28. For his fires, not being worshipped by offerings of new grain and of an animal, seek to devour his vital spirits, (because they are) greedy for new grain and flesh.

29. No guest must stay in his house without being honoured, according to his ability, with a seat, food, a couch, water, or roots and fruits.

30. Let him not honour, even by a greeting, heretics, men who follow forbidden occupations, men who live like cats, rogues, logicians, (arguing against the Veda,) and those who live like herons.

31. Those who have become Snatakas after studying the Veda, or after completing their vows, (and) householders, who are Srotriyas, one must worship by (gifts of food) sacred to gods and manes, but one must avoid those who are different.

32. A householder must give (as much food) as he is able (to spare) to those who do not cook for themselves, and to all beings one must distribute (food) without detriment (to one's own interest).

33. A Snataka who pines with hunger, may beg wealth of a king, of one for whom he sacrifices, and of a pupil, but not of others; that is a settled rule.

34. A Snataka who is able (to procure food) shall never waste himself with hunger, nor shall he wear old or dirty clothes, if he possesses property.

35. Keeping his hair, nails, and beard clipped, subduing his passions by austerities, wearing white garments and (keeping himself) pure, he shall be always engaged in studying the Veda and (such acts as are) conducive to his welfare.

36. He shall carry a staff of bamboo, a pot full of water, a sacred string, a bundle of Kusa grass, and (wear) two bright golden ear-rings.

37. Let him never look at the sun, when he sets or rises, is eclipsed or reflected in water, or stands in the middle of the sky.

38. Let him not step over a rope to which a calf is tied, let him not run when it rains, and let him not look at his own image in water; that is a settled rule.

39. Let him pass by (a mound of) earth, a cow, an idol, a Brahmana, clarified butter, honey, a crossway, and well-known trees, turning his right hand towards them.

40. Let him, though mad with desire, not approach his wife when her courses appear; nor let him sleep with her in the same bed.

41. For the wisdom, the energy, the strength, the sight, and the vitality of a man who approaches a woman covered with menstrual excretions, utterly perish.

42. If he avoids her, while she is in that condition, his wisdom, energy, strength, sight, and vitality will increase.

43. Let him not eat in the company of his wife, nor look at her, while she eats, sneezes, yawns, or sits at her ease.

44. A Brahmana who desires energy must not look at (a woman) who applies collyrium to her eyes, has anointed or uncovered herself or brings forth (a child).

45. Let him not eat, dressed with one garment only; let him not bathe naked; let him not void urine on a road, on ashes, or in a cow-pen,

46. Nor on ploughed land, in water, on an altar of bricks, on a mountain, on the ruins of a temple, nor ever on an ant-hill,

47. Nor in holes inhabited by living creatures, nor while he walks or stands, nor on reaching the bank of a river, nor on the top of a mountain.

48. Let him never void faeces or urine, facing the wind, or a fire, or looking towards a Brahmana, the sun, water, or cows.

49. He may ease himself, having covered (the ground) with sticks, clods, leaves, grass, and the like, restraining his speech, (keeping himself) pure, wrapping up his body, and covering his head.

50. Let him void faeces and urine, in the daytime turning to the north, at night turning towards the south, during the two twilights in the same (position) as by day.

51. In the shade or in darkness a Brahmana may, both by day and at night, do it, assuming any position he pleases; likewise when his life is in danger.

52. The intellect of (a man) who voids urine against a fire, the sun, the moon, in water, against a Brahmana, a cow, or the wind, perishes.

53. Let him not blow a fire with his mouth; let him not look at a naked woman; let him not throw any impure substance into the fire, and let him not warm his feet at it.

54. Let him not place (fire) under (a bed or the like); nor step over it, nor place it (when he sleeps) at the foot-(end of his bed); let him not torment living creatures.

55. Let him not eat, nor travel, nor sleep during the twilight; let him not scratch the ground; let him not take off his garland.

56. Let him not throw urine or faeces into the water, nor saliva, nor (clothes) defiled by impure substances, nor any other (impurity), nor blood, nor poisonous things.

57. Let him not sleep alone in a deserted dwelling; let him not wake (a superior) who is sleeping; let him not converse with a menstruating woman; nor let him go to a sacrifice, if he is not chosen (to be officiating priest).

58. Let him keep his right arm uncovered in a place where a sacred fire is kept, in a cow-pen, in the presence of Brahmanas, during the private recitation of the Veda, and at meals.

59. Let him not interrupt a cow who is suckling (her calf), nor tell anybody of it. A wise man, if he sees a rainbow in the sky, must not point it out to anybody.

60. Let him not dwell in a village where the sacred law is not obeyed, nor (stay) long where diseases are endemic; let him not go alone on a journey, nor reside long on a mountain.

61. Let him not dwell in a country where the rulers are Sudras, nor in one which is surrounded by unrighteous men, nor in one which has become subject to heretics, nor in one swarming with men of the lowest castes.

62. Let him not eat anything from which the oil has been extracted; let him not be a glutton; let him not eat very early (in the morning), nor very late (in the evening), nor (take any food) in the evening, if he has eaten (his fill) in the morning.

63. Let him not exert himself without a purpose; let him not drink water out of his joined palms; let him not eat food (placed) in his lap; let him not show (idle) curiosity.

64. Let him not dance, nor sing, nor play musical instruments, nor slap (his limbs), nor grind his teeth, nor let him make uncouth noises, though he be in a passion.

65. Let him never wash his feet in a vessel of white brass; let him not eat out of a broken (earthen) dish, nor out of one that (to judge) from its appearance (is) defiled.

66. Let him not use shoes, garments, a sacred string, ornaments, a garland, or a water-vessel which have been used by others.

67. Let him not travel with untrained beasts of burden, nor with (animals) that are tormented by hunger or disease, or whose horns, eyes, and hoofs have been injured, or whose tails have been disfigured.

68. Let him always travel with (beasts) which are well broken in, swift, endowed with lucky marks, and perfect in colour and form, without urging them much with the goad.

69. The morning sun, the smoke rising from a (burning) corpse, and a broken seat must be avoided. Let him not clip his nails or hair, and not tear his nails with his teeth.

70. Let him not crush earth or clods, nor tear off grass with his nails; let him not do anything that is useless or will have disagreeable results in the future.

71. A man who crushes clods, tears off grass, or bites his nails, goes soon to perdition, likewise an informer and he who neglects (the rules of) purification.

72. Let him not wrangle; let him not wear a garland over (his hair). To ride on the back of cows (or of oxen) is anyhow a blamable act.

73. Let him not enter a walled village or house except by the gate, and by night let him keep at a long distance from the roots of trees.

74. Let him never play with dice, nor himself take off his shoes; let him not eat, lying on a bed, nor what has been placed in his hand or on a seat.

75. Let him not eat after sunset any (food) containing sesamum grains; let him never sleep naked, nor go anywhere unpurified (after meals).

76. Let him eat while his feet are (yet) wet (from the ablution), but let him not go to bed with wet feet. He who eats while his feet are (still) wet, will attain long life.

77. Let him never enter a place, difficult of access, which is impervious to his eye; let him not look at urine or ordure, nor cross a river (swimming) with his arms.

78. Let him not step on hair, ashes, bones, potsherds, cotton-seed or chaff, if he desires long life.

79. Let him not stay together with outcasts, nor with Kandalas, nor with Pukkasas, nor with fools, nor with overbearing men, nor with low-caste men, nor with Antyavasayins.

80. Let him not give to a Sudra advice, nor the remnants (of his meal), nor food offered to the gods; nor let him explain the sacred law (to such a man), nor impose (upon him) a penance.

81. For he who explains the sacred law (to a Sudra) or dictates to him a penance, will sink together with that (man) into the hell (called) Asamvrita.

82. Let him not scratch his head with both hands joined; let him not touch it while he is impure, nor bathe without (submerging) it.

83. Let him avoid (in anger) to lay hold of (his own or other men's) hair, or to strike (himself or others) on the head. When he has bathed (submerging) his head, he shall not touch any of his limbs with oil.

84. Let him not accept presents from a king who is not descended from the Kshatriya race, nor from butchers, oil-manufacturers, and publicans, nor from those who subsist by the gain of prostitutes.

85. One oil-press is as (bad) as ten slaughter-houses, one tavern as (bad as) ten oil-presses, one brothel as (bad as) ten taverns, one king as (bad as) ten brothels.

86. A king is declared to be equal (in wickedness) to a butcher who keeps a hundred thousand slaughter-houses; to accept presents from him is a terrible (crime).

87. He who accepts presents from an avaricious king who acts contrary to the Institutes (of the sacred law), will go in succession to the following twenty-one hells:

88. Tamisra, Andhatamisra, Maharaurava, Raurava, the Kalasutra hell, Mahanaraka,

89. Samgivana, Mahaviki, Tapana, Sampratapana, Samghata, Sakakola, Kudmala, Putimrittika,

90. Lohasanku, Rigisha, Pathin, the (flaming) river, Salmala, Asipatravana, and Lohakaraka.

91. Learned Brahmanas, who know that, who study the Veda and desire bliss after death, do not accept presents from a king.

92. Let him wake in the muhurta, sacred to Brahman, and think of (the acquisition of) spiritual merit and wealth, of the bodily fatigue arising therefrom, and of the true meaning of the Veda.

93. When he has risen, has relieved the necessities of nature and carefully purified himself, let him stand during the morning twilight, muttering for a long time (the Gayatri), and at the proper time (he must similarly perform) the evening (devotion).

94. By prolonging the twilight devotions, the sages obtained long life, wisdom, honour, fame, and excellence in Vedic knowledge.

95. Having performed the Upakarman according to the prescribed rule on (the full moon of the month) Sravana, or on that of Praushthapada (Bhadrapada), a Brahmana shall diligently study the Vedas during four months and a half.

96. When the Pushya-day (of the month Pausha), or the first day of the bright half of Magha has come, a Brahmana shall perform in the forenoon the Utsargana of the Vedas.

97. Having performed the Utsarga outside (the village), as the Institutes (of the sacred law) prescribe, he shall stop reading during two days and the intervening night, or during that day (of the Utsarga) and (the following) night.

98. Afterwards he shall diligently recite the Vedas during the bright (halves of the months), and duly study all the Angas of the Vedas during the dark fortnights.

99. Let him not recite (the texts) indistinctly, nor in the presence of Sudras; nor let him, if in the latter part of the night he is tired with reciting the Veda, go again to sleep.

100. According to the rule declared above, let him recite the daily (portion of the) Mantras, and a zealous Brahmana, (who is) not in distress, (shall study) the Brahmana and the Mantrasamhita.

101. Let him who studies always avoid (reading) on the following occasions when the Veda-study is forbidden, and (let) him who teaches pupils according to the prescribed rule (do it likewise).

102. Those who know the (rules of) recitation declare that in the rainy season the Veda-study must be stopped on these two (occasions), when the wind is audible at night, and when it whirls up the dust in the day-time.

103. Manu has stated, that when lightning, thunder, and rain (are observed together), or when large fiery meteors fall on all sides, the recitation must be interrupted until the same hour (on the next day, counting from the occurrence of the event).

104. When one perceives these (phenomena) all together (in the twilight), after the sacred fires have been made to blaze (for the performance of the Agnihotra), then one must know the recitation of the Veda to be forbidden, and also when clouds appear out of season.

105. On (the occasion of) a preternatural sound from the sky, (of) an earthquake, and when the lights of heaven are surrounded by a halo, let him know that (the Veda-study must be) stopped until the same hour (on the next day), even if (these phenomena happen) in the (rainy) season.

106. But when lightning and the roar of thunder (are observed) after the sacred fires have been made to blaze, the stoppage shall last as long as the light (of the sun or of the stars is visible); if the remaining (above-named phenomenon, rain, occurs, the reading shall cease), both in the day-time and at night.

107. For those who wish to acquire exceedingiy great merit, a continual interruption of the Veda-study (is prescribed) in villages and in towns, and (the Veda-study must) always (cease) when any kind of foul smell (is perceptible).

108. In a village where a corpse lies, in the presence of a (man who lives as unrighteously as a) Sudra, while (the sound of) weeping (is heard), and in a crowd of men the (recitation of the Veda must be) stopped.

109. In water, during the middle part of the night, while he voids excrements, or is impure, and after he has partaken of a funeral dinner, a man must not even think in his heart (of the sacred texts).

110. A learned Brahmana shall not recite the Veda during three days, when he has accepted an invitation to a (funeral rite) in honour of one ancestor (ekoddishta), or when the king has become impure through a birth or death in his family (sutaka), or when Rahu by an eclipse makes the moon impure.

111. As long as the smell and the stains of the (food given) in honour of one ancestor remain on the body of a learned Brahmana, so long he must not recite the Veda.

112. While lying on a bed, while his feet are raised (on a bench), while he sits on his hams with a cloth tied round his knees, let him not study, nor when he has eaten meat or food given by a person impure on account of a birth or a death,

113. Nor during a fog, nor while the sound of arrows is audible, nor during both the twilights, nor on the new-moon day, nor on the fourteenth and the eighth (days of each half-month), nor on the full-moon day.

114. The new-moon day destroys the teacher, the fourteenth (day) the pupil, the eighth and the full-moon days (destroy all remembrance of) the Veda; let him therefore avoid (reading on) those (days).

115. A Brahmana shall not recite (the Veda) during a dust-storm, nor while the sky is preternaturally red, nor while jackals howl, nor while the barking of dogs, the braying of donkeys, or the grunting of camels (is heard), nor while (he is seated) in a company.

116. Let him not study near a burial-ground, nor near a village, nor in a cow-pen, nor dressed in a garment which he wore during conjugal intercourse, nor after receiving a present at a funeral sacrifice.

117. Be it an animal or a thing inanimate, whatever be the (gift) at a Sraddha, let him not, having just accepted it, recite the Veda; for the hand of a Brahmana is his mouth.

118. When the village has been beset by robbers, and when an alarm has been raised by fire, let him know that (the Veda-study must be) interrupted until the same hour (on the next day), and on (the occurrence of) all portents.

119. On (the occasion of) the Upakarman and (of) the Vedotsarga an omission (of the Veda-study) for three days has been prescribed, but on the Ashtakas and on the last nights of the seasons for a day and a night.

120. Let him not recite the Veda on horseback, nor on a tree, nor on an elephant, nor in a boat (or ship), nor on a donkey, nor on camel, nor standing on barren ground, nor riding in a carriage,

121. Nor during a verbal altercation, nor during a mutual assault, nor in a camp, nor during a battle, nor when he has just eaten, nor during an indigestion, nor after vomiting, nor with sour eructations,

122. Nor without receiving permission from a guest (who stays in his house), nor while the wind blows vehemently, nor while blood flows from his body, nor when he is wounded by a weapon.

123. Let him never recite the Rig-veda or the Yagur-veda while the Saman (melodies) are heard; (let him stop all Veda-study for a day and a night) after finishing a Veda or after reciting an Aranyaka.

124. The Rig-veda is declared to be sacred to the gods, the Yagur-veda sacred to men, and the Sama-veda sacred to the manes; hence the sound of the latter is impure (as it were).

125. Knowing this, the learned daily repeat first in due order the essence of the three (Vedas) and afterwards the (text of the) Veda.

126. Know that (the Veda-study must be) interrupted for a day and a night, when cattle, a frog, a cat, a dog, a snake, an ichneumon, or a rat pass between (the teacher and his pupil).

127. Let a twice-born man always carefully interrupt the Veda-study on two (occasions, viz.) when the place where he recites is impure, and when he himself is unpurified.

128. A twice-born man who is a Snataka shall remain chaste on the new-moon day, on the eighth (lunar day of each half-month), on the full-moon day, and on the fourteenth, even (if they fall) in the period (proper for conjugal intercourse).

129. Let him not bathe (immediately) after a meal, nor when he is sick, nor in the middle of the night, nor frequently dressed in all his garments, nor in a pool which he does not perfectly know.

130. Let him not intentionally step on the shadow of (images of) the gods, of a Guru, of a king, of a Snataka, of his teacher, of a reddish-brown animal, or of one who has been initiated to the performance of a Srauta sacrifice (Dikshita).

131. At midday and at midnight, after partaking of meat at a funeral dinner, and in the two twilights let him not stay long on a cross-road.

132. Let him not step intentionally on things used for cleansing the body, on water used for a bath, on urine or ordure, on blood, on mucus, and on anything spat out or vomited.

133. Let him not show particular attention to an enemy, to the friend of an enemy, to a wicked man, to a thief, or to the wife of another man.

134. For in this world there is nothing so detrimental to long life as criminal conversation with another man's wife.

135. Let him who desires prosperity, indeed, never despise a Kshatriya, a snake, and a learned Brahmana, be they ever so feeble.

136. Because these three, when treated with disrespect, may utterly destroy him; hence a wise man must never despise them.

137. Let him not despise himself on account of former failures; until death let him seek fortune, nor despair of gaining it.

138. Let him say what is true, let him say what is pleasing, let him utter no disagreeable truth, and let him utter no agreeable falsehood; that is the eternal law.

139. (What is) well, let him call well, or let him say 'well' only; let him not engage in a useless enmity or dispute with anybody.

140. Let him not journey too early in the morning, nor too late in the evening, nor just during the midday (heat), nor with an unknown (companion), nor alone, nor with Sudras.

141. Let him not insult those who have redundant limbs or are deficient in limbs, nor those destitute of knowledge, nor very aged men, nor those who have no beauty or wealth, nor those who are of low birth.

142. A Brahmana who is impure must not touch with his hand a cow, a Brahmana, or fire; nor, being in good health, let him look at the luminaries in the sky, while he is impure.

143. If he has touched these, while impure, let him always sprinkle with his hand water on the organs of sensation, all his limbs, and the navel.

144. Except when sick he must not touch the cavities (of the body) without a reason, and he must avoid (to touch) the hair on the secret (parts).

145. Let him eagerly follow the (customs which are) auspicious and the rule of good conduct, be careful of purity, and control all his organs, let him mutter (prayers) and, untired, daily offer oblations in the fire.

146. No calamity happens to those who eagerly follow auspicious customs and the rule of good conduct, to those who are always careful of purity, and to those who mutter (sacred texts) and offer burnt-oblations.

147. Let him, without tiring, daily mutter the Veda at the proper time; for they declare that to be one's highest duty; (all) other (observances) are called secondary duties.

148. By daily reciting the Veda, by (the observance of the rules of) purification, by (practising) austerities, and by doing no injury to created beings, one (obtains the faculty of) remembering former births.

149. He who, recollecting his former existences, again recites the Veda, gains endless bliss by the continual study of the Veda.

150. Let him always offer on the Parva-days oblations to Savitri and such as avert evil omens, and on the Ashtakas and Anvashtakas let him constantly worship the manes.

151. Far from his dwelling let him remove urine (and ordure), far (let him remove) the water used for washing his feet, and far the remnants of food and the water from his bath.

152. Early in the morning only let him void faeces, decorate (his body), bathe, clean his teeth, apply collyrium to his eyes, and worship the gods.

153. But on the Parva-days let him go to visit the (images of the) gods, and virtuous Brahmanas, and the ruler (of the country), for the sake of protection, as well as his Gurus.

154. Let him reverentially salute venerable men (who visit him), give them his own seat, let him sit near them with joined hands and, when they leave, (accompany them), walking behind them.

155. Let him, untired, follow the conduct of virtuous men, connected with his occupations, which has been fully declared in the revealed texts and in the sacred tradition (Smriti) and is the root of the sacred law.

156. Through virtuous conduct he obtains long life, through virtuous conduct desirable offspring, through virtuous conduct imperishable wealth; virtuous conduct destroys (the effect of) inauspicious marks.

157. For a man of bad conduct is blamed among people, constantly suffers misfortunes, is afflicted with diseases, and short-lived.

158. A man who follows the conduct of the virtuous, has faith and is free from envy, lives a hundred years, though he be entirely destitute of auspicious marks.

159. Let him carefully avoid all undertakings (the success of) which depends on others; but let him eagerly pursue that (the accomplishment of) which depends on himself.

160. Everything that depends on others (gives) pain, everything that depends on oneself (gives) pleasure; know that this is the short definition of pleasure and pain.

161. When the performance of an act gladdens his heart, let him perform it with diligence; but let him avoid the opposite.

162. Let him never offend the teacher who initiated him, nor him who explained the Veda, nor his father and mother, nor (any other) Guru, nor cows, nor Brahmanas, nor any men performing austerities.

163. Let him avoid atheism, cavilling at the Vedas, contempt of the gods, hatred, want of modesty, pride, anger, and harshness.

164. Let him, when angry, not raise a stick against another man, nor strike (anybody) except a son or a pupil; those two he may beat in order to correct them.

165. A twice-born man who has merely threatened a Brahmana with the intention of (doing him) a corporal injury, will wander about for a hundred years in the Tamisra hell.

166. Having intentionally struck him in anger, even with a blade of grass, he will be born during twenty-one existences in the wombs (of such beings where men are born in punishment of their) sins.

167. A man who in his folly caused blood to flow from the body of a Brahmana who does not attack him, will suffer after death exceedingly great pain.

168. As many particles of dust as the blood takes up from the ground, during so many years the spiller of the blood will be devoured by other (animals) in the next world.

169. A wise man should therefore never threaten a Brahmana, nor strike him even with a blade of grass, nor cause his blood to flow.

170. Neither a man who (lives) unrighteously, nor he who (acquires) wealth (by telling) falsehoods, nor he who always delights in doing injury, ever attain happiness in this world.

171. Let him, though suffering in consequence of his righteousness, never turn his heart to unrighteousness; for he will see the speedy overthrow of unrighteous, wicked men.

172. Unrighteousness, practised in this world, does not at once produce its fruit, like a cow; but, advancing slowly, it cuts off the roots of him who committed it.

173. If (the punishment falls) not on (the offender) himself, (it falls) on his sons, if not on the sons, (at least) on his grandsons; but an iniquity (once) committed, never fails to produce fruit to him who wrought it.

174. He prospers for a while through unrighteousness, then he gains great good fortune, next he conquers his enemies, but (at last) he perishes (branch and) root.

175. Let him always delight in truthfulness, (obedience to) the sacred law, conduct worthy of an Aryan, and purity; let him chastise his pupils according to the sacred law; let him keep his speech, his arms, and his belly under control.

176. Let him avoid (the acquisition of) wealth and (the gratification of his) desires, if they are opposed to the sacred law, and even lawful acts which may cause pain in the future or are offensive to men.

177. Let him not be uselessly active with his hands and feet, or with his eyes, nor crooked (in his ways), nor talk idly, nor injure others by deeds or even think of it.

178. Let him walk in that path of holy men which his fathers and his grandfathers followed; while he walks in that, he will not suffer harm.

179. With an officiating or a domestic priest, with a teacher, with a maternal uncle, a guest and a dependant, with infants, aged and sick men, with learned men, with his paternal relatives, connexions by marriage and maternal relatives,

180. With his father and his mother, with female relatives, with a brother, with his son and his wife, with his daughter and with his slaves, let him not have quarrels.

181. If he avoids quarrels with these persons, he will be freed from all sins, and by suppressing (all) such (quarrels) a householder conquers all the following worlds.

182. The teacher is the lord of the world of Brahman, the father has power over the world of the Lord of created beings (Pragapati), a guest rules over the world of Indra, and the priests over the world of the gods.

183. The female relatives (have power) over the world of the Apsarases, the maternal relatives over that of the Visve

Devas, the connexions by marriage over that of the waters, the mother and the maternal uncle over the earth.

184. Infants, aged, poor and sick men must be considered as rulers of the middle sphere, the eldest brother as equal to one's father, one's wife and one's son as one's own body,

185. One's slaves as one's shadow, one's daughter as the highest object of tenderness; hence if one is offended by (any one of) these, one must bear it without resentment.

186. Though (by his learning and sanctity) he may be entitled to accept presents, let him not attach himself (too much) to that (habit); for through his accepting (many) presents the divine light in him is soon extinguished.

187. Without a full knowledge of the rules, prescribed by the sacred law for the acceptance of presents, a wise man should not take anything, even though he may pine with hunger.

188. But an ignorant (man) who accepts gold, land, a horse, a cow, food, a dress, sesamum-grains, (or) clarified butter, is reduced to ashes like (a piece of) wood.

189. Gold and food destroy his longevity, land and a cow his body, a horse his eye (sight), a garment his skin, clarified butter his energy, sesamum-grains his offspring.

190. A Brahmana who neither performs austerities nor studies the Veda, yet delights in accepting gifts, sinks with the (donor into hell), just as (he who attempts to cross over in) a boat made of stone (is submerged) in the water.

191. Hence an ignorant (man) should be afraid of accepting any presents; for by reason of a very small (gift) even a fool sinks (into hell) as a cow into a morass.

192. (A man) who knows the law should not offer even water to a Brahmana who acts like a cat, nor to a Brahmana who acts like a heron, nor to one who is unacquainted with the Veda.

193. For property, though earned in accordance with prescribed rules, which is given to these three (persons), causes in the next world misery both to the giver and to the recipient.

194. As he who (attempts to) cross water in a boat of stone sinks (to the bottom), even so an ignorant donor and an ignorant donee sink low.

195. (A man) who, ever covetous, displays the flag of virtue, (who is) a hypocrite, a deceiver of the people, intent on doing injury, (and) a detractor (from the merits) of all men, one must know to be one who acts like a cat.

196. That Brahmana, who with downcast look, of a cruel disposition, is solely intent on attaining his own ends, dishonest and falsely gentle, is one who acts like a heron.

197. Those Brahmanas who act like herons, and those who display the characteristics of cats, fall in consequence of that wicked mode of acting into (the hell called) Andhatamisra.

198. When he has committed a sin, let him not perform a penance under the pretence (that the act is intended to gain) spiritual merit, (thus) hiding his sin under (the pretext of) a vow and deceiving women and Sudras.

199. Such Brahmanas are reprehended after death and in this (life) by those who expound the Veda, and a vow, performed under a false pretence, goes to the Rakshasas.

200. He who, without being a student, gains his livelihood by (wearing) the dress of a student, takes upon himself the guilt of (all) students and is born again in the womb of an animal.

201. Let him never bathe in tanks belonging to other men; if he bathes (in such a one), he is tainted by a portion of the guilt of him who made the tank.

202. He who uses without permission a carriage, a bed, a seat, a well, a garden or a house belonging to an (other man), takes upon himself one fourth of (the owner's) guilt.

203. Let him always bathe in rivers, in ponds, dug by the gods (themselves), in lakes, and in waterholes or springs.

204. A wise man should constantly discharge the paramount duties (called yama), but not always the minor ones (called niyama); for he who does not discharge the former, while he obeys the latter alone, becomes an outcast.

205. A Brahmana must never eat (a dinner given) at a sacrifice that is offered by one who is not a Srotriya, by one

who sacrifices for a multitude of men, by a woman, or by a eunuch.

206. When those persons offer sacrificial viands in the fire, it is unlucky for holy (men) it displeases the gods; let him therefore avoid it.

207. Let him never eat (food given) by intoxicated, angry, or sick (men), nor that in which hair or insects are found, nor what has been touched intentionally with the foot,

208. Nor that at which the slayer of a learned Brahmana has looked, nor that which has been touched by a menstruating woman, nor that which has been pecked at by birds or touched by a dog,

209. Nor food at which a cow has smelt, nor particularly that which has been offered by an invitation to all comers, nor that (given) by a multitude or by harlots, nor that which is declared to be had by a learned (man),

210. Nor the food (given) by a thief, a musician, a carpenter, a usurer, one who has been initiated (for the performance of a Srauta sacrifice), a miser, one bound with fetters,

211. By one accused of a mortal sin (Abhisasta), a hermaphrodite, an unchaste woman, or a hypocrite, nor (any sweet thing) that has turned sour, nor what has been kept a whole night, nor (the food) of a Sudra, nor the leavings (of another man),

212. Nor (the food given) by a physician, a hunter, a cruel man, one who eats the fragments (of another's meal), nor the food of an Ugra, nor that prepared for a woman in childbed, nor that (given at a dinner) where (a guest rises) prematurely (and) sips water, nor that (given by a woman) whose ten days of impurity have not elapsed,

213. Nor (food) given without due respect, nor (that which contains) meat eaten for no sacred purpose, nor (that given) by a female who has no male (relatives), nor the food of an enemy, nor that (given) by the lord of a town, nor that (given) by outcasts, nor that on which anybody has sneezed;

214. Nor the food (given) by an informer, by one who habitually tells falsehoods, or by one who sells (the rewards for)

sacrifices, nor the food (given) by an actor, a tailor, or an ungrateful (man),

215. By a blacksmith, a Nishada, a stage-player, a goldsmith, a basket-maker, or a dealer in weapons,

216. By trainers of hunting dogs, publicans, a washerman, a dyer, a pitiless (man), and a man in whose house (lives) a paramour (of his wife),

217. Nor (the food given) by those who knowingly bear with paramours (of their wives), and by those who in all matters are ruled by women, nor food (given by men) whose ten days of impurity on account of a death have not passed, nor that which is unpalatable.

218. The food of a king impairs his vigour, the food of a Sudra his excellence in sacred learning, the food of a goldsmith his longevity, that of a leather-cutter his fame;

219. The food of an artisan destroys his offspring, that of a washerman his (bodily) strength; the food of a multitude and of harlots excludes him from (the higher) worlds.

220. The food of a physician (is as vile as) pus, that of an unchaste woman (equal to) semen, that of a usurer (as vile as) ordure, and that of a dealer in weapons (as bad as) dirt.

221. The food of those other persons who have been successively enumerated as such whose food must not be eaten, the wise declare (to be as impure as) skin, bones, and hair.

222. If he has unwittingly eaten the food of one of those, (he must) fast for three days; if he has eaten it intentionally, or (has swallowed) semen, ordure, or urine, he must perform a Krikkhra penance.

223. A Brahmana who knows (the law) must not eat cooked food (given) by a Sudra who performs no Sraddhas; but, on failure of (other) means of subsistence, he may accept raw (grain), sufficient for one night (and day).

224. The gods, having considered (the respective merits) of a niggardly Srotriya and of a liberal usurer, declared the food of both to be equal (in quality).

225. The Lord of created beings (Pragapati) came and spake to them, 'Do not make that equal, which is unequal. The

food of that liberal (usurer) is purified by faith; (that of the) of the) other (man) is defiled by a want of faith.'

226. Let him, without tiring, always offer sacrifices and perform works of charity with faith; for offerings and charitable works made with faith and with lawfully-earned money, (procure) endless rewards.

227. Let him always practise, according to his ability, with a cheerful heart, the duty of liberality, both by sacrifices and by charitable works, if he finds a worthy recipient (for his gifts.)

228. If he is asked, let him always give something, be it ever so little, without grudging; for a worthy recipient will (perhaps) be found who saves him from all (guilt).

229. A giver of water obtains the satisfaction (of his hunger and thirst), a giver of food imperishable happiness, a giver of sesamum desirable offspring, a giver of a lamp a most excellent eyesight.

230. A giver of land obtains land, a giver of gold long life, a giver of a house most excellent mansions, a giver of silver (rupya) exquisite beauty (rupa),

231. A giver of a garment a place in the world of the moon, a giver of a horse (asva) a place in the world of the Asvins, a giver of a draught-ox great good fortune, a giver of a cow the world of the sun;

232. A giver of a carriage or of a bed a wife, a giver of protection supreme dominion, a giver of grain eternal bliss, a giver of the Veda (brahman) union with Brahman;

233. The gift of the Veda surpasses all other gifts, water, food, cows, land, clothes, sesamum, gold, and clarified butter.

234. For whatever purpose (a man) bestows any gift, for that same purpose he receives (in his next birth) with due honour its (reward).

235. Both he who respectfully receives (a gift), and he who respectfully bestows it, go to heaven; in the contrary case (they both fall) into hell.

236. Let him not be proud of his austerities; let him not utter a falsehood after he has offered a sacrifice; let him not

speak ill of Brahmanas, though he be tormented (by them); when he has bestowed (a gift), let him not boast of it.

237. By falsehood a sacrifice becomes vain, by self-complacency (the reward for) austerities is lost, longevity by speaking evil of Brahmanas, and (the reward of) a gift by boasting.

238. Giving no pain to any creature, let him slowly accumulate spiritual merit, for the sake (of acquiring) a companion to the next world, just as the white ant (gradually raises its) hill.

239. For in the next world neither father, nor mother, nor wife, nor sons, nor relations stay to be his companions; spiritual merit alone remains (with him).

240. Single is each being born; single it dies; single it enjoys (the reward of its) virtue; single (it suffers the punishment of its) sin.

241. Leaving the dead body on the ground like a log of wood, or a clod of earth, the relatives depart with averted faces; but spiritual merit follows the (soul).

242. Let him therefore always slowly accumulate spiritual merit, in order (that it may be his) companion (after death); for with merit as his companion he will traverse a gloom difficult to traverse.

243. (That companion) speedily conducts the man who is devoted to duty and effaces his sins by austerities, to the next world, radiant and clothed with an ethereal body.

244. Let him, who desires to raise his race, ever form connexions with the most excellent (men), and shun all low ones.

245. A Brahmana who always connects himself with the most excellent (ones), and shuns all inferior ones, (himself) becomes most distinguished; by an opposite conduct he becomes a Sudra.

246. He who is persevering, gentle, (and) patient, shuns the company of men of cruel conduct, and does no injury (to living creatures), gains, if he constantly lives in that manner, by controlling his organs and by liberality, heavenly bliss.

247. He may accept from any (man), fuel, water, roots, fruit, food offered without asking, and honey, likewise a gift (which consists in) a promise of protection.

248. The Lord of created beings (Pragapati) has declared that alms freely offered and brought (by the giver himself) may be accepted even from a sinful man, provided (the gift) had not been (asked for or) promised beforehand.

249. During fifteen years the manes do not eat (the food) of that man who disdains a (freely-offered gift), nor does the fire carry his offerings (to the gods).

250. A couch, a house, Kusa grass, perfumes, water, flowers, jewels, sour milk, grain, fish, sweet milk, meat, and vegetables let him not reject, (if they are voluntarily offered.)

251. He who desires to relieve his Gurus and those whom he is bound to maintain, or wishes to honour the gods and guests, may accept (gifts) from anybody; but he must not satisfy his (own hunger) with such (presents).

252. But if his Gurus are dead, or if he lives separate from them in (another) house, let him, when he seeks a subsistence, accept (presents) from good men alone.

253. His labourer in tillage, a friend of his family, his cow-herd, his slave, and his barber are, among Sudras, those whose food he may eat, likewise (a poor man) who offers himself (to be his slave).

254. As his character is, as the work is which he desires to perform, and as the manner is in which he means to serve, even so (a voluntary slave) must offer himself.

255. He who describes himself to virtuous (men), in a manner contrary to truth, is the most sinful (wretch) in this world; he is a thief who makes away with his own self.

256. All things (have their nature) determined by speech; speech is their root, and from speech they proceed; but he who is dishonest with respect to speech, is dishonest in everything.

257. When he has paid, according to the law, his debts to the great sages, to the manes, and to the gods, let him make over everything to his son and dwell (in his house), not caring for any worldly concerns.

258. Alone let him constantly meditate in solitude on that which is salutary for his soul; for he who meditates in solitude attains supreme bliss.

259. Thus have been declared the means by which a Brahmana householder must always subsist, and the summary of the ordinances for a Snataka, which cause an increase of holiness and are praiseworthy.

260. A Brahmana who, being learned in the lore of the Vedas, conducts himself in this manner and daily destroys his sins, will be exalted in Brahman's world.

1. The sages, having heard the duties of a Snataka thus declared, spoke to great-souled Bhrigu, who sprang from fire:

2. 'How can Death have power over Brahmanas who know the sacred science, the Veda, (and) who fulfil their duties as they have been explained (by thee), O Lord? '

3. Righteous Bhrigu, the son of Manu, (thus) answered the great sages: 'Hear, (in punishment) of what faults Death seeks to shorten the lives of Brahmanas!'

4. 'Through neglect of the Veda-study, through deviation from the rule of conduct, through remissness (in the fulfilment of duties), and through faults (committed by eating forbidden) food, Death becomes eager to shorten the lives of Brahmanas.'

5. Garlic, leeks and onions, mushrooms and (all plants), springing from impure (substances), are unfit to be eaten by twice-born men.

6. One should carefully avoid red exudations from trees and (juices) flowing from incisions, the Selu (fruit), and the thickened milk of a cow (which she gives after calving).

7. Rice boiled with sesamum, wheat mixed with butter, milk and sugar, milk-rice and flour-cakes which are not prepared for a sacrifice, meat which has not been sprinkled with water while sacred texts were recited, food offered to the gods and sacrificial viands,

8. The milk of a cow (or other female animal) within ten days after her calving, that of camels, of one-hoofed animals, of sheep, of a cow in heat, or of one that has no calf with her,

9. (The milk) of all wild animals excepting buffalo-cows, that of women, and all (substances turned) sour must be avoided.

10. Among (things turned) sour, sour milk, and all (food) prepared of it may be eaten, likewise what is extracted from pure flowers, roots, and fruit.

11. Let him avoid all carnivorous birds and those living in villages, and one-hoofed animals which are not specially permitted (to be eaten), and the Tittibha (Parra Jacana),

12. The sparrow, the Plava, the Hamsa, the Brahmani duck, the village-cock, the Sarasa crane, the Raggudala, the woodpecker, the parrot, and the starling,

13. Those which feed striking with their beaks, web-footed birds, the Koyashti, those which scratch with their toes, those which dive and live on fish, meat from a slaughter-house and dried meat,

14. The Baka and the Balaka crane, the raven, the Khangaritaka, (animals) that eat fish, village-pigs, and all kinds of fishes.

15. He who eats the flesh of any (animal) is called the eater of the flesh of that (particular creature), he who eats fish is an eater of every (kind of) flesh; let him therefore avoid fish.

16. (But the fish called) Pathina and (that called) Rohita may be eaten, if used for offerings to the gods or to the manes; (one may eat) likewise Ragivas, Simhatundas, and Sasalkas on all (occasions).

17. Let him not eat solitary or unknown beasts and birds, though they may fall under (the categories of) eatable (creatures), nor any five-toed (animals).

18. The porcupine, the hedgehog, the iguana, the rhinoceros, the tortoise, and the hare they declare to be eatable; likewise those (domestic animals) that have teeth in one jaw only, excepting camels.

19. A twice-born man who knowingly eats mushrooms, a village-pig, garlic, a village-cock, onions, or leeks, will become an outcast.

20. He who unwittingly partakes of (any of) these six, shall perform a Samtapana (Krikkhra) or the lunar penance

(Kandrayana) of ascetics; in case (he who has eaten) any other (kind of forbidden food) he shall fast for one day (and a night).

21. Once a year a Brahmana must perform a Krikkhra penance, in order to atone for unintentionally eating (forbidden food) but for intentionally (eating forbidden food he must perform the penances prescribed) specially.

22. Beasts and birds recommended (for consumption) may be slain by Brahmanas for sacrifices, and in order to feed those whom they are bound to maintain; for Agastya did this of old.

23. For in ancient (times) the sacrificial cakes were (made of the flesh) of eatable beasts and birds at the sacrifices offered by Brahmanas and Kshatriyas.

24. All lawful hard or soft food may be eaten, though stale, (after having been) mixed with fatty (substances), and so may the remains of sacrificial viands.

25. But all preparations of barley and wheat, as well as preparations of milk, may be eaten by twice-born men without being mixed with fatty (substances), though they may have stood for a long time.

26. Thus has the food, allowed and forbidden to twice-born men, been fully described; I will now propound the rules for eating and avoiding meat.

27. One may eat meat when it has been sprinkled with water, while Mantras were recited, when Brahmanas desire (one's doing it), when one is engaged (in the performance of a rite) according to the law, and when one's life is in danger.

28. The Lord of creatures (Pragapati) created this whole (world to be) the sustenance of the vital spirit; both the immovable and the movable (creation is) the food of the vital spirit.

29. What is destitute of motion is the food of those endowed with locomotion; (animals) without fangs (are the food) of those with fangs, those without hands of those who possess hands, and the timid of the bold.

30. The eater who daily even devours those destined to be his food, commits no sin; for the creator himself created both

the eaters and those who are to be eaten (for those special purposes).

31. 'The consumption of meat (is befitting) for sacrifices,' that is declared to be a rule made by the gods; but to persist (in using it) on other (occasions) is said to be a proceeding worthy of Rakshasas.

32. He who eats meat, when he honours the gods and manes, commits no sin, whether he has bought it, or himself has killed (the animal), or has received it as a present from others.

33. A twice-born man who knows the law, must not eat meat except in conformity with the law; for if he has eaten it unlawfully, he will, unable to save himself, be eaten after death by his (victims).

34. After death the guilt of one who slays deer for gain is not as (great) as that of him who eats meat for no (sacred) purpose.

35. But a man who, being duly engaged (to officiate or to dine at a sacred rite), refuses to eat meat, becomes after death an animal during twenty-one existences.

36. A Brahmana must never eat (the flesh of animals unhallowed by Mantras; but, obedient to the primeval law, he may eat it, consecrated with Vedic texts.

37. If he has a strong desire (for meat) he may make an animal of clarified butter or one of flour, (and eat that); but let him never seek to destroy an animal without a (lawful) reason.

38. As many hairs as the slain beast has, so often indeed will he who killed it without a (lawful) reason suffer a violent death in future births.

39. Svayambhu (the Self-existent) himself created animals for the sake of sacrifices; sacrifices (have been instituted) for the good of this whole (world); hence the slaughtering (of beasts) for sacrifices is not slaughtering (in the ordinary sense of the word).

40. Herbs, trees, cattle, birds, and (other) animals that have been destroyed for sacrifices, receive (being reborn) higher existences.

41. On offering the honey-mixture (to a guest), at a sacrifice and at the rites in honour of the manes, but on these occasions only, may an animal be slain; that (rule) Manu proclaimed.

42. A twice-born man who, knowing the true meaning of the Veda, slays an animal for these purposes, causes both himself and the animal to enter a most blessed state.

43. A twice-born man of virtuous disposition, whether he dwells in (his own) house, with a teacher, or in the forest, must never, even in times of distress, cause an injury (to any creature) which is not sanctioned by the Veda.

44. Know that the injury to moving creatures and to those destitute of motion, which the Veda has prescribed for certain occasions, is no injury at all; for the sacred law shone forth from the Veda.

45. He who injures innoxious beings from a wish to (give) himself pleasure, never finds happiness, neither living nor dead.

46. He who does not seek to cause the sufferings of bonds and death to living creatures, (but) desires the good of all (beings), obtains endless bliss.

47. He who does not injure any (creature), attains without an effort what he thinks of, what he undertakes, and what he fixes his mind on.

48. Meat can never be obtained without injury to living creatures, and injury to sentient beings is detrimental to (the attainment of) heavenly bliss; let him therefore shun (the use of) meat.

49. Having well considered the (disgusting) origin of flesh and the (cruelty of) fettering and slaying corporeal beings, let him entirely abstain from eating flesh.

50. He who, disregarding the rule (given above), does not eat meat like a Pisaka, becomes dear to men, and will not be tormented by diseases.

51. He who permits (the slaughter of an animal), he who cuts it up, he who kills it, he who buys or sells (meat), he who cooks it, he who serves it up, and he who eats it, (must all be considered as) the slayers (of the animal).

52. There is no greater sinner than that (man) who, though not worshipping the gods or the manes, seeks to increase (the bulk of) his own flesh by the flesh of other (beings).

53. He who during a hundred years annually offers a horse-sacrifice, and he who entirely abstains from meat, obtain the same reward for their meritorious (conduct).

54. By subsisting on pure fruit and roots, and by eating food fit for ascetics (in the forest), one does not gain (so great) a reward as by entirely avoiding (the use of) flesh.

55. 'Me he (mam sah)' will devour in the next (world), whose flesh I eat in this (life); the wise declare this (to be) the real meaning of the word 'flesh' (mamsah).

56. There is no sin in eating meat, in (drinking) spirituous liquor, and in carnal intercourse, for that is the natural way of created beings, but abstention brings great rewards.

57. I will now in due order explain the purification for the dead and the purification of things as they are prescribed for the four castes (varna).

58. When (a child) dies that has teethed, or that before teething has received (the sacrament of) the tonsure (Kudakarana) or (of the initiation), all relatives (become) impure, and on the birth (of a child) the same (rule) is prescribed.

59. It is ordained (that) among Sapindas the impurity on account of a death (shall last) ten days, (or) until the bones have been collected, (or) three days or one day only.

60. But the Sapinda-relationship ceases with the seventh person (in the ascending and descending lines), the Samanodaka-relationship when the (common) origin and the (existence of a common family)- name are no (longer) known.

61. As this impurity on account of a death is prescribed for (all) Sapindas, even so it shall be (held) on a birth by those who desire to be absolutely pure.

62. (Or while) the impurity on account of a death is common to all (Sapindas), that caused by a birth (falls) on the parents alone; (or) it shall fall on the mother alone, and the father shall become pure by bathing;

63. But a man, having spent his strength, is purified merely by bathing; after begetting a child (on a remarried female), he shall retain the impurity during three days.

64. Those who have touched a corpse are purified after one day and night (added to) three periods of three days; those who give libations of water, after three days.

65. A pupil who performs the Pitrimedha for his deceased teacher, becomes also pure after ten days, just like those who carry the corpse out (to the burial-ground).

66. (A woman) is purified on a miscarriage in as many (days and) nights as months (elapsed after conception), and a menstruating female becomes pure by bathing after the menstrual secretion has ceased (to flow).

67. (On the death) of children whose tonsure (Kudakarman) has not been performed, the (Sapindas) are declared to become pure in one (day and) night; (on the death) of those who have received the tonsure (but not the initiation, the law) ordains (that) the purification (takes place) after three days.

68. A child that has died before the completion of its second year, the relatives shall carry out (of the village), decked (with flowers, and bury it) in pure ground, without collecting the bones (afterwards).

69. Such (a child) shall not be burnt with fire, and no libations of water shall be offered to it; leaving it like a (log of) wood in the forest, (the relatives) shall remain impure during three days only.

70. The relatives shall not offer libations to (a child) that has not reached the third year; but if it had teeth, or the ceremony of naming it (Namakarman) had been performed, (the offering of water is) optional.

71. If a fellow-student has died, the Smriti prescribes an impurity of one day; on a birth the purification of the Samanodakas is declared (to take place) after three (days and) nights.

72. (On the death) of females (betrothed but) not married (the bridegroom and his) relatives are purified after three days,

and the paternal relatives become pure according to the same rule.

73. Let (mourners) eat food without factitious salt, bathe during three days, abstain from meat, and sleep separate on the ground.

74. The above rule regarding impurity on account of a death has been prescribed (for cases where the kinsmen live) near (the deceased); (Sapinda) kinsmen and (Samanodaka) relatives must know the following rule (to refer to cases where deceased lived) at a distance (from them).

75. He who may hear that (a relative) residing in a distant country has died, before ten (days after his death have elapsed), shall be impure for the remainder of the period of ten (days and) nights only.

76. If the ten days have passed, he shall be impure during three (days and) nights; but if a year has elapsed (since the occurrence of the death), he becomes pure merely by bathing.

77. A man who hears of a (Sapinda) relative's death, or of the birth of a son after the ten days (of impurity have passed), becomes pure by bathing, dressed in his garments.

78. If an infant (that has not teethed), or a (grownup relative who is) not a Sapinda, die in a distant country, one becomes at once pure after bathing in one's clothes.

79. If within the ten days (of impurity) another birth or death happens, a Brahmana shall remain impure only until the (first) period of ten days has expired.

80. They declare that, when the teacher (akarya) has died, the impurity (lasts) three days; if the (teacher's) son or wife (is dead, it lasts) a day and a night; that is a settled (rule).

81. For a Srotriya who resides with (him out of affection), a man shall be impure for three days; for a maternal uncle, a pupil, an officiating priest, or a maternal relative, for one night together with the preceding and following days.

82. If the king in whose realm he resides is dead, (he shall be impure) as long as the light (of the sun or stars shines), but for (an intimate friend) who is not a Srotriya (the impurity

lasts) for a whole day, likewise for a Guru who knows the Veda and the Angas.

83. A Brahmana shall be pure after ten days, a Kshatriya after twelve, a Vaisya after fifteen, and a Sudra is purified after a month.

84. Let him not (unnecessarily) lengthen the period of impurity, nor interrupt the rites to be performed with the sacred fires; for he who performs that (Agnihotra) rite will not be impure, though (he be) a (Sapinda) relative.

85. When he has touched a Kandala, a menstruating woman, an outcast, a woman in childbed, a corpse, or one who has touched a (corpse), he becomes pure by bathing.

86. He who has purified himself by sipping water shall, on seeing any impure (thing or person), always mutter the sacred texts, addressed to Surya, and the Pavamani (verses).

87. A Brahmana who has touched a human bone to which fat adheres, becomes pure by bathing; if it be free from fat, by sipping water and by touching (afterwards) a cow or looking at the sun.

88. He who has undertaken the performance of a vow shall not pour out libations (to the dead) until the vow has been completed; but when he has offered water after its completion, he becomes pure in three days only.

89. Libations of water shall not be offered to those who (neglect the prescribed rites and may be said to) have been born in vain, to those born in consequence of an illegal mixture of the castes, to those who are ascetics (of heretical sects), and to those who have committed suicide,

90. To women who have joined a heretical sect, who through lust live (with many men), who have caused an abortion, have killed their husbands, or drink spirituous liquor.

91. A student does not break his vow by carrying out (to the place of cremation) his own dead teacher (akarya), sub-teacher (upadhyaya), father, mother, or Guru.

92. Let him carry out a dead Sudra by the southern gate of the town, but (the corpses of) twice-born men, as is proper, by the western, northern, or eastern (gates).

93. The taint of impurity does not fall on kings, and those engaged in the performance of a vow, or of a Sattra; for the (first are) seated on the throne of Indra, and the (last two are) ever pure like Brahman.

94. For a king, on the throne of magnanimity, immediate purification is prescribed, and the reason for that is that he is seated (there) for the protection of (his) subjects.

95. (The same rule applies to the kinsmen) of those who have fallen in a riot or a battle, (of those who have been killed) by lightning or by the king, and (of those who perished fighting) for cows and Brahmanas, and to those whom the king wishes (to be pure).

96. A king is an incarnation of the eight guardian deities of the world, the Moon, the Fire, the Sun, the Wind, Indra, the Lords of wealth and water (Kubera and Varuna), and Yama.

97. Because the king is pervaded by those lords of the world, no impurity is ordained for him; for purity and impurity of mortals is caused and removed by (those) lords of the world.

98. By him who is slain in battle with brandished weapons according to the law of the Kshatriyas, a (Srauta) sacrifice is instantly completed, and so is the period of impurity (caused by his death); that is a settled rule.

99. (At the end of the period of impurity) a Brahmana who has performed the necessary rites, becomes pure by touching water, a Kshatriya by touching the animal on which he rides, and his weapons, a Vaisya by touching his goad or the nose-string (of his oxen), a Sudra by touching his staff.

100. Thus the purification (required) on (the death of) Sapindas has been explained to you, O best of twice-born men; hear now the manner in which men are purified on the death of any (relative who is) not a Sapinda.

101. A Brahmana, having carried out a dead Brahmana who is not a Sapinda, as (if he were) a (near) relative, or a near relative of his mother, becomes pure after three days;

102. But if he eats the food of the (Sapindas of the deceased), he is purified in ten days, (but) in one day, if he does not eat their food nor dwells in their house.

103. Having voluntarily followed a corpse, whether (that of) a paternal kinsman or (of) a stranger, he becomes pure by bathing, dressed in his clothes, by touching fire and eating clarified butter.

104. Let him not allow a dead Brahmana to be carried out by a Sudra, while men of the same caste are at hand; for that burnt-offering which is defiled by a Sudra's touch is detrimental to (the deceased's passage to) heaven.

105. The knowledge (of Brahman) austerities, fire, (holy) food, earth, (restraint of) the internal organ, water, smearing (with cowdung), the wind, sacred rites, the sun, and time are the purifiers of corporeal (beings).

106. Among all modes of purification, purity in (the acquisition of) wealth is declared to be the best; for he is pure who gains wealth with clean hands, not he who purifies himself with earth and water.

107. The learned are purified by a forgiving disposition, those who have committed forbidden actions by liberality, secret sinners by muttering (sacred texts), and those who best know the Veda by austerities.

108. By earth and water is purified what ought to be made pure, a river by its current, a woman whose thoughts have been impure by the menstrual secretion, a Brahmana by abandoning the world (samnyasa).

109. The body is cleansed by water, the internal organ is purified by truthfulness, the individual soul by sacred learning and austerities, the intellect by (true) knowledge.

110. Thus the precise rules for the purification of the body have been declared to you; hear now the decision (of the law) regarding the purification of the various (inanimate) things.

111. The wise ordain that all (objects) made of metal, gems, and anything made of stone are to be cleansed with ashes, earth, and water.

112. A golden vessel which shows no stains, becomes pure with water alone, likewise what is produced in water (as shells and coral), what is made of stone, and a silver (vessel) not enchased.

113. From the union of water and fire arose the glittering gold and silver; those two, therefore, are best purified by (the elements) from which they sprang.

114. Copper, iron, brass, pewter, tin, and lead must be cleansed, as may be suitable (for each particular case), by alkaline (substances), acids or water.

115. The purification prescribed for all (sorts of) liquids is by passing two blades of Kusa grass through them, for solid things by sprinkling (them with water), for (objects) made of wood by planing them.

116. At sacrifices the purification of (the Soma cups called) Kamasas and Grahas, and of (other) sacrificial vessels (takes place) by rubbing (them) with the hand, and (afterwards) rinsing (them with water).

117. The Karu and (the spoons called) Sruk and Sruva must be cleaned with hot water, likewise (the wooden sword, called) Sphya, the winnowing-basket (Surpa), the cart (for bringing the grain), the pestle and the mortar.

118. The manner of purifying large quantities of grain and of cloth is to sprinkle them with water; but the purification of small quantities is prescribed (to take place) by washing them.

119. Skins and (objects) made of split cane must be cleaned like clothes; vegetables, roots, and fruit like grain;

120. Silk and woollen stuffs with alkaline earth; blankets with pounded Arishta (fruit); Amsupattas with Bel fruit; linen cloth with (a paste of) yellow mustard.

121. A man who knows (the law) must purify conch-shells, horn, bone and ivory, like linen cloth, or with a mixture of cow's urine and water.

122. Grass, wood, and straw become pure by being sprinkled (with water), a house by sweeping and smearing (it with cowdung or whitewash), an earthen (vessel) by a second burning.

123. An earthen vessel which has been defiled by spirituous liquor, urine, ordure, saliva, pus or blood cannot be purified by another burning.

124. Land is purified by (the following) five (modes, viz.) by sweeping, by smearing (it with cowdung), by sprinkling (it

with cows' urine or milk), by scraping, and by cows staying (on it during a day and night).

125. (Food) which has been pecked at by birds, smelt at by cows, touched (with the foot), sneezed on, or defiled by hair or insects, becomes pure by scattering earth (over it).

126. As long as the (foul) smell does not leave an (object) defiled by impure substances, and the stain caused by them (does not disappear), so long must earth and water be applied in cleansing (inanimate) things.

127. The gods declared three things (to be) pure to Brahmanas, that (on which) no (taint is) visible, what has been washed with water, and what has been commended (as pure) by the word (of a Brahmana).

128. Water, sufficient (in quantity) in order to slake the thirst of a cow, possessing the (proper) smell, colour, and taste, and unmixed with impure substances, is pure, if it is collected on (pure) ground.

129. The hand of an artisan is always pure, so is (every vendible commodity) exposed for sale in the market, and food obtained by begging which a student holds (in his hand) is always fit for use; that is a settled rule.

130. The mouth of a woman is always pure, likewise a bird when he causes a fruit to fall; a calf is pure on the flowing of the milk, and a dog when he catches a deer.

131. Manu has declared that the flesh (of an animal) killed by dogs is pure, likewise (that) of a (beast) slain by carnivorous (animals) or by men of low caste (Dasyu), such as Kandalas.

132. All those cavities (of the body) which lie above the navel are pure, (but) those which are below the navel are impure, as well as excretions that fall from the body.

133. Flies, drops of water, a shadow, a cow, a horse, the rays of the sun, dust, earth, the wind, and fire one must know to be pure to the touch.

134. In order to cleanse (the organs) by which urine and faeces are ejected, earth and water must be used, as they may be required, likewise in removing the (remaining ones among) twelve impurities of the body.

135. Oily exudations, semen, blood, (the fatty substance of the) brain, urine, faeces, the mucus of the nose, ear-wax, phlegm, tears, the rheum of the eyes, and sweat are the twelve impurities of human (bodies).

136. He who desires to be pure, must clean the organ by one (application of) earth, the anus by (applying earth) three (times), the (left) hand alone by (applying it) ten (times), and both (hands) by (applying it) seven (times).

137. Such is the purification ordained for householders; (it shall be) double for students, treble for hermits, but quadruple for ascetics.

138. When he has voided urine or faeces, let him, after sipping water, sprinkle the cavities, likewise when he is going to recite the Veda, and always before he takes food.

139. Let him who desires bodily purity first sip water three times, and then twice wipe his mouth; but a woman and a Sudra (shall perform each act) once (only).

140. Sudras who live according to the law, shall each month shave (their heads); their mode of purification (shall be) the same as that of Vaisyas, and their food the fragments of an Aryan's meal.

141. Drops (of water) from the mouth which do not fall on a limb, do not make (a man) impure, nor the hair of the moustache entering the mouth, nor what adheres to the teeth.

142. Drops which trickle on the feet of him who offers water for sipping to others, must be considered as equal to (water collected on the ground; they render him not impure.

143. He who, while carrying anything in any manner, is touched by an impure (person or thing), shall become pure, if he performs an ablution, without putting down that object.

144. He who has vomited or purged shall bathe, and afterwards eat clarified butter; but if (the attack comes on) after he has eaten, let him only sip water; bathing is prescribed for him who has had intercourse with a woman.

145. Though he may be (already) pure, let him sip water after sleeping, sneezing, eating, spitting, telling untruths, and drinking water, likewise when he is going to study the Veda.

146. Thus the rules of personal purification for men of all castes, and those for cleaning (inanimate) things, have been fully declared to you: hear now the duties of women.

147. By a girl, by a young woman, or even by an aged one, nothing must be done independently, even in her own house.

148. In childhood a female must be subject to her father, in youth to her husband, when her lord is dead to her sons; a woman must never be independent.

149. She must not seek to separate herself from her father, husband, or sons; by leaving them she would make both (her own and her husband's) families contemptible.

150. She must always be cheerful, clever in (the management of her) household affairs, careful in cleaning her utensils, and economical in expenditure.

151. Him to whom her father may give her, or her brother with the father's permission, she shall obey as long as he lives, and when he is dead, she must not insult (his memory).

152. For the sake of procuring good fortune to (brides), the recitation of benedictory texts (svastyayana), and the sacrifice to the Lord of creatures (Pragapati) are used at weddings; (but) the betrothal (by the father or guardian) is the cause of (the husband's) dominion (over his wife).

153. The husband who wedded her with sacred texts, always gives happiness to his wife, both in season and out of season, in this world and in the next.

154. Though destitute of virtue, or seeking pleasure (elsewhere), or devoid of good qualities, (yet) a husband must be constantly worshipped as a god by a faithful wife.

155. No sacrifice, no vow, no fast must be performed by women apart (from their husbands); if a wife obeys her husband, she will for that (reason alone) be exalted in heaven.

156. A faithful wife, who desires to dwell (after death) with her husband, must never do anything that might displease him who took her hand, whether he be alive or dead.

157. At her pleasure let her emaciate her body by (living on) pure flowers, roots, and fruit; but she must never even mention the name of another man after her husband has died.

158. Until death let her be patient (of hardships), self-controlled, and chaste, and strive (to fulfil) that most excellent duty which (is prescribed) for wives who have one husband only.

159. Many thousands of Brahmanas who were chaste from their youth, have gone to heaven without continuing their race.

160. A virtuous wife who after the death of her husband constantly remains chaste, reaches heaven, though she have no son, just like those chaste men.

161. But a woman who from a desire to have offspring violates her duty towards her (deceased) husband, brings on herself disgrace in this world, and loses her place with her husband (in heaven).

162. Offspring begotten by another man is here not (considered lawful), nor (does offspring begotten) on another man's wife (belong to the begetter), nor is a second husband anywhere prescribed for virtuous women.

163. She who cohabits with a man of higher caste, forsaking her own husband who belongs to a lower one, will become contemptible in this world, and is called a remarried woman (parapurva).

164. By violating her duty towards her husband, a wife is disgraced in this world, (after death) she enters the womb of a jackal, and is tormented by diseases (the punishment of) her sin.

165. She who, controlling her thoughts, words, and deeds, never slights her lord, resides (after death) with her husband (in heaven), and is called a virtuous (wife).

166. In reward of such conduct, a female who controls her thoughts, speech, and actions, gains in this (life) highest renown, and in the next (world) a place near her husband.

167. A twice-born man, versed in the sacred law, shall burn a wife of equal caste who conducts herself thus and dies before him, with (the sacred fires used for) the Agnihotra, and with the sacrificial implements.

168. Having thus, at the funeral, given the sacred fires to his wife who dies before him, he may marry again, and again kindle (the fires).

169. (Living) according to the (preceding) rules, he must never neglect the five (great) sacrifices, and, having taken a wife, he must dwell in (his own) house during the second period of his life.

1. A twice-born Snataka, who has thus lived according to the law in the order of householders, may, taking a firm resolution and keeping his organs in subjection, dwell in the forest, duly (observing the rules given below).

2. When a householder sees his (skin) wrinkled, and (his hair) white, and. the sons of his sons, then he may resort to the forest.

3. Abandoning all food raised by cultivation, and all his belongings, he may depart into the forest, either committing his wife to his sons, or accompanied by her.

4. Taking with him the sacred fire and the implements required for domestic (sacrifices), he may go forth from the village into the forest and reside there, duly controlling his senses.

5. Let him offer those five great sacrifices according to the rule, with various kinds of pure food fit for ascetics, or with herbs, roots, and fruit.

6. Let him wear a skin or a tattered garment; let him bathe in the evening or in the morning; and let him always wear (his hair in) braids, the hair on his body, his beard, and his nails (being unclipped).

7. Let him perform the Bali-offering with such food as he eats, and give alms according to his ability; let him honour those who come to his hermitage with alms consisting of water, roots, and fruit.

8. Let him be always industrious in privately reciting the Veda; let him be patient of hardships, friendly (towards all), of collected mind, ever liberal and never a receiver of gifts, and compassionate towards all living creatures.

9. Let him offer, according to the law, the Agnihotra with three sacred fires, never omitting the new-moon and full-moon sacrifices at the proper time.

10. Let him also offer the Nakshatreshti, the Agrayana, and the Katurmasya (sacrifices), as well as the Turayana and likewise the Dakshayana, in due order.

11. With pure grains, fit for ascetics, which grow in spring and in autumn, and which he himself has collected, let him severally prepare the sacrificial cakes (purodasa) and the boiled messes (karu), as the law directs.

12. Having offered those most pure sacrificial viands, consisting of the produce of the forest, he may use the remainder for himself, (mixed with) salt prepared by himself.

13. Let him eat vegetables that grow on dry land or in water, flowers, roots, and fruits, the productions of pure trees, and oils extracted from forest-fruits.

14. Let him avoid honey, flesh, and mushrooms growing on the ground (or elsewhere, the vegetables called) Bhustrina, and Sigruka, and the Sleshmantaka fruit.

15. Let him throw away in the month of Asvina the food of ascetics, which he formerly collected, likewise his worn-out clothes and his vegetables, roots, and fruit.

16. Let him not eat anything (grown on) ploughed (land), though it may have been thrown away by somebody, nor roots and fruit grown in a village, though (he may be) tormented (by hunger).

17. He may eat either what has been cooked with fire, or what has been ripened by time; he either may use a stone for grinding, or his teeth may be his mortar.

18. He may either at once (after his daily meal) cleanse (his vessel for collecting food), or lay up a store sufficient for a month, or gather what suffices for six months or for a year.

19. Having collected food according to his ability, he may either eat at night (only), or in the day-time (only), or at every fourth meal-time, or at every eighth.

20. Or he may live according to the rule of the lunar penance (Kandrayana, daily diminishing the quantity of his food) in the bright (half of the month) and (increasing it) in the dark (half); or he may eat on the last days of each fortnight, once (a day only), boiled barley-gruel.

21. Or he may constantly subsist on flowers, roots, and fruit alone, which have been ripened by time and have fallen spontaneously, following the rule of the (Institutes) of Vikhanas.

22. Let him either roll about on the ground, or stand during the day on tiptoe, (or) let him alternately stand and sit down; going at the Savanas (at sunrise, at midday, and at sunset) to water in the forest (in order to bathe).

23. In summer let him expose himself to the heat of five fires, during the rainy season live under the open sky, and in winter be dressed in wet clothes, (thus) gradually increasing (the rigour of) his austerities.

24. When he bathes at the three Savanas (sunrise, midday, and sunset), let him offer libations of water to the manes and the gods, and practising harsher and harsher austerities, let him dry up his bodily frame.

25. Having reposited the three sacred fires in himself, according to the prescribed rule, let him live without a fire, without a house, wholly silent, subsisting on roots and fruit,

26. Making no effort (to procure) things that give pleasure, chaste, sleeping on the bare ground, not caring for any shelter, dwelling at the roots of trees.

27. From Brahmanas (who live as) ascetics, let him receive alms, (barely sufficient) to support life, or from other householders of the twice-born (castes) who reside in the forest.

28. Or (the hermit) who dwells in the forest may bring (food) from a village, receiving it either in a hollow dish (of leaves), in (his naked) hand, or in a broken earthen dish, and may eat eight mouthfuls.

29. These and other observances must a Brahmana who dwells in the forest diligently practise, and in order to attain complete (union with) the (supreme) Soul, (he must study) the various sacred texts contained in the Upanishads,

30. (As well as those rites and texts) which have been practised and studied by the sages (Rishis), and by Brahmana householders, in order to increase their knowledge (of Brahman), and their austerity, and in order to sanctify their bodies;

31. Or let him walk, fully determined and going straight on, in a north-easterly direction, subsisting on water and air, until his body sinks to rest.

32. A Brahmana, having got rid of his body by one of those modes practised by the great sages, is exalted in the world of Brahman, free from sorrow and fear.

33. But having thus passed the third part of (a man's natural term of) life in the forest, he may live as an ascetic during the fourth part of his existence, after abandoning all attachment to worldly objects.

34. He who after passing from order to order, after offering sacrifices and subduing his senses, becomes, tired with (giving) alms and offerings of food, an ascetic, gains bliss after death.

35. When he has paid the three debts, let him apply his mind to (the attainment of) final liberation; he who seeks it without having paid (his debts) sinks downwards.

36. Having studied the Vedas in accordance with the rule, having begat sons according to the sacred law, and having offered sacrifices according to his ability, he may direct his mind to (the attainment of) final liberation.

37. A twice-born man who seeks final liberation, without having studied the Vedas, without having begotten sons, and without having offered sacrifices, sinks downwards.

38. Having performed the Ishti, sacred to the Lord of creatures (Pragapati), where (he gives) all his property as the sacrificial fee, having reposited the sacred fires in himself, a Brahmana may depart from his house (as an ascetic).

39. Worlds, radiant in brilliancy, become (the portion) of him who recites (the texts regarding) Brahman and departs from his house (as an ascetic), after giving a promise of safety to all created beings.

40. For that twice-born man, by whom not the smallest danger even is caused to created beings, there will be no danger from any (quarter), after he is freed from his body.

41. Departing from his house fully provided with the means of purification (Pavitra), let him wander about absolutely silent, and caring nothing for enjoyments that may be offered (to him).

42. Let him always wander alone, without any companion, in order to attain (final liberation), fully understanding that the solitary (man, who) neither forsakes nor is forsaken, gains his end.

43. He shall neither possess a fire, nor a dwelling, he may go to a village for his food, (he shall be) indifferent to everything, firm of purpose, meditating (and) concentrating his mind on Brahman.

44. A potsherd (instead of an alms-bowl), the roots of trees (for a dwelling), coarse worn-out garments, life in solitude and indifference towards everything, are the marks of one who has attained liberation.

45. Let him not desire to die, let him not desire to live; let him wait for (his appointed) time, as a servant (waits) for the payment of his wages.

46. Let him put down his foot purified by his sight, let him drink water purified by (straining with) a cloth, let him utter speech purified by truth, let him keep his heart pure.

47. Let him patiently bear hard words, let him not insult anybody, and let him not become anybody's enemy for the sake of this (perishable) body.

48. Against an angry man let him not in return show anger, let him bless when he is cursed, and let him not utter speech, devoid of truth, scattered at the seven gates.

49. Delighting in what refers to the Soul, sitting (in the postures prescribed by the Yoga), independent (of external help), entirely abstaining from sensual enjoyments, with himself for his only companion, he shall live in this world, desiring the bliss (of final liberation).

50. Neither by (explaining) prodigies and omens, nor by skill in astrology and palmistry, nor by giving advice and by the exposition (of the Sastras), let him ever seek to obtain alms.

51. Let him not (in order to beg) go near a house filled with hermits, Brahmanas, birds, dogs, or other mendicants.

52. His hair, nails, and beard being clipped, carrying an alms-bowl, a staff, and a water-pot, let him continually wander about, controlling himself and not hurting any creature.

53. His vessels shall not be made of metal, they shall be free from fractures; it is ordained that they shall be cleansed with water, like (the cups, called) Kamasa, at a sacrifice.

54. A gourd, a wooden bowl, an earthen (dish), or one made of split cane, Manu, the son of Svayambhu, has declared (to be) vessels (suitable) for an ascetic.

55. Let him go to beg once (a day), let him not be eager to obtain a large quantity (of alms); for an ascetic who eagerly seeks alms, attaches himself also to sensual enjoyments.

56. When no smoke ascends from (the kitchen), when the pestle lies motionless, when the embers have been extinguished, when the people have finished their meal, when the remnants in the dishes have been removed, let the ascetic always go to beg.

57. Let him not be sorry when he obtains nothing, nor rejoice when he obtains (something), let him (accept) so much only as will sustain life, let him not care about the (quality of his) utensils.

58. Let him disdain all (food) obtained in consequence of humble salutations, (for) even an ascetic who has attained final liberation, is bound (with the fetters of the Samsara) by accepting (food given) in consequence of humble salutations.

59. By eating little, and by standing and sitting in solitude, let him restrain his senses, if they are attracted by sensual objects.

60. By the restraint of his senses, by the destruction of love and hatred, and by the abstention from injuring the creatures, he becomes fit for immortality.

61. Let him reflect on the transmigrations of men, caused by their sinful deeds, on their falling into hell, and on the torments in the world of Yama,

62. On the separation from their dear ones, on their union with hated men, on their being overpowered by age and being tormented with diseases,

63. On the departure of the individual soul from this body and its new birth in (another) womb, and on its wanderings through ten thousand millions of existences,

64. On the infliction of pain on embodied (spirits), which is caused by demerit, and the gain of eternal bliss, which is caused by the attainment of their highest aim, (gained through) spiritual merit.

65. By deep meditation let him recognise the subtile nature of the supreme Soul, and its presence in all organisms, both the highest and the lowest.

66. To whatever order he may be attached, let him, though blemished (by a want of the external marks), fulfil his duty, equal-minded towards all creatures; (for) the external mark (of the order) is not the cause of (the acquisition of) merit.

67. Though the fruit of the Kataka tree (the clearing-nut) makes water clear, yet the (latter) does not become limpid in consequence of the mention of the (fruit's) name.

68. In order to preserve living creatures, let him always by day and by night, even with pain to his body, walk, carefully scanning the ground.

69. In order to expiate (the death) of those creatures which he unintentionally injures by day or by night, an ascetic shall bathe and perform six suppressions of the breath.

70. Three suppressions of the breath even, performed according to the rule, and accompanied with the (recitation of the) Vyahritis and of the syllable Om, one must know to be the highest (form of) austerity for every Brahmana.

71. For as the impurities of metallic ores, melted in the blast (of a furnace), are consumed, even so the taints of the organs are destroyed through the suppression of the breath.

72. Let him destroy the taints through suppressions of the breath, (the production of) sin by fixed attention, all sensual attachments by restraining (his senses and organs), and all qualities that are not lordly by meditation.

73. Let him recognise by the practice of meditation the progress of the individual soul through beings of various kinds, (a progress) hard to understand for unregenerate men.

74. He who possesses the true insight (into the nature of the world), is not fettered by his deeds; but he who is destitute of that insight, is drawn into the circle of births and deaths.

75. By not injuring any creatures, by detaching the senses (from objects of enjoyment), by the rites prescribed in the Veda, and by rigorously practising austerities, (men) gain that state (even) in this (world).

76-77. Let him quit this dwelling, composed of the five elements, where the bones are the beams, which is held together by tendons (instead of cords), where the flesh and the blood are the mortar, which is thatched with the skin, which is foul-smelling, filled with urine and ordure, infested by old age and sorrow, the seat of disease, harassed by pain, gloomy with passion, and perishable.

78. He who leaves this body, (be it by necessity) as a tree (that is torn from) the river-bank, or (freely) like a bird (that) quits a tree, is freed from the misery (of this world, dreadful like) a shark.

79. Making over (the merit of his own) good actions to his friends and (the guilt of) his evil deeds to his enemies, he attains the eternal Brahman by the practice of meditation.

80. When by the disposition (of his heart) he becomes indifferent to all objects, he obtains eternal happiness both in this world and after death.

81. He who has in this manner gradually given up all attachments and is freed from all the pairs (of opposites), reposes in Brahman alone.

82. All that has been declared (above) depends on meditation; for he who is not proficient in the knowledge of that

which refers to the Soul reaps not the full reward of the performance of rites.

83. Let him constantly recite (those texts of) the Veda which refer to the sacrifice, (those) referring to the deities, and (those) which treat of the Soul and are contained in the concluding portions of the Veda (Vedanta).

84. That is the refuge of the ignorant, and even that (the refuse) of those who know (the meaning of the Veda); that is (the protection) of those who seek (bliss in) heaven and of those who seek endless (beatitude).

85. A twice-born man who becomes an ascetic, after the successive performance of the above-mentioned acts, shakes off sin here below and reaches the highest Brahman.

86. Thus the law (valid) for self-restrained ascetics has been explained to you; now listen to the (particular) duties of those who give up (the rites prescribed by) the Veda.

87. The student, the householder, the hermit, and the ascetic, these (constitute) four separate orders, which all spring from (the order of) householders.

88. But all (or) even (any of) these orders, assumed successively in accordance with the Institutes (of the sacred law), lead the Brahmana who acts by the preceding (rules) to the highest state.

89. And in accordance with the precepts of the Veda and of the Smriti, the housekeeper is declared to be superior to all of them; for he supports the other three.

90. As all rivers, both great and small, find a resting-place in the ocean, even so men of all orders find protection with householders

91. By twice-born men belonging to (any of) these four orders, the tenfold law must be ever carefully obeyed.

92. Contentment, forgiveness, self-control, abstention from unrighteously appropriating anything, (obedience to the rules of) purification, coercion of the organs, wisdom, knowledge (of the supreme Soul), truthfulness, and abstention from anger, (form) the tenfold law.

93. Those Brahmanas who thoroughly study the tenfold law, and after studying obey it, enter the highest state.

94. A twice-born man who, with collected mind, follows the tenfold law and has paid his (three) debts, may, after learning the Vedanta according to the prescribed rule, become an ascetic.

95. Having given up (the performance of) all rites, throwing off the guilt of his (sinful) acts, subduing his organs and having studied the Veda, he may live at his ease under the protection of his son.

96. He who has thus given up (the performance of) all rites, who is solely intent on his own (particular) object, (and) free from desires, destroys his guilt by his renunciation and obtains the highest state.

97. Thus the fourfold holy law of Brahmanas, which after death (yields) imperishable rewards, has been declared to you; now learn the duty of kings.

1. I will declare the duties of kings, (and) show how a king should conduct himself, how he was created, and how (he can obtain) highest success.

2. A Kshatriya, who has received according to the rule the sacrament prescribed by the Veda, must duly protect this whole (world).

3. For, when these creatures, being without a king, through fear dispersed in all directions, the Lord created a king for the protection of this whole (creation),

4. Taking (for that purpose) eternal particles of Indra, of the Wind, of Yama, of the Sun, of Fire, of Varuna, of the Moon, and of the Lord of wealth (Kubera).

5. Because a king has been formed of particles of those lords of the gods, he therefore surpasses all created beings in lustre;

6. And, like the sun, he burns eyes and hearts; nor can anybody on earth even gaze on him.

7. Through his (supernatural) power he is Fire and Wind, he Sun and Moon, he the Lord of justice (Yama), he Kubera, he Varuna, he great Indra.

8. Even an infant king must not be despised, (from an idea) that he is a (mere) mortal; for he is a great deity in human form.

9. Fire burns one man only, if he carelessly approaches it, the fire of a king's (anger) consumes the (whole) family, together with its cattle and its hoard of property.

10. Having fully considered the purpose, (his) power, and the place and the time, he assumes by turns many (different) shapes for the complete attainment of justice.

11. He, in whose favour resides Padma, the goddess of fortune, in whose valour dwells victory, in whose anger abides death, is formed of the lustre of all (gods).

12. The (man), who in his exceeding folly hates him, will doubtlessly perish; for the king quickly makes up his mind to destroy such (a man).

13. Let no (man), therefore, transgress that law which favourites, nor (his orders) which inflict pain on those in disfavour.

14. For the (king's) sake the Lord formerly created his own son, Punishment, the protector of all creatures, (an incarnation of) the law, formed of Brahman's glory.

15. Through fear of him all created beings, both the immovable and the movable, allow themselves to be enjoyed and swerve not from their duties.

16. Having fully considered the time and the place (of the offence), the strength and the knowledge (of the offender), let him justly inflict that (punishment) on men who act unjustly.

17. Punishment is (in reality) the king (and) the male, that the manager of affairs, that the ruler, and that is called the surety for the four orders' obedience to the law.

18. Punishment alone governs all created beings, punishment alone protects them, punishment watches over them while they sleep; the wise declare punishment (to be identical with) the law.

19. If (punishment) is properly inflicted after (due) consideration, it makes all people happy; but inflicted without consideration, it destroys everything.

20. If the king did not, without tiring, inflict punishment on those worthy to be punished, the stronger would roast the weaker, like fish on a spit;

21. The crow would eat the sacrificial cake and the dog would lick the sacrificial viands, and ownership would not remain with any one, the lower ones would (usurp the place of) the higher ones.

22. The whole world is kept in order by punishment, for a guiltless man is hard to find; through fear of punishment the whole world yields the enjoyments (which it owes).

23. The gods, the Danavas, the Gandharvas, the Rakshasas, the bird and snake deities even give the enjoyments (due from them) only, if they are tormented by (the fear of) punishment.

24. All castes (varna) would be corrupted (by intermixture), all barriers would be broken through, and all men would rage (against each other) in consequence of mistakes with respect to punishment.

25. But where Punishment with a black hue and red eyes stalks about, destroying sinners, there the subjects are not disturbed, provided that he who inflicts it discerns well.

26. They declare that king to be a just inflicter of punishment, who is truthful, who acts after due consideration, who is wise, and who knows (the respective value of) virtue, pleasure, and wealth.

27. A king who properly inflicts (punishment), prospers with respect to (those) three (means of happiness); but he who is voluptuous, partial, and deceitful will be destroyed, even through the (unjust) punishment (which he inflicts).

28. Punishment (possesses) a very bright lustre, and is hard to be administered by men with unimproved minds; it strikes down the king who swerves from his duty, together with his relatives.

29. Next it will afflict his castles, his territories, the whole world together with the movable and immovable (creation), likewise the sages and the gods, who (on the failure of offerings) ascend to the sky.

30. (Punishment) cannot be inflicted justly by one who has no assistant, (nor) by a fool, (nor) by a covetous man, (nor) by one whose mind is unimproved, (nor) by one addicted to sensual pleasures.

31. By him who is pure (and) faithful to his promise, who acts according to the Institutes (of the sacred law), who has good assistants and is wise, punishment can be (justly) inflicted.

32. Let him act with justice in his own domain, with rigour chastise his enemies, behave without duplicity towards his friends, and be lenient towards Brahmanas.

33. The fame of a king who behaves thus, even though he subsist by gleaning, is spread in the world, like a drop of oil on water.

34. But the fame of a king who acts in a contrary manner and who does not subdue himself, diminishes in extent among men like a drop of clarified butter in water.

35. The king has been created (to be) the protector of the castes (varna) and orders, who, all according to their rank, discharge their several duties.

36. Whatever must be done by him and by his servants for the protection of his people, that I will fully declare to you in due order.

37. Let the king, after rising early in the morning, worship Brahmanas who are well versed in the threefold sacred science and learned (in polity), and follow their advice.

38. Let him daily worship aged Brahmanas who know the Veda and are pure; for he who always worships aged men, is honoured even by Rakshasas.

39. Let him, though he may already be modest, constantly learn modesty from them; for a king who is modest never perishes.

40. Through a want of modesty many kings have perished, together with their belongings; through modesty even hermits in the forest have gained kingdoms.

41. Through a want of humility Vena perished, likewise king Nahusha, Sudas, the son of Pigavana, Sumukha, and Nemi.

42. But by humility Prithu and Manu gained sovereignty, Kubera the position of the Lord of wealth, and the son of Gadhi the rank of a Brahmana.

43. From those versed in the three Vedas let him learn the threefold (sacred science), the primeval science of government, the science of dialectics, and the knowledge of the (supreme) Soul; from the people (the theory of) the (various) trades and professions.

44. Day and night he must strenuously exert himself to conquer his senses; for he (alone) who has conquered his own senses, can keep his subjects in obedience.

45. Let him carefully shun the ten vices, springing from love of pleasure, and the eight, proceeding from wrath, which (all) end in misery.

46. For a king who is attached to the vices springing from love of pleasure, loses his wealth and his virtue, but (he who is given) to those arising from anger, (loses) even his life.

47. Hunting, gambling, sleeping by day, censoriousness, (excess with) women, drunkenness, (an inordinate love for) dancing, singing, and music, and useless travel are the tenfold set (of vices) springing from love of pleasure.

48. Tale-bearing, violence, treachery, envy, slandering, (unjust) seizure of property, reviling, and assault are the eightfold set (of vices) produced by wrath.

49. That greediness which all wise men declare to be the root even of both these (sets), let him carefully conquer; both sets (of vices) are produced by that.

50. Drinking, dice, women, and hunting, these four (which have been enumerated) in succession, he must know to be the most pernicious in the set that springs from love of pleasure.

51. Doing bodily injury, reviling, and the seizure of property, these three he must know to be the most pernicious in the set produced by wrath.

52. A self-controlled (king) should know that in this set of seven, which prevails everywhere, each earlier-named vice is more abominable (than those named later).

53. (On a comparison) between vice and death, vice is declared to be more pernicious; a vicious man sinks to the nethermost (hell), he who dies, free from vice, ascends to heaven.

54. Let him appoint seven or eight ministers whose ancestors have been royal servants, who are versed in the sciences, heroes skilled in the use of weapons and descended from (noble) families and who have been tried.

55. Even an undertaking easy (in itself) is (sometimes) hard to be accomplished by a single man; how much (harder is it for a king), especially (if he has) no assistant, (to govern) a kingdom which yields great revenues.

56. Let him daily consider with them the ordinary (business, referring to) peace and war, (the four subjects called) sthana, the revenue, the (manner of) protecting (himself and his kingdom), and the sanctification of his gains (by pious gifts).

57. Having (first) ascertained the opinion of each (minister) separately and (then the views) of all together, let him do what is (most) beneficial for him in his affairs.

58. But with the most distinguished among them all, a learned Brahmana, let the king deliberate on the most important affairs which relate to the six measures of royal policy.

59. Let him, full of confidence, always entrust to that (official) all business; having taken his final resolution with him, let him afterwards begin to act.

60. He must also appoint other officials, (men) of integrity, (who are) wise, firm, well able to collect money, and well tried.

61. As many persons as the due performance of his business requires, so many skilful and clever (men), free from sloth, let him appoint.

62. Among them let him employ the brave, the skilful, the high-born, and the honest in (offices for the collection of) revenue, (e.g.) in mines, manufactures, and storehouses, (but) the timid in the interior of his palace.

63. Let him also appoint an ambassador who is versed in all sciences, who understands hints, expressions of the face and gestures, who is honest, skilful, and of (noble) family.

64. (Such) an ambassador is commended to a king (who is) loyal, honest, skilful, possessing a good memory, who knows the (proper) place and time (for action, who is) handsome, fearless, and eloquent.

65. The army depends on the official (placed in charge of it), the due control (of the subjects) on the army, the treasury and the (government of) the realm on the king, peace and its opposite (war) on the ambassador.

66. For the ambassador alone makes (kings') allies and separates allies; the ambassador transacts that business by which (kings) are disunited or not.

67. With respect to the affairs let the (ambassador) explore the expression of the countenance, the gestures and actions of the (foreign king) through the gestures and actions of his confidential (advisers), and (discover) his designs among his servants.

68. Having learnt exactly (from his ambassador) the designs of the foreign king, let (the king) take such measures that he does not bring evil on himself.

69. Let him settle in a country which is open and has a dry climate, where grain is abundant, which is chiefly (inhabited) by Aryans, not subject to epidemic diseases (or similar troubles), and pleasant, where the vassals are obedient and his own (people easily) find their livelihood.

70. Let him build (there) a town, making for his safety a fortress, protected by a desert, or a fortress built of (stone and) earth, or one protected by water or trees, or one (formed by an encampment of armed) men or a hill-fort.

71. Let him make every effort to secure a hill-fort, for amongst all those (fortresses mentioned) a hill-fort is distinguished by many superior qualities.

72. The first three of those (various kinds of fortresses) are inhabited by wild beasts, animals living in holes and aquatic animals, the last three by monkeys, men, and gods respectively.

73. As enemies do not hurt these (beings, when they are) sheltered by (their) fortresses, even so foes (can) not injure a king who has taken refuge in his fort.

74. One bowman, placed on a rampart, is a match in battle for one hundred (foes), one hundred for ten thousand; hence it is prescribed (in the Sastras that a king will posses) a fortress.

75. Let that (fort) be well supplied with weapons, money, grain and beasts of burden, with Brahmanas, with artisans, with engines, with fodder, and with water.

76. Let him cause to be built for himself, in the centre of it, a spacious palace, (well) protected, habitable in every season, resplendent (with whitewash), supplied with water and trees.

77. Inhabiting that, let him wed a consort of equal caste (varna), who possesses auspicious marks (on her body), and is born in a great family, who is charming and possesses beauty and excellent qualities.

78. Let him appoint a domestic priest (purohita) and choose officiating priests (ritvig); they shall perform his domestic rites and the (sacrifices) for which three fires are required.

79. A king shall offer various (Srauta) sacrifices at which liberal fees (are distributed), and in order to acquire merit, he shall give to Brahmanas enjoyments and wealth.

80. Let him cause the annual revenue in his kingdom to be collected by trusty (officials), let him obey the sacred law in (his transactions with) the people, and behave like a father towards all men.

81. For the various (branches of business) let him appoint intelligent supervisors; they shall inspect all (the acts) of those men who transact his business.

82. Let him honour those Brahmanas who have returned from their teacher's house (after studying the Veda); for that (money which is given) to Brahmanas is declared to be an imperishable treasure for kings.

83. Neither thieves nor foes can take it, nor can it be lost; hence an imperishable store must be deposited by kings with Brahmanas.

84. The offering made through the mouth of a Brahmana, which is neither spilt, nor falls (on the ground), nor ever perishes, is far more excellent than Agnihotras.

85. A gift to one who is not a Brahmana (yields) the ordinary (reward; a gift) to one who calls himself a Brahmana, a double (reward); a gift to a well-read Brahmana, a hundred-thousandfold (reward); (a gift) to one who knows the Veda and the Angas (Vedaparaga, a reward) without end.

86. For according to the particular qualities of the recipient and according to the faith (of the giver) a small or a great reward will be obtained for a gift in the next world.

87. A king who, while he protects his people, is defied by (foes), be they equal in strength, or stronger, or weaker, must not shrink from battle, remembering the duty of Kshatriyas.

88. Not to turn back in battle, to protect the people, to honour the Brahmanas, is the best means for a king to secure happiness.

89. Those kings who, seeking to slay each other in battle, fight with the utmost exertion and do not turn back, go to heaven.

90. When he fights with his foes in battle, let him not strike with weapons concealed (in wood), nor with (such as are) barbed, poisoned, or the points of which are blazing with fire.

91. Let him not strike one who (in flight) has climbed on an eminence, nor a eunuch, nor one who joins the palms of his hands (in supplication), nor one who (flees) with flying hair, nor one who sits down, nor one who says 'I am thine;'

92. Nor one who sleeps, nor one who has lost his coat of mail, nor one who is naked, nor one who is disarmed, nor one who looks on without taking part in the fight, nor one who is fighting with another (foe);

93. Nor one whose weapons are broken, nor one afflicted (with sorrow), nor one who has been grievously wounded, nor one who is in fear, nor one who has turned to flight; (but in all these cases let him) remember the duty (of honourable warriors).

94. But the (Kshatriya) who is slain in battle, while he turns back in fear, takes upon himself all the sin of his master, whatever (it may be);

95. And whatever merit (a man) who is slain in flight may have gained for the next (world), all that his master takes.

96. Chariots and horses, elephants, parasols, money, grain, cattle, women, all sorts of (marketable) goods and valueless metals belong to him who takes them (singly) conquering (the possessor).

97. A text of the Veda (declares) that (the soldiers) shall present a choice portion (of the booty) to the king; what has not been taken singly, must be distributed by the king among all the soldiers.

98. Thus has been declared the blameless, primeval law for warriors; from this law a Kshatriya must not depart, when he strikes his foes in battle.

99. Let him strive to gain what he has not yet gained; what he has gained let him carefully preserve; let him augment what he preserves, and what he has augmented let him bestow on worthy men.

100. Let him know that these are the four means for securing the aims of human (existence); let him, without ever tiring, properly employ them.

101. What he has not (yet) gained, let him seek (to gain) by (his) army; what he has gained, let him protect by careful attention; what he has protected, let him augment by (various modes of) increasing it; and what he has augmented, let him liberally bestow (on worthy men).

102. Let him be ever ready to strike, his prowess constantly displayed, and his secrets constantly concealed, and let him constantly explore the weaknesses of his foe.

103. Of him who is always ready to strike, the whole world stands in awe; let him therefore make all creatures subject to himself even by the employment of force.

104. Let him ever act without guile, and on no account treacherously; carefully guarding himself, let him always fathom the treachery which his foes employ.

105. His enemy must not know his weaknesses, but he must know the weaknesses of his enemy; as the tortoise (hides

its limbs), even so let him secure the members (of his government against treachery), let him protect his own weak points.

106. Let him plan his undertakings (patiently meditating) like a heron; like a lion, let him put forth his strength; like a wolf, let him snatch (his prey); like a hare, let him double in retreat.

107. When he is thus engaged in conquest, let him subdue all the opponents whom he may find, by the (four) expedients, conciliation and the rest.

108. If they cannot be stopped by the three first expedients, then let him, overcoming them by force alone, gradually bring them to subjection.

109. Among the four expedients, conciliation and the rest, the learned always recommend conciliation and (the employment of) force for the prosperity of kingdoms.

110. As the weeder plucks up the weeds and preserves the corn, even so let the king protect his kingdom and destroy his opponents.

111. That king who through folly rashly oppresses his kingdom, (will), together with his relatives, ere long be deprived of his life and of his kingdom.

112. As the lives of living creatures are destroyed by tormenting their bodies, even so the lives of kings are destroyed by their oppressing their kingdoms.

113. In governing his kingdom let him always observe the (following) rules; for a king who governs his kingdom well, easily prospers.

114. Let him place a company of soldiers, commanded (by a trusty officer), the midst of two, three, five or hundreds of villages, (to be) a protection of the kingdom.

115. Let him appoint a lord over (each) village, as well as lords of ten villages, lords of twenty, lords of a hundred, and lords of a thousand.

116. The lord of one village himself shall inform the lord of ten villages of the crimes committed in his village, and the ruler of ten (shall make his report) to the ruler of twenty.

117. But the ruler of twenty shall report all such (matters) to the lord of a hundred, and the lord of a hundred shall himself give information to the lord of a thousand.

118. Those (articles) which the villagers ought to furnish daily to the king, such as food, drink, and fuel, the lord of one village shall obtain.

119. The ruler of ten (villages) shall enjoy one kula (as much land as suffices for one family), the ruler of twenty five kulas, the superintendent of a hundred villages (the revenues of) one village, the lord of a thousand (the revenues of) a town.

120. The affairs of these (officials), which are connected with (their) villages and their separate business, another minister of the king shall inspect, (who must be) loyal and never remiss;

121. And in each town let him appoint one superintendent of all affairs, elevated in rank, formidable, (resembling) a planet among the stars.

122. Let that (man) always personally visit by turns all those (other officials); let him properly explore their behaviour in their districts through spies (appointed to) each.

123. For the servants of the king, who are appointed to protect (the people), generally become knaves who seize the property of others; let him protect his subjects against such (men).

124. Let the king confiscate the whole property of those (officials) who, evil-minded, may take money from suitors, and banish them.

125. For women employed in the royal service and for menial servants, let him fix a daily maintenance, in proportion to their position and to their work.

126. One pana must be given (daily) as wages to the lowest, six to the highest, likewise clothing every six months and one drona of grain every month.

127. Having well considered (the rates of) purchase and (of) sale, (the length of) the road, (the expense for) food and condiments, the charges of securing the goods, let the king make the traders pay duty.

128. After (due) consideration the king shall always fix in his realm the duties and taxes in such a manner that both he himself and the man who does the work receive (their due) reward.

129. As the leech, the calf, and the bee take their food little by little, even so must the king draw from his realm moderate annual taxes.

130. A fiftieth part of (the increments on) cattle and gold may be taken by the king, and the eighth, sixth, or twelfth part of the crops.

131. He may also take the sixth part of trees, meat, honey, clarified butter, perfumes, (medical) herbs, substances used for flavouring food, flowers, roots, and fruit;

132. Of leaves, pot-herbs, grass, (objects) made of cane, skins, of earthen vessels, and all (articles) made of stone.

133. Though dying (with want), a king must not levy a tax on Srotriyas, and no Srotriya, residing in his kingdom, must perish from hunger.

134. The kingdom of that king, in whose dominions a Srotriya pines with hunger, will even, ere long, be afflicted by famine.

135. Having ascertained his learning in the Veda and (the purity of) his conduct, the king shall provide for him means of subsistence in accordance with the sacred law, and shall protect him in every way, as a father (protects) the lawful son of his body.

136. Whatever meritorious acts (such a Brahmana) performs under the full protection of the king, thereby the king's length of life, wealth, and kingdom increase.

137. Let the king make the common inhabitants of his realm who live by traffic, pay annually some trifle, which is called a tax.

138. Mechanics and artisans, as well as Sudras who subsist by manual labour, he may cause to work (for himself) one (day) in each month.

139. Let him not cut up his own root (by levying no taxes), nor the root of other (men) by excessive greed; for by cutting up his own root (or theirs), he makes himself or them wretched.

140. Let the king, having carefully considered (each) affair, be both sharp and gentle; for a king who is both sharp and gentle is highly respected.

141. When he is tired with the inspection of the business of men, let him place on that seat (of justice) his chief minister, (who must be) acquainted with the law, wise, self-controlled, and descended from a (noble) family.

142. Having thus arranged all the affairs (of) his (government), he shall zealously and carefully protect his subjects.

143. That (monarch) whose subjects are carried off by robbers (Dasyu) from his kingdom, while they loudly call (for help), and he and his servants are (quietly) looking on, is a dead and not a living (king).

144. The highest duty of a Kshatriya is to protect his subjects, for the king who enjoys the rewards, just mentioned, is bound to (discharge that) duty.

145. Having risen in the last watch of the night, having performed (the rite of) personal purification, having, with a collected mind, offered oblations in the fire, and having worshipped Brahmanas, he shall enter the hall of audience which must possess the marks (considered) auspicious (for a dwelling).

146. Tarrying there, he shall gratify all subjects (who come to see him by a kind reception) and afterwards dismiss them; having dismissed his subjects, he shall take counsel with his ministers.

147. Ascending the back of a hill or a terrace, (and) retiring (there) in a lonely place, or in a solitary forest, let him consult with them unobserved.

148. That king whose secret plans other people, (though) assembled (for the purpose), do not discover, (will) enjoy the whole earth, though he be poor in treasure.

149. At the time of consultation let him cause to be removed idiots, the dumb, the blind, and the deaf, animals, very aged men, women, barbarians, the sick, and those deficient in limbs.

150. (Such) despicable (persons), likewise animals, and particularly women betray secret council; for that reason he must be careful with respect to them.

151. At midday or at midnight, when his mental and bodily fatigues are over, let him deliberate, either with himself alone or with his (ministers), on virtue, pleasure, and wealth,

152. On (reconciling) the attainment of these (aims) which are opposed to each other, on bestowing his daughters in marriage, and on keeping his sons (from harm),

153. On sending ambassadors, on the completion of undertakings (already begun), on the behaviour of (the women in) his harem, and on the doings of his spies.

154. On the whole eightfold business and the five classes (of spies), on the goodwill or enmity and the conduct of the circle (of neighbours he must) carefully (reflect).

155. On the conduct of the middlemost (prince), on the doings of him who seeks conquest, on the behaviour of the neutral (king), and (on that) of the foe (let him) sedulously (meditate).

156. These (four) constituents (prakriti, form), briefly (speaking), the foundation of the circle (of neighbours); besides, eight others are enumerated (in the Institutes of Polity) and (thus) the (total) is declared to be twelve.

157. The minister, the kingdom, the fortress, the treasury, and the army are five other (constituent elements of the circle); for, these are mentioned in connexion with each (of the first twelve; thus the whole circle consists), briefly (speaking, of) seventy-two (constituent parts).

158. Let (the king) consider as hostile his immediate neighbour and the partisan of (such a) foe, as friendly the immediate neighbour of his foe, and as neutral (the king) beyond those two.

159. Let him overcome all of them by means of the (four) expedients, conciliation and the rest, (employed) either singly or conjointly, (or) by bravery and policy (alone).

160. Let him constantly think of the six measures of royal policy (guna, viz.) alliance, war, marching, halting, dividing the army, and seeking protection.

161. Having carefully considered the business (in hand), let him resort to sitting quiet or marching, alliance or war, dividing his forces or seeking protection (as the case may require).

162. But the king must know that there are two kinds of alliances and of wars, (likewise two) of both marching and sitting quiet, and two (occasions for) seeking protection.)

163. An alliance which yields present and future advantages, one must know to be of two descriptions, (viz.) that when one marches together (with an ally) and the contrary (when the allies act separately).

164. War is declared to be of two kinds, (viz.) that which is undertaken in season or out of season, by oneself and for one's own purposes, and (that waged to avenge) an injury done to a friend.

165. Marching (to attack) is said to be twofold, (viz. that undertaken) by one alone when an urgent matter has suddenly arisen, and (that undertaken) by one allied with a friend.

166. Sitting quiet is stated to be of two kinds, (viz. that incumbent) on one who has gradually been weakened by fate or in consequence of former acts, and (that) in favour of a friend.

167. If the army stops (in one place) and its master (in another) in order to effect some purpose, that is called by those acquainted with the virtues of the measures of royal policy, the twofold division of the forces.

168. Seeking refuge is declared to be of two kinds, (first) for the purpose of attaining an advantage when one is harassed by enemies, (secondly) in order to become known among the virtuous (as the protege of a powerful king).

169. When (the king) knows (that) at some future time his superiority (is) certain, and (that) at the time present (he will suffer) little injury, then let him have recourse to peaceful measures.

170. But when he thinks all his subjects to be exceedingly contented, and (that he) himself (is) most exalted (in power), then let him make war.

171. When he knows his own army to be cheerful in disposition and strong, and (that) of his enemy the reverse, then let him march against his foe.

172. But if he is very weak in chariots and beasts of burden and in troops, then let him carefully sit quiet, gradually conciliating his foes.

173. When the king knows the enemy to be stronger in every respect, then let him divide his army and thus achieve his purpose.

174. But when he is very easily assailable by the forces of the enemy, then let him quickly seek refuge with a righteous, powerful king.

175. That (prince) who will coerce both his (disloyal) subjects and the army of the foe, let him ever serve with every effort like a Guru.

176. When, even in that (condition), he sees (that) evil is caused by (such) protection, let him without hesitation have recourse to war.

177. By all (the four) expedients a politic prince must arrange (matters so) that neither friends, nor neutrals, nor foes are superior to himself.

178. Let him fully consider the future and the immediate results of all undertakings, and the good and bad sides of all past (actions).

179. He who knows the good and the evil (which will result from his acts) in the future, is quick in forming resolutions for the present, and understands the consequences of past (actions), will not be conquered.

180. Let him arrange everything in such a manner that no ally, no neutral or foe may injure him; that is the sum of political wisdom.

181. But if the king undertakes an expedition against a hostile kingdom, then let him gradually advance, in the following manner, against his foe's capital.

182. Let the king undertake his march in the fine month Margasirsha, or towards the months of Phalguna and Kaitra, according to the (condition of his) army.

183. Even at other times, when he has a certain prospect of victory, or when a disaster has befallen his foe, he may advance to attack him.

184. But having duly arranged (all affairs) in his original (kingdom) and what relates to the expedition, having secured a basis (for his operations) and having duly dispatched his spies;

185. Having cleared the three kinds of roads, and (having made) his sixfold army (efficient), let him leisurely proceed in the manner prescribed for warfare against the enemy's capital.

186. Let him be very much on his guard against a friend who secretly serves the enemy and against (deserters) who return (from the enemy's camp); for such (men are) the most dangerous foes.

187. Let him march on his road, arraying (his troops) like a staff (i.e. in an oblong), or like a waggon (i.e. in a wedge), or like a boar (i.e. in a rhombus), or like a Makara (i.e. in two triangles, with the apices joined), or like a pin (i.e. in a long line), or like a Garuda (i.e. in a rhomboid with far-extended wings).

188. From whatever (side) he apprehends danger, in that (direction) let him extend his troops, and let him always himself encamp in an array, shaped like a lotus.

189. Let him allot to the commander-in-chief, to the (subordinate) general, (and to the superior officers) places in all directions, and let him turn his front in that direction whence he fears danger.

190. On all sides let him place troops of soldiers, on whom he can rely, with whom signals have been arranged, who are expert both in sustaining a charge and in charging, fearless and loyal.

191. Let him make a small number of soldiers fight in close order, at his pleasure let him extend a large number in loose ranks; or let him make them fight, arranging (a small number) in the needle-array, (and a large number) in the thunderbolt-array.

192. On even ground let him fight with chariots and horses, in water-bound places with boats and elephants, on (ground) covered with trees and shrubs with bows, on hilly ground with swords, targets, (and other) weapons.

193. (Men born in) Kurukshetra, Matsyas, Pankalas, and those born in Surasena, let him cause to fight in the van of the battle, as well as (others who are) tall and light.

194. After arranging his troops, he should encourage them (by an address) and carefully inspect them; he should also mark the behaviour (of the soldiers) when they engage the enemy.

195. When he has shut up his foe (in a town), let him sit encamped, harass his kingdom, and continually spoil his grass, food, fuel, and water.

196. Likewise let him destroy the tanks, ramparts, and ditches, and let him assail the (foe unawares) and alarm him at night.

197. Let him instigate to rebellion those who are open to such instigations, let him be informed of his (foe's) doings, and, when fate is propitious, let him fight without fear, trying to conquer.

198. He should (however) try to conquer his foes by conciliation, by (well-applied) gifts, and by creating dissension, used either separately or conjointly, never by fighting, (if it can be avoided.)

199. For when two (princes) fight, victory and defeat in the battle are, as experience teaches, uncertain; let him therefore avoid an engagement.

200. (But) if even those three before-mentioned expedients fail, then let him, duly exerting himself, fight in such a manner that he may completely conquer his enemies.

201. When he has gained victory, let him duly worship the gods and honour righteous Brahmanas, let him grant exemptions, and let him cause promises of safety to be proclaimed.

202. But having fully ascertained the wishes of all the (conquered), let him place there a relative of the (vanquished ruler on the throne), and let him impose his conditions.

203. Let him make authoritative the lawful (customs) of the (inhabitants), just as they are stated (to be), and let him honour the (new king) and his chief servants with precious gifts.

204. The seizure of desirable property which causes displeasure, and its distribution which causes pleasure, are both recommendable, (if they are) resorted to at the proper time.

205. All undertakings (in) this (world) depend both on the ordering of fate and on human exertion; but among these two (the ways of) fate are unfathomable; in the case of man's work action is possible.

206. Or (the king, bent on conquest), considering a friend, gold, and land (to be) the triple result (of an expedition), may, using diligent care, make peace with (his foe) and return (to his realm).

207. Having paid due attention to any king in the circle (of neighbouring states) who might attack him in the rear, and to his supporter who opposes the latter, let (the conqueror) secure the fruit of the expedition from (the prince whom he attacks), whether (he may have become) friendly or (remained) hostile.

208. By gaining gold and land a king grows not so much in strength as by obtaining a firm friend, (who), though weak, (may become) powerful in the future.

209. A weak friend (even) is greatly commended, who is righteous (and) grateful, whose people are contented, who is attached and persevering in his undertakings.

210. The wise declare him (to be) a most dangerous foe, who is wise, of noble race, brave, clever, liberal, grateful, and firm.

211. Behaviour worthy of an Aryan, knowledge of men, bravery, a compassionate disposition, and great liberality are the virtues of a neutral (who may be courted).

212. Let the king, without hesitation, quit for his own sake even a country (which is) salubrious, fertile, and causing an increase of cattle.

213. For times of need let him preserve his wealth; at the expense of his wealth let him preserve his wife; let him at all events preserve himself even by (giving up) his wife and his wealth.

214. A wise (king), seeing that all kinds of misfortunes violently assail him at the same time, should try all (the four) expedients, be it together or separately, (in order to save himself.)

215. On the person who employs the expedients, on the business to be accomplished, and on all the expedients collectively, on these three let him ponder and strive to accomplish his ends.

216. Having thus consulted with his ministers on all these (matters), having taken exercise, and having bathed afterwards, the king may enter the harem at midday in order to dine.

217. There he may eat food, (which has been prepared) by faithful, incorruptible (servants) who know the (proper) time (for dining), which has been well examined (and hallowed) by sacred texts that destroy poison.

218. Let him mix all his food with medicines (that are) antidotes against poison, and let him always be careful to wear gems which destroy poison.

219. Well-tried females whose toilet and ornaments have been examined, shall attentively serve him with fans, water, and perfumes.

220. In like manner let him be careful about his carriages, bed, seat, bath, toilet, and all his ornaments.

221. When he has dined, he may divert himself with his wives in the harem; but when he has diverted himself, he must, in due time, again think of the affairs of state.

222. Adorned (with his robes of state), let him again inspect his fighting men, all his chariots and beasts of burden, the weapons and accoutrements.

223. Having performed his twilight-devotions, let him, well armed, hear in an inner apartment the doings of those who make secret reports and of his spies.

224. But going to another secret apartment and dismissing those people, he may enter the harem, surrounded by female (servants), in order to dine again.

225. Having eaten there something for the second time, and having been recreated by the sound of music, let him go to rest and rise at the proper time free from fatigue.

226. A king who is in good health must observe these rules; but, if he is indisposed, he may entrust all this (business) to his servants.

1. A king, desirous of investigating law cases, must enter his court of justice, preserving a dignified demeanour, together with Brahmanas and with experienced councillors.

2. There, either seated or standing, raising his right arm, without ostentation in his dress and ornaments, let him examine the business of suitors,

3. Daily (deciding) one after another (all cases) which fall under the eighteen titles (of the law) according to principles drawn from local usages. and from the Institutes of the sacred law.

4. Of those (titles) the first is the non-payment of debts, (then follow), (2) deposit and pledge, (3) sale without ownership, (4) concerns among partners, and (5) resumption of gifts,

5. (6) Non-payment of wages, (7) non-performance of agreements, (8) rescission of sale and purchase, (9) disputes between the owner (of cattle) and his servants,

6. (10) Disputes regarding boundaries, (11) assault and (12) defamation, (13) theft, (14) robbery and violence, (15) adultery,

7. (16) Duties of man and wife, (17) partition (of inheritance), (18) gambling and betting; these are in this world the eighteen topics which give rise to lawsuits.

8. Depending on the eternal law, let him decide the suits of men who mostly contend on the titles just mentioned.

9. But if the king does not personally investigate the suits, then let him appoint a learned Brahmana to try them.

10. That (man) shall enter that most excellent court, accompanied by three assessors, and fully consider (all) causes (brought) before the (king), either sitting down or standing.

11. Where three Brahmanas versed in the Vedas and the learned (judge) appointed by the king sit down, they call that the court of (four-faced) Brahman.

12. But where justice, wounded by injustice, approaches and the judges do not extract the dart, there (they also) are wounded (by that dart of injustice).

13. Either the court must not be entered, or the truth must be spoken; a man who either says nothing or speaks falsely, becomes sinful.

14. Where justice is destroyed by injustice, or truth by falsehood, while the judges look on, there they shall also be destroyed.

15. 'Justice, being violated, destroys; justice, being preserved, preserves: therefore justice must not be violated, lest violated justice destroy us.'

16. For divine justice (is said to be) a bull (vrisha); that (man) who violates it (kurute 'lam) the gods consider to be (a man despicable like) a Sudra (vrishala); let him, therefore, beware of violating justice.

17. The only friend who follows men even after death is justice; for everything else is lost at the same time when the body (perishes).

18. One quarter of (the guilt of) an unjust (decision) falls on him who committed (the crime), one quarter on the (false) witness, one quarter on all the judges, one quarter on the king.

19. But where he who is worthy of condemnation is condemned, the king is free from guilt, and the judges are saved (from sin); the guilt falls on the perpetrator (of the crime alone).

20. A Brahmana who subsists only by the name of his caste (gati), or one who merely calls himself a Brahmana (though his origin be uncertain), may, at the king's pleasure, interpret the law to him, but never a Sudra.

21. The kingdom of that monarch, who looks on while a Sudra settles the law, will sink (low), like a cow in a morass.

22. That kingdom where Sudras are very numerous, which is infested by atheists and destitute of twice-born (inhabitants), soon entirely perishes, afflicted by famine and disease.

23. Having occupied the seat of justice, having covered his body, and having worshipped the guardian deities of the world, let him, with a collected mind, begin the trial of causes.

24. Knowing what is expedient or inexpedient, what is pure justice or injustice, let him examine the causes of suitors according to the order of the castes (varna).

25. By external signs let him discover the internal disposition of men, by their voice, their colour, their motions, their aspect, their eyes, and their gestures.

26. The internal (working of the) mind is perceived through the aspect, the motions, the gait, the gestures, the speech, and the changes in the eye and of the face.

27. The king shall protect the inherited (and other) property of a minor, until he has returned (from his teacher's house) or until he has passed his minority.

28. In like manner care must be taken of barren women, of those who have no sons, of those whose family is extinct, of wives and widows faithful to their lords, and of women afflicted with diseases.

29. A righteous king must punish like thieves those relatives who appropriate the property of such females during their lifetime.

30. Property, the owner of which has disappeared, the king shall cause to be kept as a deposit during three years; within the period of three years the owner may claim it, after (that term) the king may take it.

31. He who says, 'This belongs to me,' must be examined according to the rule; if he accurately describes the shape, and the number (of the articles found) and so forth, (he is) the owner, (and) ought (to receive) that property.

32. But if he does not really know the time and the place (where it was) lost, its colour, shape, and size, he is worthy of a fine equal (in value) to the (object claimed).

33. Now the king, remembering the duty of good men, may take one-sixth part of property lost and afterwards found, or one-tenth, or at least one-twelfth.

34. Property lost and afterwards found (by the king's servants) shall remain in the keeping of (special) officials; those whom the king may convict of stealing it, he shall cause to be slain by an elephant.

35. From that man who shall truly say with respect to treasure-trove, 'This belongs to me,' the king may take one-sixth or one-twelfth part.

36. But he who falsely says (so), shall be fined in one-eighth of his property, or, a calculation of (the value of) the treasure having been made, in some smaller portion (of that).

37. When a learned Brahmana has found treasure, deposited in former (times), he may take even the whole (of it); for he is master of everything.

38. When the king finds treasure of old concealed in the ground-let him give one half to Brahmanas and place the (other) half in his treasury.

39. The king obtains one half of ancient hoards and metals (found) in the ground, by reason of (his giving) protection, (and) because he is the lord of the soil.

40. Property stolen by thieves must be restored by the king to (men of) all castes (varna); a king who uses such (property) for himself incurs the guilt of a thief.

41. (A king) who knows the sacred law, must inquire into the laws of castes (gati), of districts, of guilds, and of families, and (thus) settle the peculiar law of each.

42. For men who follow their particular occupations and abide by their particular duty, become dear to people, though they may live at a distance.

43. Neither the king nor any servant of his shall themselves cause a lawsuit to be begun, or hush up one that has been brought (before them) by (some) other (man).

44. As a hunter traces the lair of a (wounded) deer by the drops of blood, even so the king shall discover on which side the right lies, by inferences (from the facts).

45. When engaged in judicial proceedings he must pay full attention to the truth, to the object (of the dispute), (and) to himself, next to the witnesses, to the place, to the time, and to the aspect.

46. What may have been practised by the virtuous, by such twice-born men as are devoted to the law, that he shall establish as law, if it be not opposed to the (customs of) countries, families, and castes (gati).

47. When a creditor sues (before the king) for the recovery of money from a debtor, let him make the debtor pay the sum which the creditor proves (to be due).

48. By whatever means a creditor may be able to obtain possession of his property, even by those means may he force the debtor and make him pay.

49. By moral suasion, by suit of law, by artful management, or by the customary proceeding, a creditor may recover property lent; and fifthly, by force.

50. A creditor who himself recovers his property from his debtor, must not be blamed by the king for retaking what is his own.

51. But him who denies a debt which is proved by good evidence, he shall order to pay that debt to the creditor and a small fine according to his circumstances.

52. On the denial (of a debt) by a debtor who has been required in court to pay it, the complainant must call (a witness) who was present (when the loan was made), or adduce other evidence.

53. (The plaintiff) who calls a witness not present at the transaction, who retracts his statements, or does not perceive that his statements (are) confused or contradictory;

54. Or who having stated what he means to prove afterwards varies (his case), or who being questioned on a fact duly stated by himself does not abide by it;

55. Or who converses with the witnesses in a place improper for such conversation; or who declines to answer a question, properly put, or leaves (the court);

56. Or who, being ordered to speak, does not answer, or does not prove what he has alleged; or who does not know what is the first (point), and what the second, fails in his suit.

57. Him also who says 'I have witnesses,' and, being ordered to produce them, produces them not, the judge must on these (same) grounds declare to be non-suited.

58. If a plaintiff does not speak, he may be punished corporally or fined according to the law; if (a defendant) does not plead within three fortnights, he has lost his cause.

59. In the double of that sum which (a defendant) falsely denies or on which (the plaintiff) falsely declares, shall those two (men) offending against justice be fined by the king.

60. (A defendant) who, being brought (into court) by the creditor, (and) being questioned, denies (the debt), shall be convicted (of his falsehood) by at least three witnesses (who must depose) in the presence of the Brahmana (appointed by) the king.

61. I will fully declare what kind of men may be made witnesses in suits by creditors, and in what manner those (witnesses) must give true (evidence).

62. Householders, men with male issue, and indigenous (inhabitants of the country, be they) Kshatriyas, Vaisyas, or Sudras, are competent, when called by a suitor, to give evidence,

not any persons whatever (their condition may be) except in cases of urgency.

63. Trustworthy men of all the (four) castes (varna) may be made witnesses in lawsuits, (men) who know (their) whole duty, and are free from covetousness; but let him reject those (of an) opposite (character).

64. Those must not be made (witnesses) who have an interest in the suit, nor familiar (friends), companions, and enemies (of the parties), nor (men) formerly convicted (of perjury), nor (persons) suffering under (severe) illness, nor (those) tainted (by mortal sin).

65. The king cannot be made a witness, nor mechanics and actors, nor a: Srotriya, nor a student of the Veda, nor (an ascetic) who has given up (all) connexion (with the world),

66. Nor one wholly dependent, nor one of bad fame, nor a Dasyu, nor one who follows forbidden occupations, nor an aged (man), nor an infant, nor one (man alone), nor a man of the lowest castes, nor one deficient in organs of sense,

67. Nor one extremely grieved, nor one intoxicated, nor a madman, nor one tormented by hunger or thirst, nor one oppressed by fatigue, nor one tormented by desire, nor a wrathful man, nor a thief.

68. Women should give evidence for women, and for twice-born men twice-born men (of the) same (kind), virtuous Sudras for Sudras, and men of the lowest castes for the lowest.

69. But any person whatsoever, who has personal knowledge (of an act committed) in the interior apartments (of a house), or in a forest, or of (a crime causing) loss of life, may give evidence between the parties.

70. On failure (of qualified witnesses, evidence) may given (in such cases) by a woman, by an infant, by an aged man, by a pupil, by a relative, by a slave, or by a hired servant.

71. But the (judge) should consider the evidence of infants, aged and diseased men, who (are apt to) speak untruly, as untrustworthy, likewise that of men with disordered minds.

72. In all cases of violence, of theft and adultery, of defamation and assault, he must not examine the (competence of) witnesses (too strictly).

73. On a conflict of the witnesses the king shall accept (as true) the evidence of the) majority; if (the conflicting parties are) equal in number, (that of) those distinguished by good qualities; on a difference between (equally) distinguished (witnesses, that of) the best among the twice-born.

74. Evidence in accordance with what has actually been seen or heard, is admissible; a witness who speaks truth in those (cases), neither loses spiritual merit nor wealth.

75. A witness who depọses in an assembly of honourable men (Arya) anything else but what he has seen or heard, falls after death headlong into hell and loses heaven.

76. When a man (originally) not appointed to be a witness sees or hears anything and is (afterwards) examined regarding it, he must declare it (exactly) as he saw or heard it.

77. One man who is free from covetousness may be (accepted as) witness; but not even many pure women, because the understanding of females is apt to waver, nor even many other men, who are tainted with sin.

78. What witnesses declare quite naturally, that must be received on trials; (depositions) differing from that, which they make improperly, are worthless for (the purposes of) justice.

79. The witnesses being assembled in the court in the presence of the plaintiff and of the defendant, let the judge examine them, kindly exhorting them in the following manner:

80. 'What ye know to have been mutually transacted in this matter between the two men before us, declare all that in accordance with the truth; for ye are witnesses in this (cause).

81. 'A witness who speaks the truth in his evidence, gains (after death) the most excellent regions (of bliss) and here (below) unsurpassable fame; such testimony is revered by Brahman (himself).

82. 'He who gives false evidence is firmly bound by Varuna's fetters, helpless during one hundred existences; let (men therefore) give true evidence.

83. 'By truthfulness a witness is purified, through truthfulness his merit grows, truth must, therefore, be spoken by witnesses of all castes (varna).

84. 'The Soul itself is the witness of the Soul, and the Soul is the refuge of the Soul; despise not thy own Soul, the supreme witness of men.

85. 'The wicked, indeed, say in their hearts, "Nobody sees us;" but the gods distinctly see them and the male within their own breasts.

86. 'The sky, the earth, the waters, (the male in) the heart, the moon, the sun, the fire, Yama and the wind, the night, the two twilights, and justice know the conduct of all corporeal beings.'

87. The (judge), being purified, shall ask in the forenoon the twice-born (witnesses) who (also have been) purified, (and stand) facing the north or the east, to give true evidence in the presence of (images of) the gods and of Brahmanas.

88. Let him examine a Brahmana (beginning with) 'Speak,' a Kshatriya (beginning with) 'Speak the truth,' a Vaisya (admonishing him) by (mentioning) his kine, grain, and gold, a Sudra (threatening him) with (the guilt of) every crime that causes loss of caste;

89. (Saying), 'Whatever places (of torment) are assigned (by the sages) to the slayer of a Brahmana, to the murderer of women and children, to him who betrays a friend, and to an ungrateful man, those shall be thy (portion), if thou speakest falsely.

90. '(The reward) of all meritorious deeds which thou, good man, hast done since thy birth, shall become the share of the dogs, if in thy speech thou departest from the truth.

91. 'If thou thinkest, O friend of virtue, with respect to thyself, "I am alone," (know that) that sage who witnesses all virtuous acts and all crimes, ever resides in thy heart.

92. 'If thou art not at variance with that divine Yama, the son of Vivasvat, who dwells in thy heart, thou needest neither visit the Ganges nor the (land of the) Kurus.

93. 'Naked and shorn, tormented with hunger and thirst, and deprived of sight, shall the man who gives false evidence, go with a potsherd to beg food at the door of his enemy.

94. 'Headlong, in utter darkness shall the sinful man tumble into hell, who being interrogated in a judicial inquiry answers one question falsely.

95. 'That man who in a court (of justice) gives an untrue account of a transaction (or asserts a fact) of which he was not an eye-witness, resembles a blind man who swallows fish with the bones.

96. 'The gods are acquainted with no better man in this world than him, of whom his conscious Soul has no distrust, when he gives evidence.

97. 'Learn now, O friend, from an enumeration in due order, how many relatives he destroys who gives false evidence in several particular cases.

98. 'He kills five by false Testimony regarding (small) cattle, he kills ten by false testimony regarding kine, he kills a hundred by false evidence concerning horses, and a thousand by false evidence concerning men.

99. 'By speaking falsely in a cause regarding gold, he kills the born and the unborn; by false evidence concerning land, he kills everything; beware, therefore, of false evidence concerning land.

100. 'They declare (false evidence) concerning water, concerning the carnal enjoyment of women, and concerning all gems, produced in water, or consisting of stones (to be) equally (wicked) as a lie concerning land.

101. 'Marking well all the evils (which are produced) by perjury, declare thou openly everything as (thou hast) heard or seen (it).'

102. Brahmanas who tend cattle, who trade, who are mechanics, actors (or singers), menial servants or usurers, the (judge) shall treat like Sudras.

103. In (some) cases a man who, though knowing (the facts to be) different, gives such (false evidence) from a pious motive,

does not lose heaven; such (evidence) they call the speech of the gods.

104. Whenever the death of a Sudra, of a Vaisya, of a Kshatriya, or of a Brahmana would be (caused) by a declaration of the truth, a falsehood may be spoken; for such (falsehood) is preferable to the truth.

105. Such (witnesses) must offer to Sarasvati oblations of boiled rice (karu) which are sacred to the goddess of speech, (thus) performing the best penance in order to expiate the guilt of that falsehood.

106. Or such (a witness) may offer according to the rule, clarified butter in the fire, reciting the Kushmanda texts, or the Rik, sacred to Varuna, 'Untie, O Varuna, the uppermost fetter,' or the three verses addressed to the Waters.

107. A man who, without being ill, does not give evidence in (cases of) loans and the like within three fortnights (after the summons), shall become responsible for the whole debt and (pay) a tenth part of the whole (as a fine to the king).

108. The witness to whom, within seven days after he has given evidence, happens (a misfortune through) sickness, a fire, or the death of a relative, shall be made to pay the debt and a fine.

109. If two (parties) dispute about matters for which no witnesses are available, and the (judge) is unable to really ascertain the truth, he may cause it to be discovered even by an oath.

110. Both by the great sages and the gods oaths have been taken for the purpose of (deciding doubtful) matters; and Vasishtha even swore an oath before king (Sudas), the son of Pigavana.

111. Let no wise man swear an oath falsely, even in a trifling matter; for he who swears an oath falsely is lost in this (world) and after death.

112. No crime, causing loss of caste, is committed by swearing (falsely) to women, the objects of one's desire, at marriages, for the sake of fodder for a cow, or of fuel, and in (order to show) favour to a Brahmana.

113. Let the (judge) cause a Brahmana to swear by his veracity, a Kshatriya by his chariot or the animal he rides on and by his weapons, a Vaisya by his kine, grain, and gold, and a Sudra by (imprecating on his own head the guilt) of all grievous offences (pataka).

114. Or the (judge) may cause the (party) to carry fire or to dive under water, or severally to touch the heads of his wives and children.

115. He whom the blazing fire burns not, whom the water forces not to come (quickly) up, who meets with no speedy misfortune, must be held innocent on (the strength of) his oath.

116. For formerly when Vatsa was accused by his younger brother, the fire, the spy of the world, burned not even a hair (of his) by reason of his veracity.

117. Whenever false evidence has been given in any suit, let the (judge) reverse the judgment, and whatever has been done must be (considered as) undone.

118. Evidence (given) from covetousness, distraction, terror, friendship, lust, wrath, ignorance, and childishness is declared (to be) invalid.

119. I will propound in (due) order the particular punishments for him who gives false evidence from any one of these motives.

120. (He who commits perjury) through covetousness shall be fined one thousand (panas), (he who does it) through distraction, in the lowest amercement; (if a man does it) through fear, two middling amercements shall be paid as a fine, (if he does it) through friendship, four times the amount of the lowest (amercement).

121. (He who does it) through lust, (shall pay) ten times the lowest amercement, but (he who does it) through wrath, three times the next (or second amercement); (he who does it) through ignorance, two full hundreds, but (he who does it) through childishness, one hundred (panas).

122. They declare that the wise have prescribed these fines for perjury, in order to prevent a failure of justice, and in order to restrain injustice.

123. But a just king shall fine and banish (men of) the three (lower) castes (varna) who have given false evidence, but a Brahmana he shall (only) banish.

124. Manu, the son of the Self-existent (Svayambhu), has named ten places on which punishment may be (made to fall) in the cases of the three (lower) castes (varna); but a Brahmana shall depart unhurt (from the country).

125. (These are) the organ, the belly, the tongue, the two hands, and fifthly the two feet, the eye, the nose, the two ears, likewise the (whole) body.

126. Let the (king), having fully ascertained the motive, the time and place (of the offence), and having considered the ability (of the criminal to suffer) and the (nature of the) crime, cause punishment to fall on those who deserve it.

127. Unjust punishment destroys reputation among men, and fame (after death), and causes even in the next world the loss of heaven; let him, therefore, beware of (inflicting) it.

128. A king who punishes those who do not deserve it, and punishes not those who deserve it, brings great infamy on himself and (after death) sinks into hell.

129. Let him punish first by (gentle) admonition, afterwards by (harsh) reproof, thirdly by a fine, after that by corporal chastisement.

130. But when he cannot restrain such (offenders) even by corporal punishment, then let him apply to them even all the four (modes cojointly).

131. Those technical names of (certain quantities of) copper, silver, and gold, which are generally used on earth for the purpose of business transactions among men, I will fully declare.

132. The very small mote which is seen when the sun shines through a lattice, they declare (to be) the least of (all) quantities and (to be called) a trasarenu (a floating particle of dust).

133. Know (that) eight trasarenus (are equal) in bulk (to) a liksha (the egg of a louse), three of those to one grain of black mustard (ragasarshapa), and three of the latter to a white mustard-seed.

134. Six grains of white mustard are one middle-sized barley-corn, and three barley-corns one krishnala (raktika, or gunga-berry); five krishnalas are one masha (bean), and sixteen of those one suvarna.

135. Four suvarnas are one pala, and ten palas one dharana; two krishnalas (of silver), weighed together, must be considered one mashaka of silver.

136. Sixteen of those make a silver dharana, or purana; but know (that) a karsha of copper is a karshapana, or pana.

137. Know (that) ten dharanas of silver make one satamana; four suvarnas must be considered (equal) in weight to a nishka.

138. Two hundred and fifty panas are declared (to be) the first (or lowest) amercement, five (hundred) are considered as the mean (or middlemost), but one thousand as the highest.

139. A debt being admitted as due, (the defendant) shall pay five in the hundred (as a fine), if it be denied (and proved) twice as much; that is the teaching of Manu.

140. A money-lender may stipulate as an increase of his capital, for the interest, allowed by Vasishtha, and take monthly the eightieth part of a hundred.

141. Or, remembering the duty of good men, he may take two in the hundred (by the month), for he who takes two in the hundred becomes not a sinner for gain.

142. Just two in the hundred, three, four, and five (and not more), he may take as monthly interest according to the order of the castes (varna).

143. But if a beneficial pledge (i.e. one from which profit accrues, has been given), he shall receive no interest on the loan; nor can he, after keeping (such) a pledge for a very long time, give or sell it.

144. A pledge (to be kept only) must not be used by force, (the creditor), so using it, shall give up his (whole) interest, or, (if it has been spoilt by use) he shall satisfy the (owner) by (paying its) original price; else he commits a theft of the pledge.

145. Neither a pledge nor a deposit can be lost by lapse of time; they are both recoverable, though they have remained long (with the bailee).

146. Things used with friendly assent, a cow, a camel, a riding-horse, and (a beast) made over for breaking in, are never lost (to the owner).

147. (But in general) whatever (chattel) an owner sees enjoyed by others during ten years, while, though present, he says nothing, that (chattel) he shall not recover.

148. If (the owner is) neither an idiot nor a minor and if (his chattel) is enjoyed (by another) before his eyes, it is lost to him by law; the adverse possessor shall retain that property.

149. A pledge, a boundary, the property of infants, an (open) deposit, a sealed deposit, women, the property of the king and the wealth of a Srotriya are not lost in consequence of (adverse) enjoyment.

150. The fool who uses a pledge without the permission of the owner, shall remit half of his interest, as a compensation for (such) use.

151. In money transactions interest paid at one time (not by instalments) shall never exceed the double (of the principal); on grain, fruit, wool or hair, (and) beasts of burden it must not be more than five times (the original amount).

152. Stipulated interest beyond the legal rate, being against (the law), cannot be recovered; they call that a usurious way (of lending); (the lender) is (in no case) entitled to (more than) five in the hundred.

153. Let him not take interest beyond the year, nor such as is unapproved, nor compound interest, periodical interest, stipulated interest, and corporal interest.

154. He who, unable to pay a debt (at the fixed time), wishes to make a new contract, may renew the agreement, after paying the interest which is due.

155. If he cannot pay the money (due as interest), he may insert it in the renewed (agreement); he must pay as much interest as may be due.

156. He who has made a contract to carry goods by a wheeled carriage for money and has agreed to a certain place or time, shall not reap that reward, if he does not keep to the place and the time (stipulated).

157. Whatever rate men fix, who are expert in sea-voyages and able to calculate (the profit) according to the place, the time, and the objects (carried), that (has legal force) in such cases with respect to the payment (to be made).

158. The man who becomes a surety in this (world) for the appearance of a (debtor), and produces him not, shall pay the debt out of his own property.

159. But money due by a surety, or idly promised, or lost at play, or due for spirituous liquor, or what remains unpaid of a fine and a tax or duty, the son (of the party owing it) shall not be obliged to pay.

160. This just mentioned rule shall apply to the case of a surety for appearance (only); if a surety for payment should die, the (judge) may compel even his heirs to discharge the debt.

161. On what account then is it that after the death of a surety other than for payment, whose affairs are fully known, the creditor may (in some cases) afterwards demand the debt (of the heirs)?

162. If the surety had received money (from him for whom he stood bail) and had money enough (to pay), then (the heir of him) who received it, shall pay (the debt) out of his property; that is the settled rule.

163. A contract made by a person intoxicated, or insane, or grievously disordered (by disease and so forth), or wholly dependent, by an infant or very aged man, or by an unauthorised (party) is invalid.

164. That agreement which has been made contrary to the law or to the settled usage (of the virtuous), can have no legal force, though it be established (by proofs).

165. A fraudulent mortgage or sale, a fraudulent gift or acceptance, and (any transaction) where he detects fraud, the (judge) shall declare null and void.

166. If the debtor be dead and (the money borrowed) was expended for the family, it must be paid by the relatives out of their own estate even if they are divided.

167. Should even a person wholly dependent make a contract for the behoof of the family, the master (of the house),

whether (living) in his own country or abroad, shall not rescind it.

168. What is given by force, what is enjoyed by force, also what has been caused to be written by force, and all other transactions done by force, Manu has declared void.

169. Three suffer for the sake of others, witnesses, a surety, and judges; but four enrich themselves (through others), a Brahmana, a money-lender, a merchant, and a king.

170. No king, however indigent, shall take anything that ought not to be taken, nor shall he, however wealthy, decline taking that which he ought to take, be it ever so small.

171. In consequence of his taking what ought not to be taken, or of his refusing what ought to be received, a king will be accused of weakness and perish in this (world) and after death.

172. By taking his due, by preventing the confusion of the castes (varna), and by protecting the weak, the power of the king grows, and he prospers in this (world) and after death.

173. Let the prince, therefore, like Yama, not heeding his own likings and dislikings, behave exactly like Yama, suppressing his anger and controlling himself.

174. But that evil-minded king who in his folly decides causes unjustly, his enemies soon subjugate.

175. If, subduing love and hatred, he decides the causes according to the law, (the hearts of) his subjects turn towards him as the rivers (run) towards the ocean.

176. (The debtor) who complains to the king that his creditor recovers (the debt) independently (of the court), shall be compelled by the king to pay (as a fine) one quarter (of the sum) and to his (creditor) the money (due).

177. Even by (personal) labour shall the debtor make good (what he owes) to his creditor, if he be of the same caste or of a lower one; but a (debtor) of a higher caste shall pay it gradually (when he earns something).

178. According to these rules let the king equitably decide between men, who dispute with each other the matters, which are proved by witnesses and (other) evidence.

179. A sensible man should make a deposit (only) with a person of (good) family, of good conduct, well acquainted with the law, veracious, having many relatives, wealthy, and honourable (arya).

180. In whatever manner a person shall deposit anything in the hands of another, in the same manner ought the same thing to be received back (by the owner); as the delivery (was, so must be) the re-delivery.

181. He who restores not his deposit to the depositor at his request, may be tried by the judge in the depositor's absence.

182. On failure of witnesses let the (judge) actually deposit gold with that (defendant) under some pretext or other through spies of suitable age and appearance (and afterwards demand it back).

183. If the (defendant) restores it in the manner and shape in which it was bailed, there is nothing (of that description) in his hands, for which others accuse him.

184. But if he restores not that gold, as be ought, to those (spies), then he shall be compelled by force to restore both (deposits); that is a settled rule of law.

185. An open or a sealed deposit must never be returned to a near relative (of the depositor during the latter's lifetime); for if (the recipient) dies (without delivering them), they are lost, but if he does not die, they are not lost.

186. But (a depositary) who of his own accord returns them to a near relative of a deceased (depositor), must not be harassed (about them) by the king or by the depositor's relatives.

187. And (in doubtful cases) he should try to obtain that object by friendly means, without (having recourse to) artifice, or having inquired into (depositary's) conduct, he should settle (the matter) with gentle means.

188. Such is the rule for obtaining back all those open deposits; in the case of a sealed deposit (the depositary) shall incur no (censure), unless he has taken out something.

189. (A deposit) which has been stolen by thieves or washed away by water or burned by fire, (the bailee) shall not make it good, unless he took part of it (for himself).

190. Him who appropriates a deposit and him (who asks for it) without having made it, (the judge) shall try by all (sorts of) means, and by the oaths prescribed in the Veda.

191. He who does not return a deposit and he who demands what he never bailed shall both be punished like thieves, or be compelled to pay a fine equal (to the value of the object retained or claimed).

192. The king should compel him who does not restore an open deposit, and in like manner him who retains a sealed deposit, to pay a fine equal (to its value).

193. That man who by false pretences may possess himself of another's property, shall be publicly punished by various (modes of) corporal (or capital) chastisement, together with his accomplices.

194. If a deposit of a particular description or quantity is bailed by anybody in the presence of a number (of witnesses), it must be known to be of that particular (description and quantity; the depositary) who makes a false statement (regarding it) is liable to a fine.

195. But if anything is delivered or received privately, it must be privately returned; as the bailment (was, so should be) the re-delivery.

196. Thus let the king decide (causes) concerning a deposit and a friendly loan (for use) without showing (undue) rigour to the depositary.

197. If anybody sells the property of another man, without being the owner and without the assent of the owner, the (judge) shall not admit him who is a thief, though he may not consider himself as a thief, as a witness (in any case).

198. If the (offender) is a kinsman (of the owner), he shall be fined six hundred panas; if he is not a kinsman, nor has any excuse, he shall be guilty of theft.

199. A gift or sale, made by anybody else but the owner, must be considered as null and void, according to the rule in judicial proceedings.

200. Where possession is evident, but no title is perceived, there the title (shall be) a proof (of ownership), not possession; such is the settled rule.

201. He who obtains a chattel in the market before a number (of witnesses), acquires that chattel with a clear legal title by purchase.

202. If the original (seller) be not producible, (the buyer) being exculpated by a public sale, must be dismissed by the king without punishment, but (the former owner) who lost the chattel shall receive it (back from the buyer).

203. One commodity mixed with another must not be sold (as pure), nor a bad one (as good), nor less (than the proper quantity or weight), nor anything that is not at hand or that is concealed.

204. If, after one damsel has been shown, another be given to the bridegroom, he may marry them both for the same price; that Manu ordained.

205. He who gives (a damsel in marriage), having first openly declared her blemishes, whether she be insane, or afflicted with leprosy, or have lost her virginity, is not liable to punishment.

206. If an officiating priest, chosen to perform a sacrifice, abandons his work, a share only (of the fee) in proportion to the work (done) shall be given to him by those who work with him.

207. But he who abandons his work after the sacrificial fees have been given, shall obtain his full share and cause to be performed (what remains) by another (priest).

208. But if (specific) fees are ordained for the several parts of a rite, shall he (who performs the part) receive them, or shall they all share them?

209. The Adhvaryu priest shall take the chariot, and the Brahman at the kindling of the fires (Agnyadhana) a horse, the Hotri priest shall also take a horse, and the Udgatri the cart, (used) when (the Soma) is purchased.

210. The (four) chief priests among all (the sixteen), who are entitled to one half, shall receive a moiety (of the fee), the next (four) one half of that, the set entitled to a third share, one third, and those entitled to a fourth a quarter.

211. By the application of these principles the allotment of shares must be made among those men who here (below) perform their work conjointly.

212. Should money be given (or promised) for a pious purpose by one man to another who asks for it, the gift shall be void, if the (money is) afterwards not (used) in the manner (stated).

213. But if the (recipient) through pride or greed tries to enforce (the fulfilment of the promise), he shall be compelled by the king to pay one suvarna as an expiation for his theft.

214. Thus the lawful subtraction of a gift has been fully explained; I will next propound (the law for) the non-payment of wages.

215. A hired (servant or workman) who, without being ill, out of pride fails to perform his work according to the agreement, shall be fined eight krishnalas and no wages shall be paid to him.

216. But (if he is really) ill, (and) after recovery performs (his work) according to the original agreement, he shall receive his wages even after (the lapse of) a very long time.

217. But if he, whether sick or well, does not (perform or) cause to be performed (by others) his work according to his agreement, the wages for that work shall not be given to him, even (if it be only) slightly incomplete.

218. Thus the law for the non-payment of wages has been completely stated; I will next explain the law concerning men who break an agreement.

219. If a man belonging to a corporation inhabiting a village or a district, after swearing to an agreement, breaks it through avarice, (the king) shall banish him from his realm,

220. And having imprisoned such a breaker of an agreement, he shall compel him to pay six nishkas, (each of) four suvarnas, and one satamana of silver.

221. A righteous king shall apply this law of fines in villages and castes (gati) to those who break an agreement.

222. If anybody in this (world), after buying or selling anything, repent (of his bargain), he may return or take (back) that chattel within ten days.

223. But after (the lapse of) ten days he may neither give nor cause it to be given (back); both he who takes it (back) and he who gives it (back, except by consent) shall be fined by the king six hundred (panas).

224. But the king himself shall impose a fine of ninety-six panas on him who gives a blemished damsel (to a suitor) without informing (him of the blemish).

225. But that man who, out of malice, says of a maiden, 'She is not a maiden,' shall be fined one hundred (panas), if he cannot prove her blemish.

226. The nuptial texts are applied solely to virgins, (and) nowhere among men to females who have lost their virginity, for such (females) are excluded from religious ceremonies.

227. The nuptial texts are a certain proof (that a maiden has been made a lawful) wife; but the learned should know that they (and the marriage ceremony are complete with the seventh step (of the bride around the sacred fire).

228. If anybody in this (world) repent of any completed transaction, (the king) shall keep him on the road of rectitude in accordance with the rules given above.

229. I will fully declare in accordance with the true law (the rules concerning) the disputes, (arising) from the transgressions of owners of cattle and of herdsmen.

230. During the day the responsibility for the safety (of the cattle rests) on the herdsman, during the night on the owner, (provided they are) in his house; (if it be) otherwise, the herdsman will be responsible (for them also during the night).

231. A hired herdsman who is paid with milk, may milk with the consent of the owner the best (cow) out of ten; such shall be his hire if no (other) wages (are paid).

232. The herdsman alone shall make good (the loss of a beast) strayed, destroyed by worms, killed by dogs or (by falling) into a pit, if he did not duly exert himself (to prevent it).

233. But for (an animal) stolen by thieves, though he raised an alarm, the herdsman shall not pay, provided he gives notice to his master at the proper place and time.

234. If cattle die, let him carry to his master their ears, skin, tails, bladders, tendons, and the yellow concrete bile, and let him point out their particular. marks.

235. But if goats or sheep are surrounded by wolves and the herdsman does not hasten (to their assistance), lie shall be responsible for any (animal) which a wolf may attack and kill.

236. But if they, kept in (proper) order, graze together in the forest, and a wolf, suddenly jumping on one of them, kills it, the herdsman shall bear in that case no responsibility.

237. On all sides of a village a space, one hundred dhanus or three samya-throws (in breadth), shall be reserved (for pasture), and thrice (that space) round a town.

238. If the cattle do damage to unfenced crops on that (common), the king shall in that case not punish the herdsmen.

239. (The owner of the field) shall make there a hedge over which a camel cannot look, and stop every gap through which a dog or a boar can thrust his head.

240. (If cattle do mischief) in an enclosed field near a highway or near a village, the herdsman shall be fined one hundred (panas); (but cattle), unattended by a herdsman, (the watchman in the field) shall drive away.

241. (For damage) in other fields (each head of) cattle shall (pay a fine of one (pana) and a quarter, and in all (cases the value of) the crop (destroyed) shall be made good to the owner of the field; that is the settled rule.

242. But Manu has declared that no fine shall be paid for (damage done by) a cow within ten days after her calving, by bulls and by cattle sacred to the gods, whether they are attended by a herdsman or not.

243. If (the crops are destroyed by) the husbandman's (own) fault, the fine shall amount to ten times as much as (the king's) share; but the fine (shall be) only half that amount if (the fault lay) with the servants and the farmer had no knowledge of it.

244. To these rules a righteous king shall keep in (all cases of) transgressions by masters, their cattle, and herdsmen.

245. If a dispute has arisen between two villages concerning a boundary, the king shall settle the limits in the month of Gyaishtha, when the landmarks are most distinctly visible.

246. Let him mark the boundaries (by) trees, (e.g.) Nyagrodhas, Asvatthas, Kimsukas, cotton-trees, Salas, Palmyra palms, and trees with milky juice,

247. By clustering shrubs, bamboos of different kinds, Samis, creepers and raised mounds, reeds, thickets of Kubgaka; thus the boundary will not be forgotten.

248. Tanks, wells, cisterns, and fountains should be built where boundaries meet, as well as temples,

249. And as he will see that through men's ignorance of the boundaries trespasses constantly occur in the world, let him cause to be made other hidden marks for boundaries,

250. Stones, bones, cow's hair, chaff, ashes, potsherds, dry cowdung, bricks, cinders, pebbles, and sand,

251. And whatever other things of a similar kind the earth does not corrode even after a long time, those he should cause to be buried where one boundary joins (the other).

252. By these signs, by long continued possession, and by constantly flowing streams of water the king shall ascertain the boundary (of the land) of two disputing parties.

253. If there be a doubt even on inspection of the marks, the settlement of a dispute regarding boundaries shall depend on witnesses.

254. The witnesses, (giving evidence) regarding a boundary, shall be examined concerning the landmarks in the presence of the crowd of the villagers and also of the two litigants.

255. As they, being questioned, unanimously decide, even so he shall record the boundary (in writing), together with their names.

256. Let them, putting earth on their heads, wearing chaplets (of red flowers) and red dresses, being sworn each by (the rewards for) his meritorious deeds, settle (the boundary) in accordance with the truth.

257. If they determine (the boundary) in the manner stated, they are guiltless (being) veracious witnesses; but if they determine it unjustly, they shall be compelled to pay a fine of two hundred (panas).

258. On failure of witnesses (from the two villages, men of) the four neighbouring villages, who are pure, shall make (as witnesses) a decision concerning the boundary in the presence of the king.

259. On failure of neighbours (who are) original inhabitants (of the country and can be) witnesses with respect to the boundary, (the king) may hear the evidence even of the following inhabitants of the forest.

260. (Viz.) hunters, fowlers, herdsmen, fishermen, root-diggers, snake-catchers, gleaners, and other foresters.

261. As they, being examined, declare the marks for the meeting of the boundaries (to be), even so the king shall justly cause them to be fixed between the two villages.

262. The decision concerning the boundary-marks of fields, wells, tanks, of gardens and houses depends upon (the evidence of) the neighbours.

263. Should the neighbours give false evidence, when men dispute about a boundary-mark, the king shall make each of them pay the middlemost amercement as a fine.

264. He who by intimidation possesses himself of a house, a tank, a garden, or a field, shall be fined five hundred (panas); (if he trespassed) through ignorance, the fine (shall be) two hundred (panas).

265. If the boundary cannot be ascertained (by any evidence), let a righteous king with (the intention of) benefiting

them (all), himself assign (his) land (to each); that is the settled rule.

266. Thus the law for deciding boundary (disputes) has been fully declared, I will next propound the (manner of) deciding (cases of) defamation.

267. A Kshatriya, having defamed a Brahmana, shall be fined one hundred (panas); a Vaisya one hundred and fifty or two hundred; a Sudra shall suffer corporal punishment.

268. A Brahmana shall be fined fifty (panas) for defaming a Kshatriya; in (the case of) a Vaisya the fine shall be twenty-five (panas); in (the case of) a Sudra twelve.

269. For offences of twice-born men against those of equal caste (varna, the fine shall be) also twelve (panas); for speeches which ought not to be uttered, that (and every fine shall be) double.

270. A once-born man (a Sudra), who insults a twice-born man with gross invective, shall have his tongue cut out; for he is of low origin.

271. If he mentions the names and castes (gati) of the (twice-born) with contumely, an iron nail, ten fingers long, shall be thrust red-hot into his mouth.

272. If he arrogantly teaches Brahmanas their duty, the king shall cause hot oil to be poured into his mouth and into his ears.

273. He who through arrogance makes false statements regarding the learning (of a caste-fellow), his country, his caste (gati), or the rites by which his body was sanctified, shall be compelled to pay a fine of two hundred (panas).

274. He who even in accordance with the true facts (contemptuously) calls another man one-eyed, lame, or the like (names), shall be fined at least one karshapana.

275. He who defames his mother, his father, his wife, his brother, his son, or his teacher, and he who gives not the way to his preceptor, shall be compelled to pay one hundred (panas).

276. (For mutual abuse) by a Brahmana and a Kshatriya a fine must be imposed by a discerning (king), on the Brahmana the lowest amercement, but on the Kshatriya the middlemost.

277. A Vaisya and a Sudra must be punished exactly in the same manner according to their respective castes, but the tongue (of the Sudra) shall not be cut out; that is the decision.

278. Thus the rules for punishments (applicable to cases) of defamation have been truly declared; I will next propound the decision (of cases) of assault.

279. With whatever limb a man of a low caste does hurt to (a man of the three) highest (castes), even that limb shall be cut off; that is the teaching of Manu.

280. He who raises his hand or a stick, shall have his hand cut off; he who in anger kicks with his foot, shall have his foot cut off.

281. A low-caste man who tries to place himself on the same seat with a man of a high caste, shall be branded on his hip and be banished, or (the king) shall cause his buttock to be gashed.

282. If out of arrogance he spits (on a superior), the king shall cause both his lips to be cut off; if he urines (on him), the penis; if he breaks wind (against him), the anus.

283. If he lays hold of the hair (of a superior), let the (king) unhesitatingly cut off his hands, likewise (if he takes him) by the feet, the beard, the neck, or the scrotum.

284. He who breaks the skin (of an equal) or fetches blood (from him) shall be fined one hundred (panas), he who cuts a muscle six nishkas, he who breaks a bone shall be banished.

285. According to the usefulness of the several (kinds of) trees a fine must be inflicted for injuring them; that is the settled rule.

286. If a blow is struck against men or animals in order to (give them) pain, (the judge) shall inflict a fine in proportion to the amount of pain (caused).

287. If a limb is injured, a wound (is caused), or blood (flows, the assailant) shall be made to pay (to the sufferer) the expenses of the cure, or the whole (both the usual amercement and the expenses of the cure as a) fine (to the king).

288. He who damages the goods of another, be it intentionally or unintentionally, shall give satisfaction to the (owner) and pay to the king a fine equal to the (damage).

289. In the case of (damage done to) leather, or to utensils of leather, of wood, or of clay, the fine (shall be) five times their value; likewise in the case of (damage to) flowers, roots, and fruit.

290. They declare with respect to a carriage, its driver and its owner, (that there are) ten cases in which no punishment (for damage done) can be inflicted; in other cases a fine is prescribed.

291. When the nose-string is snapped, when the yoke is broken, when the carriage turns sideways or back, when the axle or a wheel is broken,

292. When the leather-thongs, the rope around the neck or the bridle are broken, and when (the driver) has loudly called out, 'Make way,' Manu has declared (that in all these cases) no punishment (shall be inflicted).

293. But if the cart turns off (the road) through the driver's want of skill, the owner shall be fined, if damage (is done), two hundred (panas).

294. If the driver is skilful (but negligent), he alone shall be fined; if the driver is unskilful, the occupants of the carriage (also) shall be each fined one hundred (panas).

295. But if he is stopped on his way by cattle or by (another) carriage, and he causes the death of any living being, a fine shall without doubt be imposed.

296. If a man is killed, his guilt will be at once the same as (that of) a thief; for large animals such as cows, elephants, camels or horses, half of that.

297. For injuring small cattle the fine (shall be) two hundred (panas); the fine for beautiful wild quadrupeds and birds shall amount to fifty (panas).

298. For donkeys, sheep, and goats the fine shall be five mashas; but the punishment for killing a dog or a pig shall be one masha.

299. A wife, a son, a slave, a pupil, and a (younger) brother of the full blood, who have committed faults, may be beaten with a rope or a split bamboo,

300. But on the back part of the body (only), never on a noble part; he who strikes them otherwise will incur the same guilt as a thief.

301. Thus the whole law of assault (and hurt) has been declared completely; I will now explain the rules for the decision (in cases) of theft.

302. Let the king exert himself to the utmost to punish thieves; for, if he punishes thieves, his fame grows and his kingdom prospers.

303. That king, indeed, is ever worthy of honour who ensures the safety (of his subjects); for the sacrificial session (sattra, which he, as it were, performs thereby) ever grows in length, the safety (of his subjects representing) the sacrificial fee.

304. A king who (duly) protects (his subjects) receives from each and all the sixth part of their spiritual merit; if he does not protect them, the sixth part of their demerit also (will fall on him).

305. Whatever (merit a man gains by) reading the Veda, by sacrificing, by charitable gifts, (or by) worshipping (Gurus and gods), the king obtains a sixth part of that in consequence of his duly protecting (his kingdom).

306. A king who protects the created beings in accordance with the sacred law and smites those worthy of corporal punishment, daily offers (as it were) sacrifices at which hundred thousands (are given as) fees.

307. A king who does not afford protection, (yet) takes his share in kind, his taxes, tolls and duties, daily presents and fines, will (after death) soon sink into hell.

308. They declare that a king who affords no protection, (yet) receives the sixth part of the produce, takes upon himself all the foulness of his whole people.

309. Know that a king who heeds not the rules (of the law), who is an atheist, and rapacious, who does not protect (his subjects, but) devours them, will sink low (after death).

310. Let him carefully restrain the wicked by three methods,- by imprisonment by putting them in fetters, and by various (kinds of) corporal punishments.

311. For by punishing the wicked and by favouring the virtuous, kings are constantly sanctified, just as twice-born men by sacrifices.

312. A king who desires his own welfare must always forgive litigants, infants, aged and sick men, who inveigh against him.

313. He who, being abused by men in pain, pardons (them), will in reward of that (act) be exalted in heaven; but he who, (proud) of his kingly state, forgives them not, will for that (reason) sink into hell.

314. A thief shall, running, approach the king, with flying hair, confessing that theft (and saying), 'Thus have I done, punish me;'

315. (And he must) carry on his shoulder a pestle, or a club of Khadira wood, or a spear sharp at both ends, or an iron staff.

316. Whether he be punished or pardoned, the thief is freed from the (guilt of) theft; but the king, if he punishes not, takes upon himself the guilt of the thief.

317. The killer of a learned Brahmana throws his guilt on him who eats his food, an adulterous wife on her (negligent) husband, a (sinning) pupil or sacrificer on (their negligent) teacher (or priest), a thief on the king (who pardons him).

318. But men who have committed crimes and have been punished by the king, go to heaven, being pure like those who performed meritorious deeds.

319. He who steals the rope or the water-pot from a well, or damages a hut where water is distributed, shall pay one masha as a fine and restore the (article abstracted or damaged) in its (proper place).

320. On him who steals more than ten kumbhas of grain corporal punishment (shall be inflicted); in other cases he shall be fined eleven times as much, and shall pay to the (owner the value of his) property.

321. So shall corporal punishment be inflicted for stealing more than a hundred (palas) of articles sold by the weight, (i.e.) of gold, silver, and so forth, and of most excellent clothes.

322. For (stealing) more than fifty (palas) it is enacted that the hands (of the offender) shall be cut off; but in other cases, let him inflict a fine of eleven times the value.

323. For stealing men of noble family and especially women and the most precious gems, (the offender) deserves corporal (or capital) punishment.

324. For stealing large animals, weapons, or medicines, let the king fix a punishment, after considering the time and the purpose (for which they were destined).

325. For (stealing) cows belonging to Brahmanas, piercing (the nostrils of) a barren cow, and for stealing (other) cattle (belonging to Brahmanas, the offender) shall forthwith lose half his feet.

326. (For stealing) thread, cotton, drugs causing fermentation, cowdung, molasses, sour milk, sweet milk, butter-milk, water, or grass,

327. Vessels made of bamboo or other cane, salt of various kinds, earthen (vessels), earth and ashes,

328. Fish, birds, oil, clarified butter, meat, honey, and other things that come from beasts,

329. Or other things of a similar kind, spirituous liquor, boiled rice, and every kind of cooked food, the fine (shall be) twice the value (of the stolen article).

330. For flowers, green corn, shrubs, creepers, trees, and other unhusked (grain) the fine (shall be) five krishnalas.

331. For husked grain, vegetables, roots, and fruit the fine (shall be) one hundred (panas) if there is no connexion (between the owner and the thief), fifty (panas) if such a connexion exists.

332. An offence (of this description), which is committed in the presence (of the owner) and with violence, will be robbery; if (it is committed) in his absence, it will be theft; likewise if (the possession of) anything is denied after it has been taken.

333. On that man who may steal (any of) the above-mentioned articles, when they are prepared for (use), let the king inflict the first (or lowest) amercement; likewise on him who may steal (a sacred) fire out of the room (in which it is kept).

334. With whatever limb a thief in any way commits (an offence) against men, even of that (the king) shall deprive him in order to prevent (a repetition of the crime).

335. Neither a father, nor a teacher, nor a friend, nor a mother, nor a wife, nor a son, nor a domestic priest must be left unpunished by a king, if they do not keep within their duty.

336. Where another common man would be fined one karshapana, the king shall be fined one thousand; that is the settled rule.

337. In (a case of) theft the guilt of a Sudra shall be eightfold, that of a Vaisya sixteenfold, that of a Kshatriya two-and-thirtyfold,

338. That of a Brahmana sixty-fourfold, or quite a hundredfold, or (even) twice four-and-sixtyfold; (each of them) knowing the nature of the offence.

339. (The taking of) roots and of fruit from trees, of wood for a (sacrificial) fire, and of grass for feeding cows, Manu has declared (to be) no theft.

340. A Brahmana, seeking to obtain property from a man who took what was not given to him, either by sacrificing for him or by teaching him, is even like a thief.

341. A twice-born man, who is travelling and whose provisions are exhausted, shall not be fined, if he takes two stalks of sugar-cane or two (esculent) roots from the field of another man.

342. He who ties up unbound or sets free tied up (cattle of other men), he who takes a slave, a horse, or a carriage will have incurred the guilt of a thief.

343. A king who punishes thieves according to these rules, will gain fame in this world and after death unsurpassable bliss.

344. A king who desires to gain the throne of Indra and imperishable eternal fame, shall not, even for a moment, neglect (to punish) the man who commits violence.

345. He who commits violence must be considered as the worst offender, (more wicked) than a defamer, than a thief, and than he who injures (another) with a staff.

346. But that king who pardons the perpetrator of violence quickly perishes and incurs hatred.

347. Neither for friendship's sake, nor for the sake of great lucre, must a king let go perpetrators of violence, who cause terror to all creatures.

348. Twice-born men may take up arms when (they are) hindered (in the fulfilment of their duties, when destruction (threatens) the twice-born castes (varna) in (evil) times,

349. In their own defence, in a strife for the fees of officiating priests, and in order to protect women and Brahmanas; he who (under such circumstances) kills in the cause of right, commits no sin.

350. One may slay without hesitation an assassin who approaches (with murderous intent), whether (he be one's) teacher, a child or an aged man, or a Brahmana deeply versed in the Vedas.

351. By killing an assassin the slayer incurs no guilt, whether (he does it) publicly or secretly; in that case fury recoils upon fury.

352. Men who commit adultery with the wives of others, the king shall cause to be marked by punishments which cause terror, and afterwards banish.

353. For by (adultery) is caused a mixture of the castes (varna) among men; thence (follows) sin, which cuts up even the roots and causes the destruction of everything.

354. A man formerly accused of (such) offences, who secretly converses with another man's wife, shall pay the first (or lowest) amercement.

355. But a man, not before accused, who (thus) speaks with (a woman) for some (reasonable) cause, shall not incur any guilt, since in him there is no transgression.

356. He who addresses the wife of another man at a Tirtha, outside the village, in a forest, or at the confluence of rivers, suffer (the punishment for) adulterous acts (samgrahana).

357. Offering presents (to a woman), romping (with her), touching her ornaments and dress, sitting with her on a bed, all (these acts) are considered adulterous acts (samgrahana).

358. If one touches a woman in a place (which ought) not (to be touched) or allows (oneself to be touched in such a spot), all (such acts done) with mutual consent are declared (to be) adulterous (samgrahana).

359. A man who is not a Brahmana ought to suffer death for adultery (samgrahana); for the wives of all the four castes even must always be carefully guarded.

360. Mendicants, bards, men who have performed the initiatory ceremony of a Vedic sacrifice, and artisans are not prohibited from speaking to married women.

361. Let no man converse with the wives of others after he has been forbidden (to do so); but he who converses (with them), in spite of a prohibition, shall be fined one suvarna.

362. This rule does not apply to the wives of actors and singers, nor (of) those who live on (the intrigues of) their own (wives); for such men send their wives (to others) or, concealing themselves, allow them to hold criminal intercourse.

363. Yet he who secretly converses with such women, or with female slaves kept by one (master), and with female ascetics, shall be compelled to pay a small fine.

364. He who violates an unwilling maiden shall instantly suffer corporal punishment; but a man who enjoys a willing maiden shall not suffer corporal punishment, if (his caste be) the same (as hers).

365. From a maiden who makes advances to a (man of) high (caste), he shall not take any fine; but her, who courts a (man of) low (caste), let him force to live confined in her house.

366. A (man of) low (caste) who makes love to a maiden (of) the highest (caste) shall suffer corporal punishment; he who addresses a maiden (on) equal (caste) shall pay the nuptial fee, if her father desires it.

367. But if any man through insolence forcibly contaminates a maiden, two of his fingers shall be instantly cut off, and he shall pay a fine of six hundred (panas).

368. A man (of) equal (caste) who defiles a willing maiden shall not suffer the amputation of his fingers, but shall pay a fine of two hundred (panas) in order to deter him from a repetition (of the offence).

369. A damsel who pollutes (another) damsel must be fined two hundred (panas), pay the double of her (nuptial) fee, and receive ten (lashes with a) rod.

370. But a woman who pollutes a damsel shall instantly have (her head) shaved or two fingers cut off, and be made to ride (through the town) on a donkey.

371. If a wife, proud of the greatness of her relatives or (her own) excellence, violates the duty which she owes to her lord, the king shall cause her to be devoured by dogs in a place frequented by many.

372. Let him cause the male offender to be burnt on a red-hot iron bed; they shall put logs under it, (until) the sinner is burned (to death).

373. On a man (once) convicted, who is (again) accused within a year, a double fine (must be inflicted); even thus (must the fine be doubled) for (repeated) intercourse with a Vratya and a Kandali.

374. A Sudra who has intercourse with a woman of a twice-born caste (varna), guarded or unguarded, (shall be punished in the following manner): if she was unguarded, he loses the part (offending) and all his property; if she was guarded, everything (even his life).

375. (For intercourse with a guarded Brahmana a Vaisya shall forfeit all his property after imprisonment for a year; a Kshatriya shall be fined one thousand (panas) and be shaved with the urine (of an ass).

376. If a Vaisya or a Kshatriya has connexion with an unguarded Brahmana, let him fine the Vaisya five hundred (panas) and the Kshatriya one thousand.

377. But even these two, if they offend with a Brahmani (not only) guarded (but the wife of an eminent man), shall be punished like a Sudra or be burnt in a fire of dry grass.

378. A Brahmana who carnally knows a guarded Brahmani against her will, shall be fined one thousand (panas); but he shall be made to pay five hundred, if he had connexion with a willing one.

379. Tonsure (of the head) is ordained for a Brahmana (instead of) capital punishment; but (men of) other castes shall suffer capital punishment.

380. Let him never slay a Brahmana, though he have committed all (possible) crimes; let him banish such an (offender), leaving all his property (to him) and (his body) unhurt.

381. No greater crime is known on earth than slaying a Brahmana; a king, therefore, must not even conceive in his mind the thought of killing a Brahmana.

382. If a Vaisya approaches a guarded female of the Kshatriya caste, or a Kshatriya a (guarded) Vaisya woman, they both deserve the same punishment as in the case of an unguarded Brahmana female.

383. A Brahmana shall be compelled to pay a fine of one thousand (panas) if he has intercourse with guarded (females of) those two (castes); for (offending with) a (guarded) Sudra female a fine of one thousand (panas shall be inflicted) on a Kshatriya or a Vaisya.

384. For (intercourse with) an unguarded Kshatriya a fine of five hundred (panas shall fall) on a Vaisya; but (for the same offence) a Kshatriya shall be shaved with the urine (of a donkey) or (pay) the same fine.

385. A Brahmana who approaches unguarded females (of the) Kshatriya or Vaisya (castes), or a Sudra female, shall be fined five hundred (panas); but (for intercourse with) a female (of the) lowest (castes), one thousand.

386. That king in whose town lives no thief, no adulterer, no defamer, no man guilty of violence, and no committer of assaults, attains the world of Sakra (Indra).

387. The suppression of those five in his dominions secures to a king paramount sovereignty among his peers and fame in the world.

388. A sacrificer who forsakes an officiating priest, and an officiating priest who forsakes a sacrificer, (each being) able to perform his work and not contaminated (by grievous crimes), must each be fined one hundred (panas).

389. Neither a mother, nor a father, nor a wife, nor a son shall be cast off; he who casts them off, unless guilty of a crime causing loss of caste, shall be fined six hundred (panas).

390. If twice-born men dispute among each other concerning the duty of the orders, a king who desires his own welfare should not (hastily) decide (what is) the law.

391. Having shown them due honor, he should, with (the assistance of) Brahmanas, first soothe them by gentle (speech) and afterwards teach them their duty.

392. A Brahmana who does not invite his next neighbour and his neighbour next but one, (though) both (he) worthy (of the honour), to a festival at which twenty Brahmanas are entertained, is liable to a fine of one masha.

393. A Srotriya who does not entertain a virtuous Srotriya at auspicious festive rites, shall be made to pay him twice (the value of) the meal and a masha of gold (as a fine to the king).

394. A blind man, an idiot, (a cripple) who moves with the help of a board, a man full seventy years old, and he who confers benefits on Srotriyas, shall not be compelled by any (king) to pay a tax.

395. Let the king always treat kindly a Srotriya, a sick or distressed man, an infant and an aged or indigent man, a man of high birth, and an honourable man (Arya).

396. A washerman shall wash (the clothes of his employers) gently on a smooth board of Salmaliwood he shall not return the clothes (of one person) for those (of another), nor allow anybody (but the owner) to wear them.

397. A weaver (who has received) ten palas (of thread), shall return (cloth weighing) one pala more; he who acts differently shall be compelled to pay a fine of twelve (panas).

398. Let the king take one-twentieth of that (amount) which men, well acquainted with the settlement of tolls and duties (and) skilful in (estimating the value of) all kinds of merchandise, may fix as the value for each saleablr commodity.

399. Let the king confiscate the whole property of (a trader) who out of greed exports goods of which the king has a monopoly or (the export of which is) forbidden.

400. He who avoids a custom-house (or a toll), he who buys or sells at an improper time, or he who makes a false statement in enumerating (his goods), shall be fined eight times (the amount of duty) which he tried to evade.

401. Let (the king) fix (the rates for) the purchase and sale of all marketable goods, having (duly) considered whence they come, whither they go, how long they have been kept, the (probable) profit and the (probable) outlay.

402. Once in five nights, or at the close of each fortnight, let the king publicly settle the prices for the (merchants).

403. All weights and measures must be duly marked, and once in six months let him re-examine them.

404. At a ferry an (empty) cart shall be made to pay one pana, a man's (load) half a pana, an animal and a woman one quarter of a (pana), an unloaded man one-half of a quarter.

405. Carts (laden) with vessels full (of merchandise) shall be made to pay toll at a ferry according to the value (of the goods), empty vessels and men without luggage some trifle.

406. For a long passage the boat-hire must be proportioned to the places and times; know that this (rule refers) to (passages along) the banks of rivers; at sea there is no settled (freight).

407. But a woman who has been pregnant two months or more, an ascetic, a hermit in the forest, and Brahmanas who are students of the Veda, shall not be made to pay toll at a ferry.

408. Whatever may be damaged in a boat by the fault of the boatmen, that shall be made good by the boatmen collectively, (each paying) his share.

409. This decision in suits (brought) by passengers (holds good only) in case the boatmen are culpably negligent on the water; in the case of (an accident) caused by (the will of) the gods, no fine can be (inflicted on them).

410. (The king) should order a Vaisya to trade, to lend money, to cultivate the land, or to tend cattle, and a Sudra to serve the twice-born castes

411. (Some wealthy) Brahmana shall compassionately support both a Kshatriya and a Vaisya, if they are distressed for a livelihood, employing them on work (which is suitable for) their (castes).

412. But a Brahmana who, because he is powerful, out of greed makes initiated (men of the) twice-born (castes) against their will do the work of slaves, shall be fined by the king six hundred (panas).

413. But a Sudra, whether bought or unbought, he may compel to do servile work; for he was created by the Self-existent (Svayambhu) to be the slave of a Brahmana.

414. A Sudra, though emancipated by his master, is not released from servitude; since that is innate in him, who can set him free from it?

415. There are slaves of seven kinds, (viz.) he who is made a captive under a standard, he who serves for his daily food, he who is born in the house, he who is bought and he who is given, he who is inherited from ancestors, and he who is enslaved by way of punishment.

416. A wife, a son, and a slave, these three are declared to have no property; the wealth which they earn is (acquired) for him to whom they belong.

417. A Brahmana may confidently seize the goods of (his) Sudra (slave); for, as that (slave) can have no property, his master may take his possessions.

418. (The king) should carefully compel Vaisyas and Sudra to perform the work (prescribed) for them; for if these two (castes) swerved from their duties, they would throw this (whole) world into confusion.

419. Let him daily look after the completion of his undertakings, his beasts of burden, and carriages, (the collection of) his revenues and the disbursements, his mines and his treasury.

420. A king who thus brings to a conclusion. all the legal business enumerated above, and removes all sin, reaches the highest state (of bliss).

5

Philosophical Development from Upanishadic Metaphysics to Scientific Realism

UPANISHADIC PHILOSOPHY

Although the Upanishadic texts (like some of the earlier Vedic texts) are primarily concerned with acquiring knowledge of the "soul", "spirit" and "god" - there are aspects of Vedic and Upanishadic literature that also point to an intuitive understanding of nature and natural processes. In addition, many of the ideas are presented in a philosophical and exploratory manner - rather than as strict definitions of inviolable truth.

Although the Upanishadic texts goaded the Upanishadic student to concentrate on comprehending the inner spirit, rational investigation of the world by other scholars was not entirely squelched, and eventually, the Upanishadic period gave way to an era which was not inimical to the development of rational ideas, even encouraging scientific observation and advanced study in the fields of logic, mathematics and the physical sciences.

Following an era when rituals and superstitions had begun to proliferate, in some ways the Upanishadic texts helped to clear the ground for greater rationalism in society. Brahmin orthodoxy and ideas of ritual purity were superseded by a spiritual perspective that eschewed sectarianism and could be practised universally, unfettered by an individual's social standing. Much of the emphasis was on discovering "spiritual truths" for oneself as opposed to mechanically accepting the testimony of established religious leaders. Although there is a thematic commonality to the Upanishadic discourses, different commentators offered subtly varying perspectives and insights.

The concept of god in Upanishadic (and even earlier Vedic) thinking was quite different from the more common definition of god as creator and dispenser of reward and punishment. The Upanishadic concept of god was more abstract and philosophical. Different texts postulated the doctrine of a universal soul that embraced all physical beings. All life emanated from this universal soul and death simply caused individual manifestations of the soul to merge or mingle back with the universal soul. The concept of a universal soul was illustrated through analogies from natural phenomenon.

"As the bees make honey by collecting the juices of distant trees, and reduce the juice into one form. And as these juices have no discrimination, so that they might say, I am the juice of this tree or that, in the same manner, all these creatures, when they have become merged in the True, know not that they are merged in the True. . . ."

"These rivers run, the eastern (like the Ganges) towards the east, the western (like the Indus) towards the west. They go from sea to sea (i.e., the clouds lift up the water from the sea to the sky and send it back as rain to the sea). They become indeed sea. And as those rivers, when they are in the sea, do not know, I am this or that river, in the same manner, all these creatures, proceeding from the True, know not that they have proceeded from the True. . . ."

In another story, the "wise" father, expounder of the Upanishadic concept of god, asks his son to dissolve salt in water, and asked him to taste it from the surface, from the middle and from the bottom. In each case, the son finds the taste to be salty. To this his father replies that the 'universal being' though invisible resides in all of us, just as the salt, though invisible is completely dissolved in the water. *(Chanddogya, VI)*

As a corollary to this theory emerged the notion that even as individual beings might refer to this universal soul - i.e. god in varied ways - by using different names and different methods of worship - all living beings were nevertheless related to each other and to the universal god, and capable of merging with the universal god. This approach thus laid the foundation for egalitarian and non-discriminatory philosophies such as Buddhism and Jainism (as well as non-sectarian streams of Hinduism) that followed the Upanishadic period. As is evident, such an approach was not incompatible with secular society, and permitted different faiths and sub-faiths to coexist in relative peace and harmony.

In the course of defining their philosophy, the scholars of the Upanishad period raised several questions that challenged mechanical theism (as was also done in some hymns from the Rig Veda and Atharva Veda). If god existed as the unique creator of the world, they wondered who created this unique creator. The logical pursuit of such a line of questioning could either lead to an infinite series of creators, or to the rejection or abandonment of this line of questioning. The common theist solution to this philosophical dilemma was to simply reject logic and demand unquestioning faith on the part of the believer. A few theists attempted to use this contradiction to their own advantage by positing that god existed precisely because "He" was indescribable by mere mortals. But, by and large, this contradiction was taken very seriously by the philosophers of the Upanishadic period. The Upanishadic philosophers attempted to resolve this contradiction by defining god as an entity that extended infinitely in all dimensions covering both space and time. This was a philosophical advance in that it attempted to come to terms with at least the most obvious challenges to the notion of god as a human-like creator and did not require the complete rejection of logic.

Another philosophical advance of the Upanishadic period was that religion was transformed from the realm of bookish parroting of scriptures to the realm of advanced intellectual debate and polemics. The Upanishadic philosophers did not lay down their conclusions as rigid doctrines or inviolable laws but as seductive parables - sometimes displaying remarkable worldly insight and analytical skill. By attempting to win over their followers through analogies from nature, and by employing the methods of abstract reasoning and debate, they created an environment where dialectical thinking and intellectual exchanges could later flourish.

In the very process of their questioning, (and albeit speculative reasoning about god), they had opened the door for rationalists and even outright atheists who took their tentative questioning about the role and the character of god as "creator" to conclusions that rejected theism entirely. But in either case, many rationalist and/or naturalist philosophical streams emerged from this initial foundation. Some were nominally theistic (but in the abstract Upanishadic vein), others were agnostic (as the early Jains), while the early Buddhists and the Lokayatas were atheists. Thus even though the Upanishads contained much that should rightly be dismissed as abstruse intellectual jugglery and philosophical mumbo-jumbo, the Upanishadic philosophers had levelled the ground for the seeds of rationalism to flourish in Indian soil.

THE VAISHESHIKA SCHOOL

The Vaisheshika school (considered to be founded by Kanada, author of the Vaisesika Sutra) was an early realistic school whose main achievement lay in it's attempt at classifying nature into like and unlike groups. It also posited that all matter was made up of tiny and indestructible particles - i.e. atoms that aggregated in different ways to form new compounds that formed the variety of matter that existed on the earth.

Their philosophy was described through the enumeration of the following concepts: *Dravya* (Substance), *Guna* (Quality), *Karma* (Action), *Samanya* (Generality), *Visesa* (Particularity), *Samavaya* (Inherence) and abhava (non-existence).

Dravya (or substance) was understood as the specific result of a particular aggregate effect - i.e. the combination of atoms in a unique way. Substances were repositories for qualities and actions. *Guna* or quality was that which resided in a *dravya*. Qualities did not however contain qualities themselves. 24 qualities were enumerated, such as - color, form, smell, touch, sound, number, magnitude, distinctions, conjunction, disjunction, nearness, remoteness, heaviness, fluidity and viscosity. (As was typical of the times, psychological attributes such as pleasure, pain, desire, aversion, effort, tendency, cognition, impression, and ethical attributes such as merit and demerit were also included in the list, i.e. - qualities that were inapplicable to inanimate objects were not treated separately)

Action or *Karma* represented physical movement. Unlike quality which was passive, *Karma* was dynamic. Action was the determinant of conjuction and disjunction. Five types of action were noted: throwing upwards or downwards, contraction, expansion and locomotion.

Satta or physical existence was viewed as being the common attribute of substance, quality and action - i.e. only existing (as opposed to imaginary) entities could have substance, qualities and be capable of action.

Samanyata or 'generality' was seen as a mental construct to create common classes of substances, qualities or actions while *Visesata* (particularity) was used to identify and separate individual items from their general classes. *Samavaya* or inherence was a relation that existed in those things that could not be separated without destroying them.

Four categories of *Abhava* as negation or non-existance were listed: *pragabhava* or prior non-existance, referring to the absence of an object before it's creation; *dhvamsabhava* or posterior negation, as the absence of an object after it had been destroyed; *anyonyabhava* or mutual non-existance, refering to an object being distinct and different from the other; *atyantabhava* or absolute non-existence, indicating non-existence in the past, present and future, citing the example of air as permanently lacking in smell - (which was presumably true in a period where air pollution must have been uncommon!).

An important contribution of the *Vaisheshika* school was a careful study of the time-relation in a chain of causes and effects. In a very rudimentary way, the school (along with other such schools) anticipated the theory of time calculus which could also be extended to space calculus.

The *Vaisheshika* school thus served as an important step in the study of science by enumerating concepts that could further the study of physics and chemistry. In addition, the the study of medical science (including veterinary science) received considerable impetus from such attempts at methodical observation and classification.

The Nyaya and related schools

The Nyaya schools complemented and built on the Vaisheshika school by elaborating on the process of accumulating valid scientific knowledge through accurate perception and generating valid inferences.

The school articulated four means of acquiring valid knowledge: *pratyaksha* or perception through one of the senses; *anumana* or inference; *upamana* or comparison with a well-known object; or *shabda* - verbal testimony.

The conditions of perception, and it's range and limits were carefully studied. *Trasarenu* - the minima sensibile (i.e. the minimum visible), *anubhuta-rupa* - the infra-sensible, *abhibhuta* - the obscured perception , and *anubhuta-vriti* - potential perception, were recognized as different types of perception.

A general methodology of ascertaining the truth (*tattva*) was described which consisted of describing a proposition (*uddesa*), the ascertainment of essential facts obtained through perception, inference or induction (*laksan or uppa-laksana*), and finally examination and verification (*pariksa* and *nirnaya*). This process could involve examples *(drishtanta),* logical arguments *(avayava),* reasoning *(tarka)* and discussion (*vada)* - , intellectual exchange, or interplay of two opposing sides in the process of arriving at a decisive conclusion. A successful application of this method could result in a *siddhanta* - i.e. established principle - (or in the case of mathematics - a theorem or theory) elucidated through proofs (*pramana*). Alternatively, it could lead to a rejection of the initial proposition.

The Nyaya school identified various types of arguments that hindered or obstructed the path of genuine scientific pursuit, suggesting perhaps, that there may have been considerable practical resistance to their unstinting devotion to truth-seeking and scientific accuracy. They list the term *jalpa* - an argument not for the sake of arriving at the truth but for the sake of seeking victory (this term was coined perhaps to distinguish exaggerated and rhetorical arguments, or hyperbole from genuine arguments); *vitanda* (or cavil) to identify arguments that were specious or frivolous, or intended to divert attention from the substance of the debate, that were put-downs intended to lower the dignity or credibility of the opponent; and *chal* - equivocation or ruse to confuse the argument. Three types of *chal* are listed: *vakchala* - or verbal equivocation where the words of the opponent are deliberately misused to mean or suggest something different than what was intended; *samanyachala* or false generalization, where the opponents arguments are deliberately and incorrectly generalized in a way to suggest that the original arguments were ridiculous or absurd; *uparachala* - misinterpreting a word which is used figuratively by taking it literally. Also mentioned is *jati,* a type of fallacious argument where an inapplicable similiarity is cited to reject an argument, or conversely an irrelevant dissimiliarity is cited to reject an argument.

The Nyaya school also recognized that intelligent and meaningful debates were not possible if certain fundamental principles and basic definitions and concepts were not mutually accepted. *Nigrahasthana* was the term used to identify disagreements based on absence of mutually acceptable first principles. An example might be a debate between a theist who rejected logic, and a non-theist who rejected faith.

The Nyaya school also listed five classes of logical fallacies (*hetvabhasa*) : *savyabhichara* or the inconclusive type which employed reasoning from which more than one conclusion could be drawn but was used to insist on a single specific conclusion; *viruddha* or contradictory, where the reasoning used actually contradicted the proposition to be established; *kalatita* - where the elapse of time had made the argument invalid; *sadhyasama,* the unproven type, where the reasoning employed rested on arguments or principles that had not been proven and require proofs themselves - i.e. this was the type of fallacy where one unproven result was merely converted into another unproven result.; and finally *prakaranasama* - where the reasoning employed provoked the very question it was designed to answer- i.e. a recursive fallacy. In this manner, the Nyaya school defined a very sophisticated school of rational philosophy where the process of scientific epistemology was analyzed threadbare and all the dangers of unscientific reasoning and propaganda ploys were skillfully exposed.

Causality

Buddhist and Jain scholars, as well as later Hindu scholars offered their own approaches to scientific reasoning. Virtually all the rational schools were concerned with describing causality and causal relationships, and recognized that effects may not have single causes but may require a group or conjunction of causes to occur. Buddhist scholars emphasized that cause and effect need not have a linear effect but that desired effects may also require the right conditions for their fruition. (That is to say that for a plant to grow successfully, it would not only need the right seed, but that it would also need the right type of soil, fertilization, sunlight and water.)

Both the Jains and the Buddhists correctly speculated that a potential for the desired effect must also be present in the cause or causal agent. (For instance, only a mango seed could produce a mango tree because only the mango seed incorporated the potential of developing into a mango tree.) As another example, one could note that something with brittle properties such as glass might break upon impact whereas something strong such as steel would survive. Thus a physical impact on substances of different properties would have different results.

The Nyaya school also recognized co-effects - i.e a series of antecedants could cause a series of effects either successive and staggered in time, or near simultaneous. Nyaya texts on causality indicate that there was an awareness that light travelled at a very high speed but the transmission of light was not instantaneous.

BUDDHIST AND JAIN ATOMIC THEORIES

The Buddhist and Jain philosophers also proposed their own variations of the atomic theory. Like the Vaisheshikas, atoms were perceived as infinitely small by the Jainas. But the Jainas went a step further by positing that the union of atoms required opposite qualities in the combining atoms - as is true in the case of electrovalent bonding. However, they erred in thinking that covalent bonding (which does not require opposite polarities in the combining atoms) could not occur. But their intuition that opposite polarities created mutual attraction and facilitated chemical reactions was correct. In the Buddhist view, matter was in fact an aggregate of rapidly recurring forces or energy waves. Their theory was illustrated with examples drawn from natural phenomenon involved with light emission. An atom was perceived as a momentary flash of light combining and separating from other atoms according to strict and definite laws of causality. Physical matter was thus seen as a denser and more concentrated form of light. Although at odds with other atomic theories of the time, their approach fit in with their general view that all things in nature were temporal, that there was constant change in nature - that degradation and renewal were continuous processes.

The Syadvada system of Jain Logic

Jain philosophers also made certain important contributions to the science of epistemology by proposing that the truth of a concept or observation could not only be true or false but indeterminate - and combinations of the above - such as true under some conditions (or true at a particular time or place - or true based on the validity of certain inferences) and false under other conditions, or true under some conditions but indeterminate under others, and so on. This led to a matrix of seven possible states of the truth (true, false, true or false, indeterminate, true or indeterminate, false or indeterminate, true or false or indeterminate).

Jaina rationalists also studied the relationship between the universal and the particular and made important points concerning generalities and individual peculiarities. They also noted that objects in the real world exist in a network of relationships with each other - and have specific attributes that mark them temporally and spatially: "Every real is thus hedged round by a network of relations and attributes, which we propose to call its system or context or universe of discourse, which demarcates it from others." Jaina philosophers also successfully synthesized earlier debates on change and permanence by positing that all objects (or parts of objects) passed through phases of "existence, persistence, and cessation" and that reality was therefore a complex combination of things relatively permanent yet also relatively changing.

These ideas thus formed the foundations of Indian science and contributed to the gradual elaboration of mathematics and astronomy, as well as agricultural and meteorological sciences. Developments in metallurgy and civil engineering also followed. Medicine and surgery perhaps received the greatest and the earliest impetus from these developments. Developments in philosophy also led to concomitant developments in the realm of art and culture.

Yet. to a considerable extent, knowledge about the progress of science and reason in Indian history is often scarce. These (and other such) historical contributions were either denied or demeaned during the process of colonization, and are only now beginning to be re-acknowledged within India and abroad. But in A. D 1068, Indian contributions to the mainstream of science were held in great esteem and readily acknowledged in some parts of the world: Here is what Said Al-Andalusi, an 11th C Spanish scholar, court historian and chronicler wrote then:

> *"Among the nations, during the course of centuries and throughout the passage of time, India was known as the mine of wisdom and the fountainhead of justice and good government and the Indians were credited with excellent intellects, exalted ideas, universal maxims, rare inventions and wonderful talents ... They have studied arithmetic and geometry. They have also acquired copious and abundant knowledge of the movements of the stars, the secrets of the celestial sphere and all other kinds of mathematical sciences. Moreover, of all the peoples they are the most learned in the science of medicine and thoroughly informed about the properties of drugs, the nature of composite elements and peculiarities of the existing things."*

6

Peoples and Languages

What was the language of the Indus Valley, present-day Pakistan, in the pre-Islamic period? Did this region have one language or many? Did it have one language family or many? In which script, or scripts, were they written? These questions cannot be answered by the linguist alone. To answer them one needs the help of the archaeologist, the historian and the anthropologist. Let us then begin with the evidence about the Indus Valley civilization brought to light by the archaeologists first.

THE INDUS VALLEY CIVILIZATION

The Indus Valley, or Harrapan, civilization was discovered in 1920-21 when engraved seals were discovered near present-day Sahiwal in Pakistani Punjab at a place called Harappa. Later Rakhal Das Banerjee, John Marshall, E.J.H Mackay and M.S.Vats carried out excavations at Mohenjodaro in Sind and discovered the buried remains of a civilization with a pictographic script. Many archaeologists , including the celebrated Sir Mortimer Wheeler, added to our knowledge of this civilization . We now know that it extended to the Yamuna along the bed of the river Ghaggar in Rajhastan, Gujrat and upto the mouths of the rivers Narbada and Tapati.

It does appear, however, that the major sites of this civilization are in Pakistan. In fact it is in Pakistan that an earlier phase of it has also been unearthed. This happened between 1955-57 when a Pakistani archaeologist, F.A.Khan, discovered a town of the pre-Indus period (c. 3300-2800 B.C) at Kot Diji in Khairpur, Sind. Such sites were also discovered by Rafique Mughal in Bahawalpur, especially in the Cholistan desert, extending the area of this culture to the whole of southern Pakistan. The area was further extended by Professor Ahmad Hasan Dani, the famous Pakistani archaeologist and Sanskritologist, when he discovered the sites of this civilization at Gumla, seven miles from Dera Ismail Khan. In fact Dani identified six cultural periods and Professor Farzand Ali Durrani , who excavated Rahman Dheri which is fourteen miles north of Dera Ismail Khan city, provided more details about the extension of this civilization in the North West Frontier Province.

Archaeologists disagree whether the Kot -Diji type of cultural artifacts constitute a separate civilization or an early phase of the same civilization. Rafique Mughal, citing evidence from the excavations at Bahawalpur and Cholistan, concluded that 'all Kot Diji-related sites *together* constitute an Early Harappan or early urban, formative phase of the Indus Civilization'. However, Parpola argues that the term is misleading because it 'suggests discontinuity, like pre-Aryan vs. Aryan'. In fact, many scholars treat the latter culture as a changed form of the earlier one. This is significant because, if the dates of the Indus Valley Culture are approximately 2300-2000 B.C, and the dates of the kot Diji one are c. 3300-2800, then the length of the period of urban civilization in South Asia have been pushed back a thousand years. The area of the early culture is given by Mughal as follows:

... the central-northern areas of Baluchistan, the greater portion of Sind and the Punjab, Kalibangan on the Indian side, and the south-western part of the Frontier Province are the regions which are likely to have been comprised within the limits of the Kot Dijian culture.

Thus , one may suggest that the area now called Pakistan had some sort of cultural similarity as early as three thousand years before the birth of Christ. Whether it also had linguistic similarity is a question which needs to be answered.

THE LANGUAGE OF THE INDUS VALLEY

Unfortunately the few symbols on the ceramics of the Kot Dijian culture have not been deciphered. F.A.Durrani, following

B.B. Lal and B.K.Thapar, suggests that these symbols may be the beginning of writing in the Indus Valley. There are, however, nearly 4,000 specimens of a script from the Indus Valley Civilization carved on stone, fragments of pottery and other objects. They have not been deciphered satisfactorily but a history of the attempts at such decipherment is available in Asko Parpola's most recent book on the subject. The script, or at least the pictographs, appear to have been uniform but that is not proof that the language too was one. In fact, as in all parts of the world, the language must have been divided in dialects or area-bound varieties. It is possible, however, that these were varieties of a language belonging to one language family. The question then is what that language family was?

Beginning from Sir John Marshall, who was the first to suggest that the language of the Indus Civilization was Dravidian , most scholars have taken the 'Dravidian hypothesis' seriously. Piero Meriggi, a scholar who contributed towards the decipherment of the Hittite hieroglyphs, opined that Brahvi, the Dravidian language spoken even now in part of Balochistan, must be the original Harappan language . However, Brahvi has changed so much and become so Balochified, as Elfenbein points out , that it cannot give clear evidence of any sort in this case. Another scholar, the Spanish Jesuit Henry Heras, 'turned more than 1,800 Indus texts into "Proto-Dravidian" sentences' but his decipherment and linguistic theories were not accepted. Later Soviet scholars headed by Yurij V. Knorozov, carried on a very rigorous computer analysis of sign distribution in the Indus texts coming to the conclusion that it belonged to the Dravidian language family · However, Kamil Zvelebil, also a Russian scholar came to the conclusion that 'the Dravidian affinity of the Proto-Indian language remains only a very attractive and quite plausible hypothesis. Indeed, the plausibility of the hypothesis is such that many people, such as Iravatham Mahadevan, a scholar of old Tamil epigraphy, have used it to offer readings of the Indus script · F.C.Southworth and D.Mc Alpin used the Dravidian roots to reconstruct the language of the Indus Valley. Walter A. Fairservis, another specialist in this area, stated with considerable certainty that 'the Harappan language was basically an early Dravidian language'. Even Parpola, after much careful and detailed sifting of the evidence, opines 'that the Harappan language is most likely to have belonged to the Dravidian family'.

THE DRAVIDIAN INFLUENCE ON PAKISTANI LANGUAGES

If the Harrapan language family was Dravidian, then the first languages of the area of present-day Pakistan was not Indo-Aryan but Dravidian. Such a claim has been made in an extreme and unsubstantiated form by Ainul Haq Faridkoti, a Pakistani philologist, in his several publications. Other scholars have used the theory of linguistic 'transfer' or 'interference' to explain the presence of Dravidian elements in the languages of present-day Pakistan which are generally said to be the daughters of Sanskrit, an Indo-Aryan language. 'Transfer' or 'interference' refers to the influence of the rules of one's first language on another language one learns later. Thus, if Pakistanis learn English, they speak it more or less according to the rules of their first language. As they get more and more exposed to the rules of English, they will speak like native speakers. However, some characteristics of the mother tongue of the speaker will remain which is what we call a Punjabi, Pashto, Sindhi or Urdu accent.

Sometimes an old language dies out and all its speakers learn a new language. But the way they use this language is influenced by the rules of their old language. The new language, then, has a 'substratum' of the old language. If we apply this theory to old Indo-Aryan we can hypothesize that the Harappan language, which was probably Dravidian, influenced old Aryan. Thus Pakistani languages have a Dravidian substratum. The evidence for the presence of this substratum, according to Bertil Tikkanen, is the presence of retroflex consonants which do not exist in Iranian or European members of the Indo-European family of languages. Another clue may be the existence of consonantal clusters in the beginning and end of words in Iranian, European , Dardic languages and even Sanskrit. Thus Sanskrit has /p r e m/ which means love. But Hindi-Urdu speakers call it /p i r e m/. They insert the vowel /i/ between the two word-initial consonants /p/ and /r/ because their own rules of pronunciation (called phonological rules) do not allow word-initial consonantal clusters. Similarly, speakers of Urdu, Punjabi and Sindhi separate consonants in word such as 'school', 'stool' and 'small' etc. It may be that this splitting of consonantal clusters comes into some of the languages of South Asia from languages older than Sanskrit. This, however, is a suggestion by the present author which needs much research by linguists for substantiation.

THE COMING OF THE INDO-ARYAN LANGUAGES

Contrary to the popular myth in Pakistan, the Aryans did not roll down the northern mountains like a tidal wave carrying all the Dravidians before them. According to some scholars they came in at least two major waves in Pakistan as well as small trickles. The first wave came 'around 2000 B.C, and the second some six centuries later'. After the second wave, when they became dominant, their language too spread over northern India. It is this language, or rather a number of dialects, which we call Old Indo Aryan for convenience. The language of the first wave, which remained confined to the Pamir mountains of Pakistan, is identified as Dardic while the second one may be called Indic.

This chart does not take the Dravidian element into account but it cannot be ignored in the face of considerable evidence. The evidence of such an element is clearer in vocabulary than in syntax or pronunciation. For instance there are Dravidian loan words in the Rigvedic language:

...including *phalam* '(ripe) fruit'... as well as *mukham* 'mouth' and *khala* - 'threshing-floor'. The Harappans used a plough, and the Rigvedic word for 'plough', *langala*, is probably derived from Proto-Dravidian * *nangal* / **nangal*.... .

The number of Dravidisms — in all aspects of the language including phonology — increased in the post-Rigvedic era. According to Burrow:

The large majority appear first in the classical language, but in its early stage, being first recorded in Panini, Patanjali, Mahabharata, Srautasutra, etc. The majority appear also in

Pali, which is important for dating since these canonical texts take us back to a period from 500-300 B.C.

According to Parpola, by 1800 B.C 'Mohenjo-daro was abandoned' and a 'cultural fragmentation in the Greater Indus Valley' took place. When this happened the Harappan language remained as a substratum in the language of the Aryan civilization of the Indus Valley of about 1200 to 1000 B.C when the *Rigveda* was largely composed in the plains of the Punjab.

THE SANSKRITIC LEGACY

Sanskrit became the elitist language of the Indus Valley from about 1000 B.C and remained in use in some domain or the other, generally religion and the state, till the Muslim conquest when Persian took its place. Thus, although the Prakrits which finally changed into the vernacular languages of the people of Pakistan were simultaneously in use as I will argue later, let us look into the development of Sanskrit first. The Rigveda itself gives importance to language which is personified as a goddess. In Esa Itkonen's translation it glorifies itself as follows:

I gave birth to the father on the head of this world. My womb is in the waters, within the ocean. From there I spread out over all creatures and touch the sky with the crown of my head.

I am the one who blows like the wind, embracing all creatures. Beyond the sky, beyond this earth, so much have I become in my greatness.

Language was sacred and change was seen as corruption. But all living languages change and the spoken languages of the people, the Prakrits, changed all the time. This threat was countered by making grammatical rules which would petrify language. The most well known of this set of rules was made by the great grammarian Panini who was born at 'Salatura' which is about twelve miles from Jahangira near the Attock bridge in the North West Frontier Province of Pakistan. In those days this village was part of Gandhara which, according to Panini, comprised 'the valley of the Kabul river, with its frontier outpost at Takshasila'. Panini's grammar contains about

4000 rules which were memorized and orally transmitted 'for a couple of hundred years' and was not written down at all. So sacred was the language of the religious texts, Sanskrit, that the grammar itself acquired a central and almost sacrosanct place in the education system of the Indus Valley Aryans.

Since Panini lived in what is now Pakistan it was the speech of the elite of this region that was considered 'correct' and it was this that he wrote about. There are, indeed, passages in the Sanskritic texts which bear this out. The following quotations from them are in Hock's translation:

(1) In the northern region, speech is spoken particularly distinct(ly). People go to the north to learn speech. Or if someone comes from there, they like to hear/ learn from him ... For this is known as the region of speech (*Kausitaki-Brahmana* 7.6).

(2) Through Pathya Svasti they recognized the northern quarter/ region. Therefore there speech speaks better, among the Kuru-Panchalas. For she is really speech (*Satapatha-Brahmana* 3.2.3.15).

Panini was not memorized in isolation. Katayayana (c.250 B.C) and Patanjali (c. 150 B.C), who wrote commentaries on his work, were also part of the canon which aspiring scholars at great centres of Brahmanical learning like Taxila had to learn.

THE EMERGENCE OF THE PRAKRITS

In all probability the Indo-Aryans did not speak one uniformly standardized language but mutually intelligible non-standardized dialects. The process of standardization must have been started by the Brahmins earlier but Panini perfected it in about 400 B.C so that this polished (*saṃskrita*) language did not change and was considered superior to the ever-changing dialects which were spoken by the people. As the elite looked down upon the uneducated people, it also held their languages in contempt. Thus the Prakrits were a sign of rusticity and illiteracy as the languages of the ordinary people are even nowadays. But the term *prakrriti* means 'root' or 'basis' according to Katre who suggests that they existed when Sanskrit was standardized. It is in the light of this insight that we can study the development of the Prakrits into the vernaculars spoken in Pakistan today.

According to George Grierson the Primary Prakrits were living languages in Vedic days. Later they were also fixed by grammarians who wrote their grammars and the living languages of the people were called Secondary Prakrits or 'Sauraseni'. When even these were fossilized by grammarians the Tertiary Prakrits or 'Apabhramasas' were born. By 1000 A.D even the tertiary Prakrits became dated and from this time onward, as we shall see, the modern Pakistani vernaculars emerged. But before we come to the actual emergence of the Pakistani languages let us look at the language of Gandhara.

THE LANGUAGE OF GANDHARA

According to A.H.Dani 'the new cultural trends of the centuries were identified in the swat, Dir, and Peshawar valleys, and because of its original location in that area, it was termed "Gandhara Grave Culture"'. This region was inhabited by the Dasas who worshipped the snake and must have spoken the Indus Valley's Dravidian languages(s) before the Aryans established their supremacy here. By the first millennium B.C, however, 'the Aryanization of most of the population of the northern areas of the subcontinent was complete'. The elite used Sanskrit as we have seen but the common people used what scholars have called 'North-Western Prakrit' or the 'language of Gandhara'. This language, opines Gankovsky, was probably made up of elements from the languages of the 'local pre-Indo-European population and Indo-Aryan tribes, as well as the Dardic and East-Iranian ethnic elements'.

Among the pre-Vedic languages the Dardic languages of the first wave of Aryans who settled down in the Pamir mountains were mentioned earlier. These languages influenced the Indo-Aryan language of Gandhara as the language of the *Gandhari Dhammapada* bears out. This Buddhist text was written in the Kharoshthi script, which was derived from Armaic and will be dealt with in more detail later, and was discovered in the Chinese Turkestan. The dates of this text is c. 269 A.D. and the language: agrees closely with the (Post-Asokan)

Kharoshthi inscriptions from N.W.India and (slightly less closely) with the Prakrit version of the Dhammapada. Moreover, it shows sufficient characteristics in common with the modern Dardic languages to be assigned definitely to that group, and among these languages it would seem to be most closely allied to Torwali.'

Torwali is still spoken in the Kohistan region of Pakistan. But Dardic is not the only influence on the Gandharan language. Another influence was Persian.

THE PERSIAN INFLUENCE

This was hardly surprising because the Gandhara region was ruled by the Persians some time in the sixth century B.C. This is evidenced in the

inscriptions of Darius in which 'clear mention has been made of *Hi (n) du,* that is, the Punjab territory, as a part of the realm'. Further evidence comes from the discovery of an Armaic-Greek inscription of Asoka, the great Buddhist ruler of around 250 B.C., a few miles west of present-day Kandahar in April 1957. Carratelli, writing on this discovery remarks:

... the region had been an old Iranian province and it is logical to assume that the tradition of the Achaeminian state language was maintained. Satrapal offices must have survived during Macedonian domination (when Greek was added) and continued their use of Armaic when the Mauryas took over. The importance of Armaic for administration purposes in the former Iranian provinces is borne out by the Taxila and the Pul-i-Durunteh inscriptions.

Armaic 'came to the fore' at 'the time of the Assyrian empire and became the principal means of communication in the Persian empire'. It was a kind of *lingua franca* in Gandhara and Bactria (part of present-day Afghanistan). King Ashoka (spelled as Asoka by other writers) used it presumably because the people of Kandahar at that time understood Armaic. However, as Gankovsky points out, the common peoples' language did not become Persianized. Even so the script in which their Prakrit was written came from the Persian empire: it was Kharoshthi.

This script, like other Middle Eastern scripts, was written from right to left and A.H.Dani gives the values of its symbols in Arabic letters in his *Kharoshthi Primer*. The script was used not only by the Iranian kings who ruled this part of the world but even by the Mauryas who succeeded them. In fact the script of the famous edicts of Ashoka at Shahbazgarhi and Mansehra (Pakistan) is Kharoshthi whereas the edicts in the rest of India are in Brahmi. This script was 'mainly prevalent in the places which are known as the North Western Province, the Punjab and the Ganges-Jumna Doab roughly from the third century A.D.' Latter the script remained in use in Chinese Turkestan for at least a century. But, whatever the script, the edicts of Ashoka are in the Prakrit of Gandhara and not in an Iranian language. Before we go on to the language of Sind, let us look at the Greek influence on the area we now call Pakistan at the linguistic level.

THE GREEK INFLUENCE ON THE LANGUAGES OF ANCIENT PAKISTAN

The Urdu word for Greek is *Yunani* (*Yunani Tib* = Greek medicine). This is 'derived from the Persian Yauna, meaning Ionian'. As the Ionian Greeks — the Greeks settled in Ionia which is present-day Turkey — were the first to be encountered by the Persians, they called them, and by extension all Greeks, Ionian or *Yunani*. From this root comes the Sanskrit word *Yavana* which one encounters in ancient Sanskrit sources including Panini's grammar. Thus, according to Agrawala, 'the yavanani lipi was known only in Gandahara and the north-west at Panini's time' [*lipi* = edict]. This is not surprising because there were Greek settlements in the Hindu Kush even when Alexander entered that area in 327 B.C. Although Alexander did not stay long in India, he left his representatives and the Greeks established their rule in Bactria.

By the third century B.C. the Mauryan kings (ruled c. 317-180 B.C.), of whom Ashoka was so illustrious an example, were losing their grip over the northern part of the subcontinent. The Greek kings of Bactria now seized the Western provinces of the Mauryas and by 180 B.C. the Greek language came to be used in some domains such as coins.

King Menander (d. 130 B.C) inherited 'western Punjab and Gandhara up to the Indus, with its capital at Taxila'. Under him 'Pushkalawati — present-day Charsadda near Peshawar— began its period of prominence as a Greek centre'. Since the coins of these Greek kings bear Kharoshthi — and sometimes Brahmi — inscriptions, it is evident that this script was never suppressed. Similarly, the local languages continued to be used. However, Greek too found a place of prominence and came to be used at least in the elitist domains. According to Woodcock:

For at least a century and a half, in fact, Greek remained not only the commercial but also the patrician lingua franca of the Kabul valley and of Gandhara at least as far as Taxila. Merchants and kings learnt it as a matter of course, as is shown by the experiences of Appolonius of Tyana when he journeyed to Taxila in 44 A.D.

By the middle of the first century B.C., Greek rule in Gandhara had come to an end except for an enclave around Peshawar. The Sakas, who were from Central Asia and spoke an Iranian tongue, came to rule Gandhara by 32 B.C. Later they left their original language and became strong supporters of Sanskrit. They did not, however, stop the use of Kharoshthi or the Greek language altogether. In fact 'the local Saka ruler of Ujjain' sent a letter to Augustus Ceasar in 24 B.C. in Greek. The Saka kings also inscribed Greek legends, as well as Kharoshthi ones, on their coins. It is also reported that 'the women of Surastra continued to use the Greek form of greetings' for quite some time. The Sakas did, however, become Indianized and language reflects this. According to Chattopadhyaya:

The inscriptions of the successors of Rudradama are also mostly written in Sanskrit. On the contrary, the inscriptions of the contemporary Satavakanus are written in Prakrit, which seems to have been the language of the common folk. The later coins of Damaghasada, son of Rudradaman, are in pure Sanskrit, and the use of Sanskrit legends on the coins was continued by his son Satyadaman also.

Rudradaman ruled about 130 A.D. and it was during his reign that the 'Sindhu-Sauvira region', which, as we shall see in more details later, has been identified with modern Sind and the lower Pakistani Punjab, was conquered from the Kushanas who had been ruling it earlier. In short, around 200 A.D. Sanskritization was being encouraged at the highest level and classical Sanskrit drama was developing. By 295 A.D. the Sakas were subordinates of the Iranian Sassanid kings and by 400 A.D. they had been replaced by the Gupta kings who also patronized Sanskrit.

According to A.H.Dani, Gandhara and the Punjab were ruled by three families by the third and the early part of the fourth century A.D. The Kidara Kushanas too penetrated up to the Hindu Kush and may have acknowledged the suzerainty of the Sassanians or Chandragupta Vikramaditya (ruled c. 375-413 A.D).

The point which is relevant for us is the increasing Indianization as Brahmi replaces Kharoshthi on coins and non-Buddhist Indian religions replace Buddhism and Jainism which had favoured the Prakrits initially. The White Huns even destroyed Gandhara, a centre of Buddhist civilization, in 450 A.D. and Sung-Yun, the Chinese traveller who visited this area in 520 A.D., found Taxila being ruled by Mihirakula (d. circa 532 A.D.) who worshipped the Hindu deity Shiva and used the Brahmi script.

In the 8-10th centuries, opines Dani, 'Taxila went into the hands of the Shahis'. The Hindu Shahis, who also ruled part of Afghanistan, probably spoke the prevalent Prakrit of the North Western part of the subcontinent. This could be a descendant of the language of Gandhara which Ashoka used about 250 B.C. Let us now come to the language of Sindh which will lead us on to the languages of Pakistan at about 1000 A.D. when Muslim rule was established in this area.

THE LANGUAGE OF SIND

Although the Arabs attacked Sindh earlier, it was Mohammad bin Qasim who conquered it and ruled it for about three years (712-715 A.D) before being recalled and killed. The north was conquered by the Turks beginning a little before 1000 A.D. when Mahmud Ghaznavi first entered northern India. However, for many centuries before the Muslim conquest, the cultural development of the northern and southern parts of Pakistan would appear to be different. However, it is not easy to assert that Sind has had a different development from the Punjab and the Frontier because it is not always easy to determine the meaning of Sind.

The countries of Sindhu and Sauvira are mentioned in the *Mahabharata* and have been taken to be roughly the present province of Sind and lower (i.e. Siraiki) Punjab. Some scholars, however, consider them 'neighbouring countries of the Punjab' with Sindhu on the west and Sauvira on the east of the Indus· A.H.Dani, however, locates Sindhu roughly in the province of Sind and Sauvira, in his opinion, 'definitely lay to the east of the river Indus much higher up.' This leads to interesting linguistic hypotheses which are best given in Dani's own words as follows:

If we accept this suggestion, it is not difficult to understand why the Sindhi language is confined to the lower Indus while Saraiki is now spoken in much the same area where *Sauvira* is located by Alberuni. With this understanding of the Saraiki-speaking area, we can now say that the very name *Saraiki* is probably a corruption of the original term Sauviraki.

At different periods in history, however, the boundaries of Sind have been shifting. The Achaeminian kings 'of 2500 years ago provide us, in their rock inscriptions, with some thirty names of sixteen Aryan provinces.

Among them, we have Hindu (Sindhu) and its adjective Hinduya (Sindhi)'. The Muslim historians, however, differentiate between Sind and Hind but their Sind extends up to northern Pakistan. For instance Ibn Khurdadba and Al-Masudi count Kandahar, Multan and Kanauj among the countries of Sind. Rashid ud Din, whose work is based upon Al-Beiruni, says:

Hind is surrounded on the east by Chin and Machin, on the west by Sind and Kabul, and on the South by the sea. On the north lie Kashmir, the country of the Turks, and mountain of Meru.

But Kashmir, according to the evidence of Hsien Tsiang, appears to have been larger than it is now. Around A.D.640, even the Punjab — or some part of it— was a dependency of that kingdom as king Kanishka ruled there and Taxila (Ta ch'a shi lo) was a 'tributary to kia-shi-mi-lo (Kasmir)'.

This evidence suggests that, for some centuries before the Arab conquest of Sind and Multan and about three centuries after it, we should look for one kind of cultural development in Sind and another kind in Kashmir, parts of Punjab and the North West Frontier Province.

In Sind the Rai dynasty and then the Brahmin Chach's line held sway till the eighth century. In Afghanistan and part of Punjab the Hindu Shahis ruled till the Turk Subuktagin defeated Jayapala around 992 A.D and wrested away all the territory west of the Indus including Peshawar. In Kashmir a certain Muslim Rajput adventurer called Shah Mir (also called Shams ud Din) ascended the throne around 1339 A.D. By this period the indigenous languages of Pakistan were emerging.

THE LANGUAGES OF PAKISTAN ON THE EVE OF THE MUSLIM CONQUEST

One of the factors which make it difficult to ascertain the names of the languages of the subcontinent is that the Muslims used to refer to all these languages as Hindi, Hindui or Hindawi. For instance, according to Al-Badaoni, the Commander of the fort of Kalinjar 'composed a poem in Hindi in praise of the Sultan [Mahmud], and sent it to him'.

Later, in the reign of Mahmud's grandson, the poets Masud Saad Salman and Ustad Abul Faraj Runi both had poetic collections of verse (*diwans*) in Hindi as well as Persian and Arabic. Both these poets lived, at least for some period of their lives, in Lahore around 1114 A.D. and if they wrote in the language of Lahore it could hardly have been what we now understand as Hindi.

Badaoni also tells us that Shamsuddin Ayaltimish 'with the assistance of Hindu pundits translated 32 stories about him which are a wonder of relation and strange circumstance, from the Hindui into the Persian tongue and called it *Nama-i-Khirad Afza.*' As this book has not been discovered so far it is impossible to say whether the original was from Kalidasa's Sanskrit as

George Ranking, the translator of Badaoni's history, suggests or some Prakrit work. Another work called the *Mujmalu-t Tawarikh* was, however, translated by Abu Salih bin Shuaib bin Jami 'into Arabic from the Hindwani language' in 1026 A.D. Here by 'Hindwani' it is probably Sanskrit which is meant.

The Muslims did, however, know the differences between some of the Indian languages and despite the generic use of the term Hindi, referred to these differences in some writings. Al-Masudi tells us, for instance, that 'the language of Sind is different from that of India', while Ibn Haikal tells us that after the Islamic conquest 'the language of Mansura, Multan, and those parts is Arabic and Sindian. In Makran they use Persian and Makranic.' In short the Sindhi language had been identified as a distinct language a little after the Muslim conquest of Southern Pakistan.

According to Grierson the mother of Sindhi was Vrachda. It was the spoken language, or Apabhramsa, 'of the country round the lower Indus.' It was also the mother of what Grierson calls Lahnda and what are now known as Siraiki and Hind Ko. According to the same author 'India had left the Prakrit stage, and had reached the stage of the tertiary Prakrits, i.e. of the modern Indo-Aryan vernaculars, by the year 1000 A.D.' .

It is possible then, as A.L.Turner opines, that Sindhi must have separated from the mass of related languages sometime between 250 B.C. and the first century A.D. John Bordie, using linguistic evidence of loss of certain words per thousand years, suggests that Sindhi and Punjabi separated between A.D.750 to 1400 and that the implosives of the Sindhi language 'came into existence prior to A.D. 1400 and subsequent to the separation of Sindhi from the mass of related languages.'

Since Siraiki too has implosive sounds, it too may have become a separate language around this period. But Siraiki shares its vocabulary, or at least a major part of the core vocabulary, with Punjabi so that the present writer is unsure whether Siraiki is a sister of Punjabi which picked up some features of the Sindhi sound-system (phonology) or a sister of Sindhi which picked up Punjabi words as Grierson suggests.

In Grierson's opinion Punjabi is the descendant of the Takka Apabhramasa of the North Central Punjab and the Upanagara Apabhramasa of the Southern Punjab. However, the language is not mentioned by this name till after the Muslim conquest. In fact the very term Punjab is from Persian (*Punj* = five and *ab* = water or river).

Since five rivers flow in this region the Persian chroniclers called it 'Punj-ab' and the name replaced the earlier names of the region. However, Amir Khusrau, writing in 1317, calls the language of Lahore not Punjabi but 'Lahori'. Khusrau also mentions Sindhi and Kashmiri but not Pashto or Balochi. It is Abul Fazal who mentions 'Afghan' (Pashto) in the *Ain-i-Akbari* in the sixteenth century.

In short, Sindhi, Punjabi, Siraiki and some form of Hind Ko as well as the Dardic languages were spoken in some form or the other in the area now comprising Pakistan.

Pashto and Balochi are not part of this article since they were only on the fringes of the boundaries of present-day Pakistan in the tenth century when the Muslim conquests took place.

However, they will be mentioned in passing here. According to Gankovsky the Pakhtuns moved in the plains of Peshawar, Kohat and Bannu in the thirteenth and fourteenth centuries, to Swat, Kurram and Panjkora as well as to Zhob, Loralai and Quetta in the fifteenth and the sixteenth centuries.

The Baluchi language, which too is descended from the Iranian branch of the Indo-European languages, is a late comer in its present location. However, in the tenth century when the Arabs ruled parts of Baluchistan, they occupied Kalat which was probably Brahvi-speaking even then. Baluchi too may have been present on the peripheries but it spread all over Pakistani Balochistan and elsewhere with the raids of the Ghaznavids and the Ghorids.

CONCLUSION

Pakistan is heir to some of the most ancient civilizations of the world. Its languages, which were part of the culture of the people of this region, too have ancient roots. These languages have not generally been used in the domains of power because the rulers of this region were generally foreigners. But the foreigners — whether Achaeminian Iranians, Greeks or Muslim Arabs, Turks and Pathans as well as the British — have also enriched the indigenous languages so that their vocabulary is multilingual and varied.

As the people of this area converted to Islam the Arabic and Persian words became part of their Islamic identity and remain so. In a sense it is their very presence as well as the Arabic-based scripts of all Pakistani languages which give them a kind of cultural unity. Linguistically, then, Pakistan faces two directions: India - because the roots of its languages are Dravidian as well as Indo-Aryan; and the Middle East - because its scripts and vocabulary owe much to Arabic and Persian. To deny any of these directions out of ideological zeal is historically incorrect to say the least.

Bibliography

Aiyar, R. Krishnaswami: *Outlines of Vedaanta*, Chetana, Bombay, 1978.

Aurobindo, Sri: *Vyasa and Valmiki*, Acharya Press, Pondicherry, 1956.

Avalon, Arthur and Ellen: *Hymns to the Goddess*, Ganesh and Co., Madras, 1964.

Basham, A.L.: *History and Doctrines of the Ajivikas*, Oxford, London, 1951.

Bhattacharji, Sukumari: *Literature in the Vedic Age*, Kali Ram Press, Calcutta, 1984.

Bhattacharya, Narendra Nath: *A Dictionary of Hindu Mythology*, Munshiram Manoharlal, Delhi, 2001.

Bose, D. N.: *Dharmashastra: Their Philosophy and Occult Secrets*, Kali Press, Calcutta, 1965.

Burke, John G.: *The New Technology and Human Values*, Warswork Publishing, California, 1966.

Chaturvedi, M.D.,: *Hinduism, The Eternal Religion*, Bharatiya Vidya Bhavan, Bombay, 1992.

Collect, S. D.: *The Life and Letter of Raju Rahmmohun Roy*, Kali Ram Press, Calcutta, 1962.

Collier, Richard: *The Great Indian Mutiny*, MacMillan, New York, 1963.

Coomaraswamy, Ananda K.: *Contemporary Indian Philosophy*, Geroge Allen & Unwin, London, 1936.

Dandekar, R.N.: *Some Aspects of the History of Hinduism*, Radhey Shayam Press, Poona. 1967.

Datta, M. R.: *The Secret Serpent*, Kali Ram Press, Calcutta, 1913.

Dhar, Niranjan: *Vedanta and Bengal Renaissance*, Minerva Associates, Calcutta, 1977.

Dimock, Edward C.: *In Praise of Krishna*, University of Chicago Press, Chicago, 1998.

Eliot Deutsch: *Advaita Vedanta: a Philosophical Reconstruction*, East-West Center Press, Honolulu, 1969

Farquhar, J.N.: *Modern Religious Movements in India*, Munshiram, New Delhi, 1967.

Frauwallner, Erich.: *History of Indian Philosophy*, Motilal, Delhi, 1973.

Garbe, R.: *The Philosophy of Ancient India*, Chicago University Press, Chicago, 1899.

Geiger, Wilhelm: *Culture of Ceylon in Medieval Times*, Wiesbaden, London, 1960.

Govinda, Lama Anagarika: *Foundations of Tibetan Mysticism*, Oxford, New York, 1969.

Grant, G. P.: *Philosophy in the Mass Age*, Copp Clark, Toronto, 1959.

Grisenold, H.D.: *Insights into Modern Hinduism*, Oxford, New York, 1934.

Harding, Elizabeth: *Kali: The Black Goddess of Dakshineshwar*, Nicolas-Hays, York Beach, 1993.

Harman, William: *The Sacred Marriage of a Hindu Goddess*, Indiana University Press, Bloomington, 1989.

Heimann, Betty: *Facets of Indian Thought*, Geroge Allen & Unwin, London, 1964.

Hopkins, Thomas J.: *The Hindu Religious Tradition*, Dickenson, California, 1971.

Jain, J.C.: *Life in Ancient India as Depicted in the Jain Canons*, Akarshan Press, Bombay, 1947.

Jain, Jyoti Prasad: *Jain Sources of the History of India*, Bhagawati Press, Delhi, 1964.

Jha, Ganganatha: *Purva-Mimamsa-Sutras of Jaimini*, Bharatiya Publ., Varanasi 1979.

Keith, Arthur Berriedale: *The Religion and Philosophy of the Veda and Upanishads*, MacMillan, Delhi, 1925.

Klostermaier, Klaus K.: *A Survey of Hinduism*, State University of New York Press, Albany, 1989.

Kottackal, Jacob: *Religion and Ethics in Advaita*, C.M.S. Press, Kottayam, 1982.

Krishnamurthy, Visvantha: *Essentials of Dharmashastra*, Narosa Pub. House, New Delhi, 1989.

Levy, John: *The Nature of Man According to Vedanta*, Routledge & Kegan Paul, London, 1956.

Mathew, Arnold: *Culture and Anarchy*, The University Press, Cambridge, 1935.

Miller, Barbara Stoller: *The Bhagavad-Gita*, Bantam Books, Varanasi, 1986.

Mitcham, C.: *Philosophy and Technology*, The Free Press, New York, 1972.

Munshi, K M.: *Glory that was Gurjaradesa*, Rawat Press, Bombay, 1955.

Narla, V.R.: *The Truth about the Gita*, Narla Institute, Hyderabad, 1988.

Piatigorsky, Alexander: *The Buddhist Philosophy of Thought*, Rowman & Allenheld, London, 1984.

Prime, Ranchor: *Hinduism and Ecology*, Motilal Banarsidass, Delhi 1994.

Ramakrishnananda, Swami: *Life of Sri Ramanuja*, Sai Kalyani Press, Madras, 1959.

Ranade, R. D.: *Mysticism in Maharashtra*, MacMillan, Delhi, 1933

Renou, Louis: *The Nature of Dharmashastra,* Walker and Co., New York, 1997.

Samsookha, Puranchand: *Lord Mahavira*, Kali Ram Press, Calcutta, 1957.

Satyapal Verma: *Role of Reason in Sankara Vedanta*, Parimal Publication, Delhi, 1992.

Sengaku Mayeda: *A Thousand Teachings: the Upadesasahasri of Sankara*, University of Tokyo Press, 1979.

Shastri, Manmatha Nath: *Outlines of Hindu Metaphysics*, Kali Ram Press, Calcutta, 1910.

Singer. Charles: *Technology and History*, Oxford University Press, London, 1952.

Sivaramamurti, C.: *Sri Lakshmi in Indian Art and Thought*, Kanak, New Delhi, 1982.

Spengler, Oswald: *Man and Technics: A Contribution to Philosophy of Life*, MacMillan, New York, 1932.

Subramaniam, Kamala: *Mahabharata*, Rawat Press, Bombay, 1971.

Tejomayananda, Swami: *Hindu Culture: An Introduction*, Chinmaya Publications, Piercy, 1993.

Thomas, P.: *Kama Kalpa or the Hindu Ritual of Love*, D. B. Taraporevala Sons, Bombay, 1965.

Usha Kapoor: *Women and Welfare : A Study of Voluntary Agencies*, Indus, New Delhi, 1995.

Utpat, V.N.: *Riddles of Buddha and Ambedkar*, Itihas Patrika Prakashan, Thane 1988.

Vable, D.: *The Arya Samaj. Hindu without Hinduism*. Vikas Publ., Delhi, 1983.

van Buitenen, J. A. B.: *The Mahabharata*, University of Chicago Press, Chicago, 1973.

Vedantavagisha, Kalivara: *Sankara and Sakyamuni*, Bangiya Sahitya Parishad Patrika (Bengali), Calcutta, 1901.

Wendy Doniger: *Siva: The Erotic Ascetic*, Oxford University Press, Delhi, 1998.

Index

E

F

G

H

I

J

K

L

M

O

P

R

S

T

U

V

W

Y

❑❑❑